D1549374

Brian Pullan

A History of Early
RENAISSANCE
ITALY

From the Mid-Thirteenth to the
Mid-Fifteenth Century

ALLEN LANE

To William and Thomas Pullan

Contents

Foreword

Pitfalls await every historian of Italy who ventures outside the period and place on which he has carried out detailed research in archives. He can venture to write about Italy as a whole only in the uneasy awareness that there is always some scholar somewhere who knows more than he does about almost every aspect of his subject. He must do so in the knowledge that in a sense the richest and most meaningful Italian history is always local history, and that generalizations can seldom be confidently offered. But for non-specialists local monographs often have little significance unless they can somehow be placed, however approximately, in a wider context in space and time. This book is an attempt to sketch a background against which original and detailed studies – some of which are listed in the bibliography – can perhaps be read with greater appreciation. More than this it cannot seek to do.

I owe many thanks to the Cambridge students who have talked to me about Italian history, and to Mr Dieter Pevsner of Penguin Books for his criticisms of the first draft of this work.

B.S.P.

Introduction

This book follows certain important themes in Italian history across a period of some 200 years from the mid-thirteenth to the mid-fifteenth century.

Historians who try to define periods are very conscious, unless their interests are restricted to very narrow themes, of trying to cut a river with a carving knife. Anyone who has had to take account of the periods defined, out of administrative necessity, within university or school courses knows that the limits and divisions appropriate to one branch of history are frequently meaningless in another; and that scrupulous attention to exact boundaries thrown across the whole stream of history can only hamstring study and inquiry. The most that can be said in favour of calling these two centuries a period in Italian history is that a historian of politics and administration, a student of the history of ideas, a specialist in economic history, and an art historian would probably concur in recognizing them as centuries of dramatic transition between two markedly different situations.

In the mid-thirteenth century Italy was the most invaded country in Europe and the battleground between Pope and Emperor, both of whom claimed a form of authority whose frontiers were the limits of western Christendom: each of them was, in the well-worn phrase, a 'universalist' power. About 1450 the Italian peninsula comprised a number of finite and fairly self-contained states, the larger entities balancing each other in precarious equilibrium. The Emperor was seldom seen in Italy and the Pope had become an Italian prince, settled at last in Rome and firmly identified with the temporal dominions of the Holy See that sprawled across the centre from the Tyrrhenean to the

Adriatic. In Italian diplomacy the prime movers were native Italian states, and although the south formed part of a Spanish empire the King of Aragon was not a lone colossus in Italian politics but one prince among several, whose ambitions could well be contained and limited by his peers. The threat of foreign intervention could never be ignored: but Italy had ceased for the time being to be the most invaded country in Europe, and had formed a culture of its own. In the thirteenth century city-states had claimed autonomy and feudal lords sought their fortunes within the loose and rickety framework of the Empire or the Papal States. By 1450, although the process was far from complete, they were being absorbed into sovereign territorial states – in some of which, however, the corporate rule of great cities was still dominant. Expanding republics and dukedoms were replacing the vicariates of the Emperor.

Between these years the Italian peninsula did not only shed its passive international role as the most invaded country in the west: it also lost its outstanding position as the home of the leader-economies of Europe and of the pioneers of the medieval commercial revolution. In the early thirteenth century, Italians had achieved their greatest worldly successes as merchants and lawyers, and Italian literature and art depended heavily on Gothic, French and Byzantine inspiration. About 1450 the peoples of northern Italy were still the most technically advanced in Europe, but their lead over other nations – Catalonia, Flanders, England, France – had become less impressive. The greatest distinction of Italians and their most exciting contribution to civilization now lay in their capacity for giving their heritage from the ancient world an entirely new meaning, in art and literature, for their own society.

This book tries to show how these changes came about. There is nothing in 1450 which marks a dramatic irruption into a new era. Between 1250 and 1450 the situation had not altered out of all recognition, and not all vestiges of the thirteenth century had been destroyed. The recovery of the ancient world had not meant the overthrow of the Christian religion, or meant its sudden replacement by antiquity as the supreme source of inspiration to the scholar or intellectual. The thirteenth century had seen the rejuvenation of the Italian Church by the order of St Francis, at the cost of some departure from the saint's ideals, at the cost of condemning his most zealous disciples as heretics. In the fifteenth century came a respectable Franciscan revival, admired and supported by the Pope himself. In the thirteenth century Italian churchmen were in the midst of a war on heresy; the fifteenth saw the beginnings of social and philanthropic movements which heralded the Catholic reformation. Not everyone will feel that the mid-fifteenth century marks the start or finish of an epoch or a cycle in Italian history: but some may agree that it offers a vantage point from which important changes can be registered, surveyed, and perhaps to some extent explained.

PART ONE

The Church, its Allies and Enemies

*c.*1250–*c.*1350

Introduction

There is a tradition that when a woman of Lombardy was giving birth to Manfred of the seed of Frederick, the forms of two women appeared in the cloudy skies over Tuscany and hung like a mist above the earth, and a great clap of thunder, as from an echoing vault, appeared to pronounce their names together. And it is plausibly held that – so far as anyone could tell – one was called Guelfa and the other Ghibellina. They wrestled and pitted their strength against each other and fought hand to hand from dawn to high noon, and now one and now the other triumphed and trampled her foe underfoot . . .

These were the words of Saba Malaspina, a Roman by birth and a functionary at the court of Pope Martin IV, writing his *History of Sicilian Affairs* for the college of cardinals in the early 1280s.

The conflicts of the Guelf and Ghibelline factions, echoing throughout the peninsula, imparted a kind of unity to thirteenth-century Italy. They made it a theatre of war. It became an arena in which innumerable local contests and rivalries seemed at intervals to be subsumed into one much vaster and more far-reaching struggle. In theory at least, a Guelf was a supporter of the Church, or rather of the temporal power of the Papacy; and a Ghibelline was a partisan of the Emperor. Thirteenth-century Italy was in a sense the most cosmopolitan country in Europe; it was the geographical point of collision between two potentates who claimed an international authority, indeed a universal power over all western Christendom.

But there was a striking contrast between the vast theoretical claims asserted by both Emperor and Pope and the comparatively flimsy foundations of their actual power. Both derived their authority in some degree from Rome, the shrunken, half-ruined city which had once been the heart and brain of the civilized world. For centuries the Emperors had been German princes, and yet they called themselves Emperors, not of the Germans, but of the Romans, and came to seek coronation at the hands of the Pope. The symbolic association of Rome with supreme and universal dominion had now survived by nearly a thousand years the physical breakdown of the Roman Empire in the west.

Legend connected Rome with the apostle St Peter, and the Popes claimed to be his heirs and to be the Vicars of Christ, the point of intersection between heaven and earth. St Peter had been the rock on which the Church was built, and had (it was claimed on the authority of Scripture) received from Christ a unique 'commission' which made him a participant in divine government: 'whatsoever you shall bind on earth shall be bound in heaven also, and whatsoever you shall loose on earth shall be loosed in heaven.' Between the mid-eleventh and the mid-thirteenth centuries the Popes had proclaimed themselves judges over Christian nations, acting as a court of final appeal not only in spiritual matters but also in some temporal affairs. In a Christian society which aimed at procuring salvation it was hard to draw the frontier between the things that were Caesar's and the things that were God's. Indeed the Popes, even if they did not blatantly flout the claims of royal or secular jurisdiction, were frequently to be accused – in Italy and elsewhere – of misusing the spiritual weapons of excommunication and interdict in order to gain material ends. In practice, the acceptance or rejection of the Pope's decisions – in Italy or other parts of Europe – was bound to depend on the local political situation, and on the existence of parties or factions which (partly out of self-interest) were prepared to side with the Pope. From such roots sprang the loose alliances of Guelf partisans in Italy, and they arose specifically out of the conflicts of successive Popes with the Emperors, kings and princes of the Swabian house of Staufen.

The Popes had long claimed that nobody, not even princes, could be excepted from the injunction 'Feed my sheep' – the all-embracing command of Christ to St Peter and hence to St Peter's successors on earth. If the Pope were to wield authority over princes, and if he were to preserve his neutrality and his position as an umpire in disputes between Christians, he needed to be a temporal prince in his own right and not to appear (as did the Patriarch in Byzantium) to be a subject or servant of any particular monarch. For several centuries the Popes had exercised some temporal power in central Italy. But it was Innocent III (1198–1216) who established the outlines of the Papal States as they were to remain until the newly united Kingdom of Italy absorbed them in 1870. By making good his claims to the March of Ancona and to the Duchy of Spoleto, Innocent helped to secure a wide sash of papal territory extending diagonally across central Italy from the Tyrrhenean to the Adriatic Sea. Rather later, in 1278, the Papacy was to obtain formal recognition of its temporal sovereignty over the province of Romagna also.

But it has to be said that at least until the sixteenth century the Pope's control over his dominions was to remain very loose. For much of the time he was unable to govern by means of officials or commissioners whom he could appoint or dismiss at will and who would be solely responsible to him. Rather, he was often compelled to accept the officials nominated by the individual towns, or to accord recognition to local potentates with landed estates and

vassal followers in the area – seigneurs who wanted their
de facto power legitimated by the formal grant of a 'vicariate'
from the Pope. Like that of the Emperor in Lombardy and
Tuscany, the Pope's dominion in central Italy was a superstructure resting on a ramshackle base, its cohesion and
effectiveness fluctuating dramatically from one generation
to another. Even in Rome itself the Pope's presence was
only intermittent and the Papacy – expelled at intervals
by local rebellions or choosing to hold court elsewhere –
was not to settle permanently in the city until 1443, in the
days of Eugenius IV.

Even outside the Papal States the Popes exercised a form
of indirect temporal power in some parts of Europe whose
kings had become their vassals and sworn fealty to the
Pope – theoretically holding their dominions of the See of
St Peter as if they formed a feudal tenure, a grant of land
in the expectation of loyal service. To the south of the Papal
States the Kingdom of Sicily (which comprised both the
island and a vast tract of the south Italian mainland) con-
stituted such a fief. In the mid-eleventh century the Popes
had granted to Norman adventurers who drove back
Saracen invaders from the south legal authority to occupy
conquered territories. Conversely, Norman warrior chieftains had sworn to respect and defend the property and
rights of St Peter. In times of crisis, long after the rule of
the Normans had passed away, the Popes were to claim
the authority to dispose of the Sicilian crown, to settle succession disputes, to exact tribute, even to deprive an errant
ruler and his descendants and transfer the throne to some
prince who promised to be more amenable. Above all the
thirteenth-century Popes were determined that the imperial
and the Sicilian crowns must never be united in the person
of the same man. For this would mean that the nascent
Papal State would be encircled and caught in a pincer; that
the Pope's territorial independence would be threatened;

that he would be able to find no counterweight to a recalcitrant Emperor; and that his lands might be used as a corridor for troops passing between south and north or vice versa. This danger had materialized at the close of the twelfth century, out of the dynastic ambitions of the Staufen princes, and it would account for much of the bitter hostility of Guelf and Ghibelline.

As did the Pope, the Emperor claimed a form of universal power, or at least a unique prestige as the doyen of European monarchs. He was the head of the Catholic laity and lord of the Kingdoms of Germany and northern Italy – of realms which formed the spinal cord of Europe and a 'power-aggregate' which straddled the Alps. The Empire in the west had arisen in the time of Charlemagne. It was then that the Papacy had resolved to find for the Holy See and for the Latin form of Christianity champions and protectors in the great warlords whose power centred in the north but could still be stretched as far south as Rome. On Christmas Day, 800, Pope Leo III had crowned Charlemagne Emperor of the Romans, and had thus helped to create between Pope and Emperor a relationship which was potentially profitable to both parties, but was fraught with innumerable difficulties. Long after the death of Charlemagne, the imperial dignity became firmly associated with the lordship of Germany and northern Italy and with coronation in Rome. Indeed, until the early sixteenth century, no German monarch was to assume the title of Emperor unless he had made the journey to Rome to receive the imperial crown. Without this he was merely a king – albeit the King of the Romans. Coronation in Rome created for the ruler of Germany a unique standing and had the power to differentiate him unmistakably from other German magnates and other European kings.

But for all his vast claims the German ruler was in a sense the most vulnerable European monarch: his lands were far-flung, he was over-stretched and over-committed, and in northern Italy he was often an absentee ruler who could only seek intermittently to make his power a reality. Unlike his counterparts in France and England he remained an elective monarch, for he depended for nomination as King on his fellow German princes, and on the Pope for promotion to the rank of Emperor. At the start of the thirteenth century Pope Innocent III made it clear that he would not consider himself automatically bound to consecrate the candidate chosen by a majority of the German princes. Nor would he allow the imperial crown to become the hereditary property of the reigning dynasty of Staufen, which the Ghibelline factions originally followed.

From the mid-twelfth century the Staufen Emperors had begun to concentrate with growing intensity on the exploitation of their Italian possessions, and this resulted in a higher incidence of territorial disputes between the Emperors and the Popes. In Lombardy and Tuscany especially, the cities had developed a very high degree of autonomy. Their leaders felt an acute consciousness of possessing rights and privileges which they were determined to defend against the claims of imperial officials striving to reassert crown prerogatives. Of course the whole of northern Italy had not become urbanized, and there were great areas, in Piedmont, or Friuli, or Liguria, still subject to feudal lords, to the Emperor's counts and marquesses. But, in the form of the cities, there were many 'non-feudal islands' in this 'feudal sea', and some of them had reduced the neighbouring landed lords to a condition of subjection. With this mosaic of feudal and urban lordships, in which the reality of local power was now concentrated, the Staufen had now to reckon. They did not govern so much as negotiate among the complexities of inter-city politics, taking advantage of local rivalries to build up a following. They were compelled to recognize the right of Lombard cities to form leagues in defence of their privileges, and they had to face the ominous possibility of an alliance between the Papacy and some of the urban communes.

A new development, which was to bring about the most prolonged and drastic confrontation between Papacy and Empire, had occurred at the close of the twelfth century. The Staufen Henry VI had married Constance, aunt to the last Norman King of Sicily, the childless William II. This union of royal families had soon resulted in a union of crowns. The Popes (now determined to extend their own temporal power) were faced with the grim prospect of encirclement. Although Innocent III did for a time withhold the imperial crown from Henry VI's heir, the child-King Frederick of Sicily, he was in practice unable to find a reliable enough alternative candidate, an Emperor who would respect the integrity of the Papal States; and he was at last driven back to the Staufen. In 1212 Frederick promised to renounce the Sicilian throne on being crowned Emperor, and recognized the Pope as feudal lord of the Kingdom; but he failed to honour this undertaking. In the 1230s and 1240s, in the days of Pope Gregory IX and Pope Innocent IV, deep-seated papal distrust of the Staufen as persecutors of the Church, and the alliance between the Popes and a formidable section of the Lombard communes, were to evoke a long and bitter struggle which in some degree involved all Italy and raised up the factions of pro-papal Guelfs and pro-imperial Ghibellines.

The name 'Guelf' was derived from the German house of Welf, a princely dynasty which was traditionally hostile to the Staufen and had once been supported by Innocent III. On the other hand, 'Ghibelline' served as a somewhat contorted Italian version of the name of the castle of Waiblingen in Swabia, which belonged to the Staufen and once provided their followers with a war-cry. In later years Italians were to offer other explanations for these familiar names – for example, a fourteenth-century Florentine believed that Ghibellines had originally been those who were making war (*gerentes bellum*) upon the Church, Guelfs those who kept faith (*gerentes fidem*) with it. But such conjectures, if more rational and plausible, seem to have been unfounded.

In practice the links between local Guelfs and Ghibellines and the super-powers of their choice were frequently somewhat tenuous. These labels were often imposed upon local polarizations, cleavages or rivalries which had existed independently of the great conflict between Pope and Emperor, and often had no very profound intellectual or social content. If the As became Guelf, their rivals the Bs instinctively turned Ghibelline, and so on. Guelfs were probably those who judged that their aspirations to power, prestige and wealth in the locality could best be served by alliance with the Pope at such times as he or his partisans were a force in the region. Ghibellines placed a similar trust in the Emperor and his followers. Inter-city rivalries were eventually to be expressed in the same way – when Florence became Guelf, such rivals as Arezzo or Pisa remained Ghibelline.

With over-simplification, one can visualize Italy in the mid-thirteenth century as essentially divided into three great segments, each of these standing in some relationship to one or both of the universalist powers within Catholic Christendom. Broadly speaking, northern Italy was imperial territory and central Italy the province of the Papal States: whilst throughout most of the first half of the century southern Italy and Sicily – officially forming a papal fief – were linked to the north by a purely personal union embodied in the Emperor Frederick II of Staufen. But within the contours of each of these sectors of Italy there was constant movement and unrest, caused especially by the rivalries of cities and landed lords existing in a highly competitive environment in the north and centre, so that local conflicts were always giving leverage to the struggle between the super-powers. In the south, however, the cities had not developed in the same way into semi-independent dwarf republics, for the south had an unusual tradition of strong monarchy, of kings prepared to assert and maintain an autocratic power over towns and barons which had much more in common with the Byzantine Empire than with any brand of kingship found elsewhere in the west. Indeed it cannot be too strongly emphasized that the temporary union of north and south was a dynastic union only: there was no merging of institutions, and there were no really strong similarities in social structure or in levels of economic development. Between north and south there were very radical contrasts in climate, land formation, urbanization and governmental traditions. Italy was and remained a subcontinent rather than a single country or state, and its peoples could not feel a strong sense of national identity based on cultural, linguistic or racial bonds. With the death of Frederick II in 1250 the peninsula was destined to become an international land of adventure for the ambitious princes of Europe.

Guelf and Ghibelline

2

In 1245 relations between Frederick II of Staufen and Pope Innocent IV deteriorated to the point at which the Pope excommunicated the King–Emperor and declared him deposed at a general council held at Lyons. Three years later this formal act of deposition, always a grave incitement to rebellion against the Staufen, became more of a reality when the imperial armies were defeated by Guelf partisans beneath the walls of Parma in Lombardy. Then, in 1250, the Emperor died excommunicate in Apulia. A prolonged interregnum began, in which there was no certain or impressive claimant either to the title of King of the Romans or to the throne of Sicily. For Italian and indeed for European history the consequences were very profound. The second half of the thirteenth century witnessed the disintegration of the Italo-German axis and of the ancient link between rule in Germany and rule in Lombardy and Tuscany. It saw the Emperor reduced to a far less significant role within the Church, whilst both in Italy and in the Church at large there was a countervailing growth in French influence. Until 1310 no German ruler was to prove willing to undertake the *Romzug* – the ritual journey to Rome for coronation, which entailed the formal assertion of the monarch's authority in Italy by his appearance in person, aspiring to bring peace, order and justice, south of the Alps.

Since the Popes had no intention of conferring the Sicilian or 'Roman' monarchies of which they disposed on any

descendant of the accursed race of Staufen, these crowns
became for a time an inviting target for ambitious princes
of the established royal houses of Europe. Younger sons and
brothers, and even one reigning monarch, from Germany,
England, Castile and France: all for a time displayed interest or staked their claims. Conrad and Manfred, the sons of
Frederick II, chose to cut their losses in Germany and to
campaign and die in defence of their Italian inheritance.
On the other hand, the would-be Kings of the Romans had
little purchase on Italian soil. Hence the old patterns of
Italo-German politics began to fade. For a time it seemed
as though success might lie with the most italianate of the
Staufen – the attractive, cultured, erratic Manfred, son of
Frederick II by a Lombard noblewoman, Bianca Lancia;
the omens at his birth were dramatically recalled by the
chronicler Malaspina. For a few years his star rose high
and burned brilliantly. He was crowned King of Sicily in
1258 – though without recognition from the papal overlord.
His influence was by no means confined to the south, for in
Lombardy he had a most formidable henchman, the Marquess Uberto Pellavicino, lord of Piacenza and some time
Captain-General of the Milanese armies. In Tuscany, his
Ghibelline partisans from Siena and Florence won a
devastating and bloody victory at Monte Aperti in 1260.
It has been suggested that the processions of flagellant
penitents that spread across the centre and north a few
weeks later may have been inspired by the sense that all
Italy now seemed overshadowed by the enemies of the
Church. In 1265 Manfred addressed an eloquent appeal
over the Pope's head to the people of Rome, calling upon
them to grant him the imperial crown; but nothing was to
come of this ambition.

At about this time there was an increase in French
influence among the cardinals, who elected the Pope, and
this was also to favour French designs on the Kingdom of

the south. In 1261 a deadlock within the college of cardinals caused them to break with long-standing tradition and choose a non-Italian Pope, the first foreigner to be elected for a hundred years. This was Jacques Pantaléon, Patriarch of Jerusalem and a native of Troyes in Champagne; it was he who, as Pope Urban IV, created a strong and lasting French party among the cardinals. Six out of the fourteen red hats he bestowed in 1261 and 1262 went to native Frenchmen, including Gui Foulquois, Archbishop of Narbonne, a servant of the French King who was to succeed as Pope Clement IV in 1265 and continue the policies of Urban. There was no question of the French monopolizing the college of cardinals, for Urban was careful not to alienate Italian support – but the French element was now weighty enough to swing the policy of the Holy See decisively towards the French royal house, and to favour the pious and implacable Charles of Anjou, younger brother of King Louis IX. It was he who would displace Manfred and take possession of the great vassal Kingdom on the southern frontiers of the Papal States.

The choice of Charles of Anjou was a realistic one, for he – unlike the English Plantagenets who had briefly entertained designs on Sicily – was capable of mustering the financial resources vital to an effective military expedition. His strength lay in the two semi-autonomous 'apanage counties' of Anjou and Maine (apanages being fiefs held on special terms from the French King by younger sons and cadet branches of the royal family); and still more in the County of Provence. Here Charles's revenues actually outstripped his expenditure in the years immediately before his expedition to southern Italy. But massive supplies of ready cash were also needed to back the enterprise, and Tuscan merchant bankers came forward to supply them – thus becoming for the first time the financial partners in a new and relatively stable Guelf alliance, which was to remain a dominant force in Italian politics at least until the 1330s.

By the early 1260s governments of Ghibelline complexion ruled in Florence and Siena, but Urban IV managed to drain away support from these regimes by threatening to take revenge on the property of their merchants in Rome and the Papal States. Many were drawn into exile, and in the autumn of 1265 these merchant bankers proved ready to gamble either on being restored to their native cities by an Angevin triumph or on suffering the total ruin which would overtake them if Charles failed. They were ready to provide a lump sum of 250,000 *livres tournois*: this was, in effect, an anticipation of revenue, for the bankers' security consisted chiefly of taxes levied on French ecclesiastical benefices by the combined authority of the Pope and King Louis IX. As further and more tangible pledges the Pope offered them the contents of his treasury, the property of some Roman churches, and his own jewels.

As it turned out, the gamble succeeded. Charles came to the south, and Manfred was defeated and killed on the field of Benevento in 1266. Two years later came the collapse of the last serious Staufen attempt at the reconquest of the whole Kingdom. Conradin, the sixteen-year-old grandson of Frederick II, was defeated and captured, and Charles of Anjou, determined to destroy the Staufen root and branch, had the pretender publicly executed in Naples. But as events in the island of Sicily were to show some years later, the descendants of the Staufen and the remnants of Ghibellinery could not be so easily stamped out.

*

For at least three generations after 1266 there survived a comparatively stable Guelf alliance. It was based on the collusion of the Pope and his Angevin vassal, with financial support from the highly developed Tuscan economy, and some degree of sympathy from towns or seigneurs in the north and centre where Guelf factions were in the ascendant. Loose and troubled as this connection was, it was still one of the few political or diplomatic bonds transcending regional differences and imparting a measure of unity to the peninsula. It is now important to examine and try to analyse the constituents of the Guelf connection – the Kingdom of Sicily, the Guelf parties elsewhere, the Pope's relations with them – in the hope of understanding where its resources came from and what pulled it together.

The Popes were of course aware of the danger that Charles of Anjou and his heirs might not accept their dependent status and might become tyrants no less redoubtable than the Staufen. They had offered Charles the crown only on carefully formulated conditions intended to curb his power – these aimed at reducing his control over the affairs of the Sicilian clergy, at forestalling any designs he might entertain on the imperial title, at obliging him to pay large sums in tribute to the Holy See, and at forbidding him to accumulate offices of profit and power on papal or imperial territory. In practice, however, this last condition proved unenforceable, and from 1268 to 1278 he held the influential posts of Senator in Rome (an office which he exercised through deputies, and which gave him a standing pretext for intervention in Roman affairs), and of imperial vicar in Tuscany. This meant that the authority and influence of the Angevin kings was never localized or successfully confined to the south. Long after the death of Charles, his grandson Robert (Robert the Wise, who reigned from 1309 to 1343) was called upon by the Popes to become 'Vicar of the Empire in all parts of Italy subject to the Empire' – for they claimed the right to appoint to imperial offices at such times as the imperial throne was vacant, and there was no recognized King of the Romans. In other words, Robert was to exercise general suzerainty over vir-

tually the whole peninsula outside the temporal states of
the Church. He was sometimes required to undertake similar
commissions even on papal territory, although his oath to
the Papacy, sworn on his accession, bound him in theory
not to do so. The Popes could find no substitute for the
Angevin King.

Moreover, the Angevins had not abandoned their French
possessions. In the north, their influence began to spread
from their hereditary County of Provence into the mountainous borderlands between France and Italy, where
Charles II (1285–1309) created an Angevin County of
Piedmont. In the early fourteenth century many towns
placed themselves under Angevin protection, vowing their
Signoria or lordship at least for a specific period to the King
or to one of his family – as in 1325 the Florentines voted the
Signoria for a ten-year stretch to Robert's son, Charles,
Duke of Calabria. It was natural that cities where Guelfs
were in the ascendant should turn for military aid and protection to the Guelf chieftains. From 1318 to 1335 Robert
held a protectorate over Genoa, which helped to secure
communications between his own French and Italian
dominions, and kept him in touch with Avignon – to which
(for reasons to be mentioned later) the papal court had now
been transferred.

The Angevin King, then, was much more than the ruler
of the south: but the Kingdom of Sicily was the economic
and military basis of his power, and it is now necessary to
consider some of its salient characteristics, going back some
distance in time in order to explain its foundations.

In theory the King of Sicily was in the mid-thirteenth
century the most nearly absolute monarch in western
Europe. Supreme judicial and administrative authority
was invested to a formidable degree in the King – instead
of being broken into fragments and distributed among city
corporations and feudal lords, as in the Empire or Papal

States. On the other hand, like all states in which authority is over-concentrated in the monarch and over-dependent upon his personal energy and acumen, Sicily was vulnerable to royal minorities and disputes over the succession, in which claimants to the crown might have to win support by granting away some of the state's power – in the form of jurisdiction over the people – to private men, baronial partisans who would treat their jurisdictional rights as a form of hereditary property. Furthermore the King's position, as both autocrat and tributary vassal of the Holy See, was highly ambiguous. None the less it was true that in the south no hydra like the Lombard cities had risen to challenge the King's authority – although in the 1250s and the 1280s Messina, Palermo and other important towns did in spells of unrest proclaim themselves communes and abortively strive to unite under the leadership of the Pope. The comparative continuity of royal government in the south had forestalled the development of the cities into miniature states.

Sicilian monarchy still rested on the foundations laid by the political genius of the Normans in the twelfth century and reconstructed by Frederick II. The first Norman kings had claimed an authority which resembled that of the autocratic Byzantine Emperor, recognizing no formal institutional limitations and no formal obligations to subjects, setting the King in isolated and holy splendour above them. In the words of a famous law of King Roger, 'There must be no dispute about judgements, resolutions or dispositions made by the King; for it is a form of sacrilege to question his judgements and acts or his statutes and resolutions, or to contest the fitness of anyone chosen and appointed by the King.' Since the Norman conquest the land had been divided into crown estate or demesne (which was subject to direct royal government), and into fiefs, lands granted in the expectation of service, which were held by the King's followers. Norman government had been characterized partly by the high proportion of royal demesne to infeudated land, especially on the island of Sicily, and by strict control over fiefs. The Normans had managed to curb some of the strong centrifugal tendencies normally present in feudalism, in that they made many grants of land which did not carry any right of hereditary succession; in that they exacted very onerous military service from their vassals; and in that they kept in their own hands the right to try serious criminal offences.

Frederick II of Staufen had developed the concept of royal autocracy still further, and had shifted the centre of government from the island to the Italian mainland. From 1220 onwards, after the civil wars which tore the Kingdom during his minority, Frederick had embarked on a determined attempt to restore order. He had striven to reconstitute crown estates and destroy private castles, and he had governed through a network of civil servants and of justiciars who were strangers to the provinces they administered. Not being powerful local lords in their own right, they could be expected to be more amenable to the King's control. The Constitutions of Melfi, a law code issued in Frederick's name and incorporating legislation of the Normans, painted an impressive picture of a symmetrical and rationally organized state. They extolled the King as an agent of divine providence for the protection of the Holy Church and the preservation of peace and justice. In theory at least, the royal will was to be the sole source of law, the King the only fount of judicial authority. Prelates, barons and knights must never presume to act as justiciars on their own tenures, but must look to the royal justiciars, and city corporations must not (as in the Italian portions of the Empire) appoint their own officials. Despite any custom which might have developed to the contrary, they were to leave the field entirely clear for the justiciars, chamberlains, bailiffs and judges appointed by the King, from whom all judicial and executive power should flow downwards to be diffused throughout the Kingdom.

The coming of the Angevins in 1266 meant that another race of conquering invaders, mostly Provençal, had now to be assimilated into an already complex, polyglot and multi-racial society. In many respects the Kingdom seemed more closely tied in its cultural and governmental traditions to Greece and north Africa than to northern Italy. The island of Sicily had owed to Arabs and Greeks the introduction of such crops as rice, sugar-cane and cotton, the lemon, the bitter orange, and the mulberry for the culture of silk-worms. Norman kings had borrowed court ceremonial and procedure from Byzantium and dignified their high functionaries with the Greek titles of Catapan, Logothete or Strategos, blending these Mediterranean imports with Norman institutions from northern Europe to form a highly eclectic structure. As late as 1270 municipal decrees on the island of Sicily were published in Latin, Greek, Arabic and Hebrew.

Naturally enough the first Angevin king was determined to insert loyal followers into positions of power, and Provençals became military and naval commanders, judges, diplomats and financial officers. Between 1269 and Charles's death in 1285 only twenty-five out of 125 provincial justiciars appointed in the Kingdom of Sicily were Italians. French became the official language of the government, although Italians were still employed in the royal secretariat and in lesser legal posts, and half the financial officials or treasurers were still Italians. Moreover, after Charles had carried out mass confiscations of land to avenge risings in favour of the Staufen pretender Conradin in 1268, nearly 700 Frenchmen or natives of Provence were endowed with fiefs. As well as confiscated land, crown estate was liberally granted out in fee to reward partisans

and secure control over rebellious communes. 160 enfeoff-
ments were made in the year 1269 alone. There was some
risk of rousing xenophobia on the part of native inhabitants
– especially in the island of Sicily, which seldom saw Charles
of Anjou, and was alienated enough to rise against him in
the prolonged rebellion which began in 1282. But the
Italian south was already accustomed to a long tradition of
invasion and foreign monarchy, and had long been a more
racially varied society than the north or centre. By the time
of King Robert, the French and Provençal nobility was
inter-marrying with the native aristocracy and forming ties
with such families as the Sanseverino, Aquino, Celano and
Ruffo. Provençal high functionaries, including the vice-
chancellor Philippe de Cabassole, Bishop of Cavaillon,
then served beside Neapolitans in the royal administration.

French and Provençal infiltration was certainly not confined to the upper levels of the feudal and administrative
hierarchies, for Charles of Anjou encouraged the immigra-
tion of peasants and artisans to the south as well. In 1273
he sought to encourage 140 Provençal peasant families, with
carpenters, masons and smiths, to settle at Lucera near
Foggia, and to provide some counterweight to the Saracen
military colony which had been implanted there by
Frederick II and might one day prove disconcertingly loyal
to his memory. Even outside the Kingdom the Guelf military
league of Tuscany recruited most of its mercenary cavalry
from France and Provence up to the 1290s – after which
time it began to rely instead on Catalans and native
Italians.

Hence the lay chieftain of the Guelf alliance was a foreign
monarch, half absolute king and half papal vassal, whose
strength was based on the yield of this complex, multi-
racial society. Though advanced politically down the road
towards centralization and rational government, the south
had made less progress economically. In the thirteenth

century the level of development was considerably lower in
the Kingdom of Sicily than in the more highly urbanized
regions of Tuscany and Lombardy. Sicily itself and the
region of Apulia now exported foodstuffs, wines and live-
stock, but not manufactured goods, and the textiles of
Tuscany or the metallurgy of Lombardy had no real
southern counterpart. Land was less intensively used, and
population was less dense: it was about 100 per square mile
in the environs of Naples, and about sixty in Sicily – falling
well short of the 200 per square mile attained during the
thirteenth century in some parts of Tuscany and of the
fertile Lombard plain. Concentration in large towns was also
far less common in the south. In the late thirteenth century,
of twenty-six Italian towns with a population of more than
20,000, only three lay south of Rome. The harbours of the
south were not badly placed geographically, but they served
chiefly to provide bases and transit-stations for the great
mercantile powers of Genoa, Pisa and Venice, and did not
form their own rich native merchant classes.

None the less it was possible for the monarchy to extract
considerable profit from such an economy by the collection
of toll revenue, by the exploitation of royal monopolies, and
by engaging in trade on its own account. Indeed, royal
policy was directed towards strengthening the state rather
than towards enriching individuals, and this meant further-
ing the ambitions of the monarch rather than contributing
to the common weal. Crown estates or royal demesne were
carefully husbanded by well-chosen royal servants, and
crown forests provided timber for the navy. The King took
full advantage of royal rights over the extraction and distribution of pitch, salt and metals. The crown could further
supplement its revenues by hiring state-owned ships to
private persons and by trafficking on its own account in
cotton, linen, silks and spices, which were stocked in the
warehouses of Bari, Barletta, Brindisi and Trani. Charles

continued the policy of promoting the construction of harbours which had already been set in motion by the Staufen,
and adopted many measures generally favourable to commerce: though he did betray a marked tendency to favour
foreign merchants (especially Venetians and Florentines)
at the expense of native enterprise. During the reign of
Robert the royal finances were in a surprisingly healthy
state – as witness the fact that between 1309 and 1330
Robert was able to forestall any increase in his inherited
debts to the Papacy for arrears of tribute, and managed to
clear the backlog altogether between 1330 and 1340. Still
more remarkably, he achieved this feat at the cost of scarcely
any increment in the principal direct taxes of the Kingdom,
which fluctuated very little between 1290 and 1348.

But the story of the Angevins was not only one of competent administration and unbroken success. For their
power was drastically weakened and their attention forcibly
diverted from the affairs of the peninsula by the prolonged
revolt of the island of Sicily, which broke out in 1282. This
frustrated the most far-reaching of Charles's ambitions, for
it was an indirect consequence of his determination to use
the Italian south as a springboard for an attack on the
Byzantine Empire. Here his purpose was to overthrow the
newly established Greek dynasty of Palaeologos and forcibly to reclaim the Christian East for the Latin or 'Catholic'
form of Christianity. In Sicily there was still a Greek population sympathetic to Byzantium, and the people had in
general been alienated by royal absenteeism and by the
King's pursuit of policies largely irrelevant to their particular interests. Moreover, the King of Aragon, the only
power in the western Mediterranean to command the vital
naval resources, was ready to contemplate intervention in
Sicily, and this was to be in a sense a continuation of the
Guelf-Ghibelline struggle. For King Peter of Aragon had
married Constance, daughter of Manfred, and he and his

wife could be seen as the only surviving heirs of the Staufen line and its ambitions. Since the failure of Conradin's expedition, their court had been a haven for refugees exiled from Sicily. Of these the most prominent was Giovanni da Procida, Manfred's former chancellor, who had risen to become chancellor of Aragon and to direct its foreign policy after Peter's accession to the throne in 1276.

It was to the Aragonese that the Sicilians turned after the explosion of the anti-French rebellion of 1282. Known (from the hour of its outbreak) as the Sicilian Vespers, it destroyed Charles's fleet at Messina, plunged the realm into years of civil war, and diverted the Angevin Kings for several future generations into fruitless efforts to recover the island. For all their dislike of the French occupation, the Sicilians were not nationalistic enough to reject the idea· of all foreign rule. Rather, they wanted another patron who would respect their cherished ancient rights more scrupulously than had the Angevin. These were described as the rights and liberties of Good King William's time, for the Sicilians were inclined to look back into a hallowed past rather than forge ahead into a utopian future, and they seem to have seen these rights chiefly in terms of freedom from heavy taxation. For some ninety years the Sicilian question remained open and uncertain, or was settled only temporarily and by uneasy compromise. Eventually, in 1295, the *Infante* Frederick of Aragon was crowned King of Sicily. Although ingenious attempts were subsequently made to arrange marriages between the Angevin and Aragonese families, with provisions for the eventual return of the crown to the Angevins, these reversionary clauses were in practice repudiated, and Aragonese kings continued to reign in Sicily. The Aragonese acquisition of Sardinia in 1324 threatened to ˙transform the western Mediterranean into a Spanish lake; and on the rare occasions on which would-be Emperors did descend into

Italy in the early fourteenth century, the Aragonese were their potential allies against the Angevin and the Guelf.

The revolt which resulted in the political detachment of Sicily from Angevin rule had further consequences to the detriment of royal authority, both on the island and on the mainland. There was a change in the balance of power between the King and the baronage, as a result of the concessions made to win support in Kingdoms riven by factional strife. Hence the foundations of Frederick II's bureaucratic monarchy were shaken, and royal control over fiefs and the administration of justice was loosened.

On the island one of the Aragonese princes, in the late thirteenth century, promised to allow childless barons to bequeath fiefs to collateral branches of their families, and this concession made it far less likely that feudal estates would revert or 'escheat' to the crown as they had formerly done. In other words, they were increasingly treated as private property, and there was a reduction in the proportion of crown estate to infeudated land. On the mainland, during the years 1283 to 1285, concessions were now made whereby the marriage arrangements of feudatories and the practice of giving portions of fiefs as dowries were freed from the regulations which had been imposed upon them by Frederick II of Staufen. At about the same time the duration of baronial military service was reduced, and barons were released from the obligation to serve the King in person or contribute towards his foreign wars. Furthermore, from the time of Frederick of Sicily onwards, the native baronage on the island acquired a monopoly of the office of justiciar, and succeeded in asserting a high degree of control over the towns, most of which had formerly been under the King's direct dominion. In addition to this the jurisdiction once exercised by the state began to slip into the hands of private persons willing to acknowledge only a tenuous obligation to it. On the island, powers of trying criminal cases were granted to senior counts as well as to members of the royal family. In particular, the counties of Modica and Geraci developed into states within a state, and could even strike their own coins.

Towards the close of the thirteenth century, parliaments on the island began to assemble more frequently and to collaborate more closely with the sovereign. They were attended by counts and barons, and also by representatives of the communes. It was the task of the parliament to correct the misconduct of royal officials, and to join with the King in making laws, which the King would then faithfully observe – 'it being most just that the King be bound to observe his own laws'. Frederick of Aragon and Sicily had to promise not to leave the island, declare war or make peace 'without the full knowledge and consent of Sicilians', and parliamentary consent was required for all new taxation.

Some Sicilians were benefiting by the revolt. The baronage was now securing a resident monarchy and manning an increasingly powerful parliament. It was guaranteed some protection against infiltration by foreigners into cherished fields of patronage, and it was enjoying much greater local autonomy. On the other hand, ninety years of intermittent warfare, from 1282 to 1372, were to inflict terrible damage upon the economy, causing extensive peasant migration, driving other peasants into brigandage and allowing irrigation works to fall into decay.

*

Even with his glory tarnished, his authority circumscribed, and his energies periodically drained into unsuccessful attempts to recapture the island, the Angevin King was still the most powerful individual in Italy. He was still the defender of the Church against its enemies and the mainstay of the Guelf alliance, whose strength and weakness were closely related to his position. But what did the name of Guelf mean in other parts of the peninsula?

In general, the labels of Guelf and Ghibelline helped to give a more far-reaching appearance to essentially local rivalries. These were rivalries between, or even within, competing clans and their followers, among urban patricians, guildsmen and landed aristocrats. The rivalries between the Monaldeschi and Filippeschi of Orvieto, the Buondelmonti and Uberti of Florence, the Cancellieri and Panciatichi of Pistoia, or the Torriani and Visconti of Milan: all these local fissures had at one time or another, superimposed upon them, the familiar party names. About 1260 Rolandino (a notary of Padua), writing his history of the March of Treviso, saw it chiefly in terms of a rivalry between families of the local aristocracy which was afterwards sucked into the mainstream of the pan-Italian contest of the Papacy and the Staufen – so that the faction of the da Romano became the 'party of the Empire', and the connection of the Estensi family the 'party of the Church and of the Marquess of Este'.

It would be difficult to establish that there was in general any strong ideological, social or economic content in either 'Guelfism' or 'Ghibellinery'. At least there seems to have been none that transcended local barriers. In a particular place such as Florence, representatives of a specific economic interest (such as banking) might be strongly attracted into the Guelf camp by the need of the Papacy and of the Angevins of Naples for the economic services of Italians who were not natives of their own states. It does seem to be broadly true that, when Frederick II died in 1250 and Ghibelline fortunes flagged, a surprising number of established local city oligarchies found themselves ousted by 'popular' régimes, which ·were probably manned by families of relative newcomers to the towns concerned; true that this situation was partially reversed when Manfred scored his great victory in 1260; and true that with the Angevin triumph of 1266 'popular' régimes tended to return to power, especially in Tuscany. But it cannot simply be inferred from this that Guelfism was plebeian or Ghibellinery aristocratic in character, for there would be disconcerting exceptions to any such rule – in Pisa, for example, the 'popular' régime of the 1250s was Ghibelline, and in Orvieto most of the Guelfs were noblemen. Furthermore local studies of the small Tuscan towns of San Gimignano and Prato have suggested that here the distribution of wealth between Guelfs and Ghibellines (as revealed by tax registers) was approximately even. Hence the struggle in these particular localities can hardly be conceived as one between haves and have-nots or between plutocracy and middle class. In San Gimignano in the late thirteenth century all households were classified by the fisc as either Guelf or Ghibelline, and separate tax-assessments drawn up. The Guelfs accounted for 46·5 per cent of taxable wealth, and the Ghibellines for 53·5 per cent.

Generally, Guelf and Ghibelline affiliations tended to become a matter of habit and tradition. But these terms could briefly assume a literal meaning, even in the fourteenth century, on the rare occasions when an imperial claimant came southwards into Italy. In and after 1310 the traditionally Guelf city of Florence organized massive and far-reaching resistance in Lombardy as well as Tuscany to Henry of Luxemburg, King of the Romans, when he came to seek coronation as Emperor in Rome. But at other times divisions within the Guelf connection itself could well appear more important and urgent, especially in Tuscany at the turn of the thirteenth century. For Tuscany the neighbouring temporal power of the Papacy sometimes appeared to be a more immediate menace than any designs on the part of a German king or of some remote descendant of the Staufen. Related to this confused situation was the notorious split between Black and White Guelfs. In Pistoia this seems to have originated in a division within the Guelf clan of Cancellieri, and in a bitter quarrel between cousins. It was the defeat of the White Guelfs in Florence, on the issue of the extension of papal power over Tuscany, that drove the poet Dante into his long exile from his native city in 1302.

It was in Tuscany, perhaps, that Guelf connections became most highly institutionalized. The triumph of Charles of Anjou in 1266, and the victory for the Church's temporal power implied in the success of its chosen candidate, created a situation in which whole cities became Guelf and persons of genuine or alleged Ghibelline sympathies were exiled or deprived of office. They were frequently driven to take refuge in rival towns, as many expatriate Florentines congregated in Arezzo, there to hatch plans to force their way back to influence and fortune in their native places. By about 1269 Charles of Anjou had built up a Guelf League spanning most of Tuscany and enlisting the support of fifteen communes. Each member of the League contributed a fixed quota to its military forces, consisting partly of civic militiamen and partly of mercenaries (especially cavalry).

Some cities contained very highly organized Guelf parties, whose heads or 'captains' occupied a specific place in the machinery of communal government; there might, indeed, be some risk of the Guelf party developing into an institution which competed with the commune and was imperfectly subordinated to it. To take the famous and comparatively well-documented case of Florence: between 1267 and 1280 the political structure of the commune was founded on party rule and party councils functioned as constitutional organs of the city. After that time the constitution was transformed and came to be based instead

upon guilds or *Arti* – though most of the rich guildsmen
tended to be Guelf, and there was no dramatic break in
political continuity. But towards the middle of the fourteenth century the identification of the Guelf party's leadership with the ruling élite which governed Florence was to
become much less exact. For the Guelf captains were then
to emerge as ultra-conservatives, clinging to the traditional
alliance with the Papacy at a time when many Florentines
had again developed misgivings about the growth of the
Pope's temporal power. Even in the third quarter of the
fourteenth century, the Guelf captains were still to prove
capable of using anti-Ghibelline legislation to proscribe
their political opponents – so that a Ghibelline was no
longer, objectively, a person of imperialist sympathies or
even one whose ancestors had entertained them. Rather he
was, subjectively, one of whom the captains disapproved.
This subjective element, stemming from personal or political
vendetta, was always liable to complicate the terminology
of rivalry in Italy.

Outside Tuscany Guelfism – if it can properly be called
an '-ism' at all – was rather less highly organized: although
the existence of a Guelf network spanning several cities was
demonstrated, for example, in the eagerness of Guelf
chieftains from Lombardy and Emilia to ensure that a Guelf
family, the Estensi, retained the lordship of Ferrara in 1264
and acquired that of Modena in 1289. On the other hand
there were prominent cities, including both Rome and
Venice, which did not commit themselves as a body to the
Guelf or the Ghibelline cause, and did not out of partisanship drive great numbers of their citizens into exile. This
was true even though the dominance of the Venetians in
the Adriatic gave them an important stake in Apulian
ports under Charles's rule, and although he was prepared
to uphold their commercial privileges and to allow them to
pay lower dues than native merchants. Although the

Venetians were prepared to lend naval support to Charles's expedition to the east in the hope of winning further commercial advantages, they were not so deeply involved in the politics of the Italian mainland as to be firmly committed to the Guelf cause or organization.

*

Although the name of Guelf implied papalism, it could be said – without being unduly paradoxical – that not all Popes were Guelf. Not all of them believed in partisan rule, in unbalanced dependence on the Guelf chieftains and unreserved endorsement of their ambitions, or indeed in progressively fostering French influence in Italy.

Admittedly some Popes were very pro-Angevin or pro-French – as was Martin IV, the reigning pontiff at the time of the Sicilian Vespers. As Simon de Brion he had been appointed a cardinal by Urban IV, and was a former chancellor of King Louis IX of France and a personal friend of Charles of Anjou; he had supervised the levy of taxes destined to finance the successful expedition of 1266. Later, in 1294, the college of cardinals, as if determined to experiment with an unworldly pontiff, elected for a brief spell Pietro di Morrone, a hermit from the Abruzzi who became Pope Celestine V. His incompetence as an administrator threatened to reduce the Papacy drastically to the status of a puppet of the Angevins. He went so far as to move the curia to Naples, and most of the dozen cardinals he created were clearly nominations of Charles II of Anjou. It is also true that when the Papacy settled at Avignon in the early fourteenth century the kings in Naples became its landlords as well as its protectors, for from 1290 to 1348 Avignon was a possession of the Angevin kings in their capacity of Counts of Provence, and it was only in 1348 that Pope Clement VI purchased Avignon for the sum of 80,000 florins.

On the other hand certain Popes were by no means eager

to rely too heavily on the Guelf connection. This was especially true in the years 1271 to 1280, when Italian Popes returned to the Holy See. They were anxious to secure some counterweight to the power of Charles in Italy, and to this end they took cautious steps towards reviving the possibility of imperial intervention in northern Italy: balanced by and balancing the Angevin, it would surely be less dangerous. For years imperial power had been paralysed by lack of agreement among the German princes, but Gregory X (1271–6) managed to bring disputes and uncertainties to an end by procuring the election of Count Rudolf of Habsburg as King of the Romans in 1273. This enabled the Pope to claim that the restoration of order in northern Italy was properly the business of Rudolf and not of Charles. As it turned out, the Habsburg proved far readier to renounce claims over Italy than to assert them. But it was the temporal power of the Holy See and not the Angevins that benefited when Nicholas III (1277–80) persuaded Rudolf to recognize the Romagna as part of the Papal States. Nicholas, too, hoped for the establishment of a balance of power between Habsburg and Angevin, and for this purpose envisaged the creation of a border Kingdom of Burgundy and Arles in which both would have had a stake. In particular places the aims of both Popes were pacific. They did not want to back the Guelf factions unreservedly and give free reign to local passions and vendettas, but rather to arbitrate between Guelfs and Ghibellines in the Romagna and Tuscany. They were prepared to make arrangements which would have led to the gradual repatriation of exiled Ghibellines: as witness, for example, the attempts at conciliation made in Florence in 1280 by Cardinal Latino Malabranca, nephew to Nicholas III.

On more than one occasion Pope and Angevin found themselves at variance on questions of religious policy. Both Gregory X and Charles of Anjou were anxious in their

several ways to effect a reunion between the Catholic and
Orthodox Churches, which had been severed by schism for
over 200 years; but Gregory was bent on peaceful reconciliation, whilst Charles became in time committed to the
plans for conquest of the Christian east which were to fold
so disastrously on the outbreak of the Vespers. Even in the
days of Robert and even when Jacques Duèse (an ex-
chancellor of the Kingdom of Sicily) reigned as Pope John
XXII, the relationship between Pope and Angevin was not
entirely a happy one. For Robert, his wife and her brother
strongly sympathized with the Franciscan Spirituals, a
small and rebellious group of rigorists who were breaking
away from the main body of their order and incurring for
their disobedience the enmity and condemnation of the
Holy See. Despite the Pope's hostility the Spirituals continued to enjoy the King's protection, and Robert was
formally received into their order just before he died. It was
partly for their sake that he took precautions to forestall
intervention in the Kingdom after his death by a papal
legate armed with full powers.

Although the Guelf connection undoubtedly existed, even
its heads were not always in harmony. It was a loose
federation based on the qualified mutual support of
politically minded spiritual lords and their largely independent royal vassals; between businessmen conscious of the
services they could export to Pope and Angevin and alert
to the advantages to be gained by collaborating with them;
between innumerable cliques of local politicians who
believed that their own interests could best be furthered,
their personal enemies dismayed, by intermittent alliances
with other partisans supposedly united to uphold the
Angevin King and the Pope's temporal power. Its foundations were in local interest. Without the purchase which
this afforded its programme, such as it was, could have
scant appeal. But the vague sense of traditional loyalties

implied in adhesion to the party of the Guelfs was one of the few bonds capable of giving a certain unity to a large part of the peninsula of Italy in the thirteenth and early fourteenth centuries.

The Withdrawal of Pope and Emperor

3

By the start of the fourteenth century the Papacy was clearly beginning to forfeit some of its traditional character as a universal authority and at the same time to abandon its close identification with Italy and with Rome. To be sure, the maintenance of the temporal power in the Papal States was never a matter of indifference to the Popes, and two very able legates, Bertrand du Poujet (1320–34) and Gil Albornoz (1353–67), were to work to rebuild it after spells of anarchy. But distrust in Tuscany of this policy of consolidation was eventually to further the collapse of the old Guelf entente, and even to contribute to the outbreak of war between Guelf Florence and the Holy See.

At the turn of the century the limitations of the Pope's claims to universal authority were dramatically revealed when the formidable Boniface VIII clashed with the French King, Philip the Fair, who was determined to exclude from his Kingdom all foreign jurisdiction that threatened to compete with and to restrict his own sovereignty. Philip contended that the monarchy automatically had a right to the taxes which had been levied on its behalf upon the French clergy by the authority of Boniface and his predecessors. Not only did Boniface, when he tried to defend the 'immunities' of the French clergy from the normal exercise of the secular power, find himself frustrated by Philip's techniques for robbing papal sanctions of effect within

France: he was also attacked and humiliated on his own territory through the French King's collusion with a rebellious family of Roman barons, the Colonna.

Within the Papal States Boniface was anxious to benefit his own family, the Caetani of Anagni: he employed his relatives both out of natural familial feeling and out of a shrewd sense that they were the people he could most thoroughly trust. He tried to place in their hands a line of castles extending across the province called the Patrimony of St Peter in Tuscany. But the ambitions of the Caetani and the Colonna collided. When war broke out in 1297 the Colonna rebels were defeated and their property confiscated. Exiled members of the clan gathered in Paris and helped to circulate ugly rumours about the Pope, even to cast doubt on the lawfulness of his election and the validity of his acts. Since his predecessor, Celestine V, had taken the unprecedented step of abdicating from the responsibilities of his high office, such doubts could easily be stirred. The climax came in 1303 when Philip's chancellor, Guillaume Nogaret, planned to kidnap the Pope, bear him off to French territory, and there force him to summon a council of the Church which would declare him deposed. Nogaret travelled to Italy to establish liaison, west of Rome, with discontented nobles who were jealous of the Caetani. Then, with the collaboration of Stefano and Sciarra Colonna, he seized the person of the Pope in his native town of Anagni. Within a few days outraged public opinion forced the conspirators to release Boniface, who retired to Rome, to die a few weeks later. But the vengeance of Philip, intended to weaken and discredit the institution of the Papacy through a relentless personal attack upon one of its occupants, pursued Boniface beyond the grave. He was now subjected to an unconcluded posthumous 'trial', for which the libellous manifestoes issued by the Colonna provided excellent material. He was charged with atheism, sodomy, sorcery and heresy – in alleged denial of the immortality of the soul, and in irreverence towards the sacrament of the Mass. By a compromise reached in 1311 Boniface was at last recognized in France as having been lawful Pope, although the evidence against him was never formally refuted.

In the years which followed the Papacy itself and the college of cardinals became heavily gallicized. Boniface's successor, Cardinal Niccolò Boccasini, Pope Benedict XI, proved to be the last Italian Pope for over seventy years. Between 1305 and 1378 all occupants of the Holy See were Frenchmen, some being natives of the continental possessions of the King of England. 113 out of the 134 cardinals appointed between 1309 and 1378 were Frenchmen, and three-quarters of them came from Mediterranean or southern France.

When Benedict XI died, division in the college of cardinals between supporters and opponents of the dead and defamed Boniface resulted in a very prolonged conclave at Perugia, and eventually in the choice of a Gascon churchman who was not a cardinal – for there were no neutral cardinals left. This was Bertrand de Got, Archbishop of Bordeaux, who became Pope Clement V. As a subject of the King of England who had owed his preferment to Boniface but could still be sensitive to pressure from the French and the Colonna, he seemed a good compromise candidate. He and his immediate successors were never to enter Italy, and in 1308 Clement transferred the court to the important town of Avignon. Under the protection of the Angevin kings, it stood on the edge of the Comtat-Venaissin, the only temporal possession of the Papacy north of the Alps.

For some time, however, the move was not regarded as permanent. Only in the 1330s did work begin on the vast buildings specifically designed to house the curia; only in

1339 were the papal archives transferred from Assisi; only in 1348 did the Popes purchase Avignon. The stay in this place could well be justified by its central position in relation to western Christianity. Now that this had expanded into Scandinavia and eastern Europe, and now that Christian civilization no longer centred upon the Mediterranean, Avignon was better placed geographically than was Rome. It also stood on the borders between France and the German Empire. More immediately, there were serious problems in France in which the Popes were eager to have some say, and conditions in central Italy were so turbulent that they could not have returned to Rome in dignity and security. For a time even Bologna seemed a better prospect as a place of residence for the Pope and his court.

None the less the Papacy (acting through its own legates or through Robert of Anjou) kept up an intense interest in Italian affairs and in the pacification of the Papal States. In the days of John XXII the greater part of papal revenue was spent on war in Italy. Between the financial years 1320–21 and 1325–6 the expenditure of the Apostolic Treasury rose from 112,490 florins to 528,857 florins, and in 1325–6 the sum of about 336,000 florins was assigned to the conduct of wars in Lombardy. But to the greatest Italian intellectuals of the fourteenth century, the divorce of the Papacy from Rome was a tragedy. Although his boyhood had been spent in the Comtat-Venaissin and although he had profited by the patronage of the court at Avignon, Petrarch did not tire of urging the Popes to return from this 'Babylon' north of the Alps. For Dante, the mild Clement V became 'a lawless shepherd of uglier deeds' even than the hated Boniface VIII, because he had made the decision to settle at Avignon.

The continued entanglement of the Popes in Italian politics did imply the survival of some form of meaningful

Guelfism, at least till the 1330s and perhaps beyond that time. Some kind of Guelf-Ghibelline polarization was also kept alive by two 'descents' into Italy made by princes who aspired to be Emperors – by Henry of Luxemburg, who was crowned in 1313 as the Emperor Henry VII, and by Ludwig of Bavaria. Despite his prolonged absence the Emperor was still regarded as a valuable source of legal authority, and as having the right to legitimate the *de facto* power of local lords who were on the make in Lombardy and Tuscany. The grant of imperial vicariates could be an advantage to them. Whilst really pursuing their own interests they could pretend to be acting as the Emperor's authorized officers, and this would give a valued air of respectability and legality to their régimes. Since these parvenu lords were prepared to pay for recognition, the sale of vicariates could become a source of considerable financial gain to the Emperor, as well as securing him partisans of moderate reliability. Hence there were strong material incentives for an imperial claimant to make the southward journey. Henry of Luxemburg was influenced partly by the fact that many German barons were bound to perform services and grant financial aid only after he had been crowned in Rome. Ludwig's German resources, parcelled and split between contentious members of his own family, the Wittelsbachs, were all too scanty, and the sale of vicariates in Italy would have been a welcome supplement to his revenue.

Some distinguished thinkers hoped to see the salvation of Italy in the revival of the Empire and in the civil power reasserting its rightful independence of clerical domination. For the exiled Dante, a universal Empire (with its heart in Christian Rome and a German ruler as honorary Roman) would represent the height of civilization and order. In 1307 he had written of Italy as a riderless horse left destitute by the Emperor, and during Henry's Italian years he

campaigned in defence of the Empire. In 1324, soon after
the death of Dante, Marsiglio Mainardini, son of a Paduan
notary, completed his treatise *The Defender of Peace*. For
some time a lecturer in natural philosophy in Paris and so
in a position to read the manifestoes of Philip the Fair's
publicists, he had also served Ghibelline lords in Verona
and Milan. He blamed the Church's fraudulent claims to
temporal power and the Emperor's consequent absence for
the disorder and confusion into which Italy had sunk. He
sought to deny the priesthood all coercive jurisdiction in
this world, arguing that Christ himself had claimed none
and had submitted to the authority of the Roman state: let
priests be content with the position of expert advisers on
spiritual matters, without power to punish those who
ignored or rejected their counsel. Inspired by the teachings
of Aristotle, Marsiglio traced all authority in the Church or
state to the people, not to divine origins, deriving it from
below and not from above. His Paduan background may
well account for some of his republicanism and anticlericalism, and he saw the Emperor as potentially the supreme
moderator in the north Italian Kingdom within which
the small emergent civic republics were contained. When
his authorship of the treatise was discovered in 1326, he was
forced to flee from Paris to the Bavarian court, and he
accompanied Ludwig on his progress to Rome during the
next two years.

In the event neither of the imperialist expeditions, on
which such high hopes were pinned, succeeded in making
any lasting impression on the face of Italy. Henry of
Luxemburg came to Italy without opposition from Clement
V in Avignon, but he did fall foul of the Guelf cities and the
Angevin King. Ludwig was not recognized by the Papacy
and was resolutely opposed by John XXII: embittered
accusations and counter-charges of heresy were exchanged
between the Pope and the imperial claimant.

With every imperial 'descent' into Italy the city communes were liable to have to defend the *de facto* gains they had made by expanding into surrounding country districts or annexing neighbouring towns. Since they could seldom show any title to these acquisitions from the Emperor, who was the ultimate source of lawful authority, they did face the threat of being deprived of them; and they feared that the coming of the Emperor might furnish a legalistic pretext for rebellion on the part of their miniature colonies. Hence, about 1310, the Florentines began a campaign to protect 'our liberty and status and that of the other communes of the Guelf party of the League of Tuscany and our other friends' – and this alliance against Henry spread rapidly eastwards to include Bologna and also certain Lombard cities. Henry began to clash with Robert of Anjou, who was accepting protectorates of towns both in Tuscany and in Piedmont, a region supposed to have been 'pacified' by Henry soon after his first entry into Italy through the pass of Mont Cenis.

Henry was often seen (and, indeed, came to see himself) as the great peacemaker who would restore order and harmony to a country in bitter internal conflict. But to many he seemed to come as the avenging angel who would shepherd exiles back to their native cities and bring confusion and discomfort upon their enemies. In practice he was inevitably suspected of coming not as an impartial peacemaker but as a faction leader, the chief of the Ghibellines. Evidence for this was not far to seek. Soon after his arrival in Piedmont he was restoring Ghibelline exiles at Chieri and Asti, and appointing Ghibellines to serve as imperial vicars. Later he allowed Verona, the most important Ghibelline city of the north, to bar its gates to Guelf exiles. When he began to raise revenue by selling long-term or life-time 'vicariates' to local lords, so that they could reign as his deputies and so make their power seem lawful, it was usually Ghibelline bosses who profited by the arrangement. Furthermore, Henry's efforts at making peace in the cities, however well intentioned, were often utopian and sometimes consisted merely of effecting formal reconciliations between leading factions and rival clans, and paying slight attention to the administrative difficulties created by the return of exiles. Added to these shortcomings was the severe irritation and heavy cost to whichever city he happened to be in, of supporting Henry's peripatetic court and army. This helped to provoke an unsuccessful rebellion which was started by the Guelf clan of Torriani in Milan in 1311, and moved Henry to some unduly harsh measures of repression.

Henry did in the end obtain his coronation in Rome at the hands of cardinals sent by Pope Clement, but his troops had to fight the Angevin garrison in the streets and he had to receive the crown in the basilica of St John Lateran – not in St Peter's itself. The expedition was terminated by the abrupt anticlimax of Henry's death at Pisa in 1313, when he left in turmoil the lands he had come to reduce to order. His most enduring action had been to bolster up the authority of Ghibelline henchmen in Lombardy by the grant of imperial titles. Matteo Visconti in Milan, the Scaligeri in Verona, the Bonacolsi in Mantua – all had received the seal of his approval, and clung to it resolutely in the years to come, although in reality they were not agents of the Emperor but local lords by virtue of their own strength and cunning.

Ludwig of Bavaria fared no better, and commanded far less solid support when he crossed the Alps in 1327. He did enjoy fleeting support from the people of Rome, to whom (as Manfred had done sixty years earlier) he appealed for coronation; and he brashly adopted the old-fashioned expedient of setting up a Pope of his own in Rome, as a counter to his distant opponent, John XXII in Avignon.

He also obtained ephemeral aid from one ruthless oppor-
tunist, Castruccio Castracani, lord of Lucca, military hope
of exiled Ghibellines from Pistoia and Genoa, and scourge
of Guelf Florence. Castruccio was determined to seek the
legitimacy and respectability, the promise of permanence,
that he could only extract from an Emperor. He got his
wish when Ludwig declared him Duke of Lucca, Pistoia
and Volterra, and Standard-Bearer of the Empire. Since
this title would protect him in theory from dismissal, it put
him on a higher plane than those other seigneurs who were
still mere vicars and no more than officers of the Empire.
But Castruccio's loyalty was not deep-seated, and he and
Ludwig began to drift apart; after the new Duke's death
support for Ludwig melted away, he retreated from Italy,
and his antiPope submitted to John XXII.

Indeed, there were signs by the 1330s that the old Guelf-
Ghibelline alignments, always flexible and based upon
local self-interest rather than general principle, were
becoming irrelevant and ceasing to have real meaning. So
were the ancient claims of the universalist, supra-national
powers round which these connections had formed. There
was even a time in the 1330s when Robert of Anjou and the
Papacy found themselves on opposite sides in a suddenly
shifting pattern of alliances. Pope Benedict XII began to
adopt a much less aggressive policy in Italy and to seek
reconciliation with traditionally Ghibelline lords whom his
predecessors had been determined to dislodge. Since the
Pope regarded the imperial throne as vacant and would not
recognize Ludwig, and since in these circumstances he was
also claiming to appoint to imperial offices, a suitable means
of wooing the Visconti of Milan or the Scaligeri of Verona
was for the Pope to grant them vicariates himself. Supra-
national authority was in decline, and although the south
and Sicily retained their traditions of foreign monarchy the
politics of the north and centre were in future years to be

shaped increasingly by the ambitions of the Visconti of Milan – a native Italian dynasty which owed little to foreign support.

The polarization of Italians round the universalist powers of the high Middle Ages was no longer giving real unity or cohesion to the complexities of Italian politics. But fantasies of restoring the world-wide authority of Rome did not expire altogether, even with the retreat of Ludwig of Bavaria. During the 1340s there arose in Rome an antiquarian revolutionary, in the strange figure of Cola di Rienzo, notary and son of an innkeeper, who exploited rumours that his real father was the Emperor Henry VII. He maintained that Rome would succeed in recovering its ancient role as head of the world if it expelled its feuding nöbles and created a just and orderly government. His ideology was based on the so-called *Lex Regia*, by which the Roman people were believed to have conferred authority on the Emperor Vespasian in the first century A.D. This inspired his announcement that the Roman people were about to reaffirm their authority over the Empire and to settle disputes between rival claimants to the supreme dignity of Emperor. He issued manifestoes summoning all Italians to unite in an immense fraternal alliance, for he was ready to extend the privileges of Roman citizenship to all the peoples of Italy and to associate them with his enterprise. Eventually, this tribune of the Roman people announced that power to elect the Emperor was to be transferred from the German college of princes to the Italians. But Cola's fantasies came to nothing, although he achieved some success in his narrower local aims of bringing Roman nobles under stricter control. Toughly opposed by an increasingly suspicious Pope, Cola di Rienzo retreated in the face of threats of banishment, excommunication and trial on charges of heresy. He abdicated in December 1347.

With his antiquarianism and the vivid inspiration he

drew from ruins and inscriptions recalling the splendours of ancient Rome, Cola has appeared to some historians as a herald of the Renaissance. But the dissolution of his dreams may equally well be seen as a token of the passing of the old order in Italy and the decline of the symbolic power of the city of Rome and its people.

The Conquest of Heresy

4

Enmity towards the Church and its official hierarchy did not only take the form of Ghibellinery. The terms 'Ghibelline' and 'heretic' were often treated as almost synonymous, and some prominent supporters of the Empire (including Marsiglio of Padua) were condemned by the Papacy as heretics. But there also existed in northern and central Italy throughout the thirteenth century deeper forms of heresy which aimed at the purification of the Church through the abandonment of its vast wealth and political concerns, and through a return to the poverty and evangelism of Christ and his apostles.

Bishops and parish clergy were in danger of failing to meet the spiritual needs of the Italian people, and the episcopate included many canon lawyers and diplomats, who were often of aristocratic birth and owed their advancement to powerful relatives rather than to piety, theological learning or spiritual vision. Prowess as a warrior did not inevitably entail neglect of a bishop's pastoral duties, and there were certainly clerics of astonishing versatility in the sees of Arezzo and Parma from time to time. But the Church's constant involvement in politics and war was deeply regretted by many observers. In the Po valley the struggle against Frederick II had created an impressive élite of militant prelates which culminated in Gregorio da Montelongo, papal legate in Lombardy from 1239, of whom the chronicler Matthew Paris wrote that 'He used the material sword, but never performed works of mercy, for he neglected prayers and fasting ... and put all his trust in money and plunder.' After mid-century the type still flourished in, for example, Raimondo della Torre, Bishop of Como and afterwards Patriarch of Aquileia, who directed Milan's foreign policy from 1264 to 1277. For fifteen years the Archbishopric of Milan itself became an object of factional struggle between the leading local families of the della Torre and the Visconti, and its rightful claimant had to suffer a long spell of exile. Elsewhere, in central Italy, the coveted status of cathedral city was sometimes used by the Papacy as a means of rewarding loyal towns, whilst rebellious ones found themselves deprived of their bishop: the episcopal dignity was switched between Osimo and Recanati in the March of Ancona on more than one occasion for largely political reasons.

For a brief spell in 1294 the Papacy itself seemed to have been rescued from worldly hands, when Pietro di Morrone, a hermit from the Abruzzi, became Pope Celestine V. But he proved hopelessly ineffective, and within a few months abdicated. Dante was soon to portray his spirit among the great crowd of the futile beyond the gates of hell,

'the shadow of that soul
who, in his cowardice, made the Great Denial'.

His renunciation of the papal office opened the way to a man of more conventional stamp, a canon lawyer of despotic temperament from Anagni in the Papal States. This was Cardinal Benedetto Caetani, Pope Boniface VIII, of whom an Aragonese diplomat remarked: 'The Pope only cares for three things and thence bends all his thoughts: that he should live long, acquire money, and enrich, magnify and exalt his own kin.'

Vividly, in the nineteenth canto of the *Inferno*, Dante saw the punishment of simoniacs, those guilty of selling and making private profit from the things of God, in the eighth circle of hell, where they were buried head downwards in fissures of rock. There he spoke with the shade of the nepotistic Pope Nicholas III, who had been so determined to exploit his tenure of the papal throne for the benefit of the Orsini family, and who in his agony foresaw the coming of Boniface VIII to be buried above him. By the time of Boniface, the mercenary character of the Roman curia was fully established. It charged heavy fees for appointment to bishoprics or abbeys by papal provision, including the so-called *servitia communia*, which were fixed at one-third of the first year's income and compelled the new prelates to borrow extensively and at high rates of interest from papal bankers. Private interviews with the Pope cost large sums, and substantial charges were made for exempting great prelates from the obligation to visit Rome in person at regular intervals. Clerical subsidies were levied throughout western Christendom, not for the purposes of crusading in the Holy Land, but to meet the financial needs of the Roman church and of its Angevin and French allies. Boniface and his defenders held that in this there could be no simony, because all papal financial transactions merely entailed the Pope's resuming control of wealth which was rightfully his.

However, the heresies of medieval Italy were not merely a reaction against corruption and worldliness on the part of the hierarchy. To a certain extent they resulted from a long process of excluding the laity from an effective role in the Catholic Church, and hence from any genuine sense of involvement with it. As the Italian historian Gioacchino Volpe argued, the reforming Papacy of the eleventh century had in some respects encouraged lay participation in the life of the Church; it had not been wholly consistent in its aim of making the Church into a self-governing corporation wholly independent of lay control. Laymen had sometimes

been invited to become judges over the clergy and to withdraw their obedience from married or simoniac priests. A
decree issued in 1059 had declared 'that no one shall hear
Mass said by a priest whom he knows without doubt to be
keeping a mistress or concubine in his house'. Hence the
validity of the sacraments had for a time been made to
depend on the moral quality of the priest offering them –
as judged by his flock. But ecclesiastical policy over the
next century showed more tendency to disenfranchise the
laity, for the newly codified canon law forbade laymen to
bring accusations against bishops or clerics, even if they
were of immoral life, and also declared that 'good and evil
priests are equally capable of offering the body of Christ'.
Laymen ceased to take part in episcopal elections, and these
might, as at Milan, be reserved to a cathedral chapter consisting entirely of noble prebendaries, with frequent election
disputes inviting the Pope's intervention. On the other hand
bodies of laymen could sometimes have a part in elections
at a lower level. They could, as in the diocese of Lucca,
influence the choice of the archpriests who took charge of
big collegiate churches or *pievi* in town and countryside.
But it is uncertain how far such processes could counteract
the tendency towards disenfranchisement.

Unorthodox movements arose whose followers first
dreamed of renewing the existing Church by a return to its
primitive condition with a fresh emphasis on the Bible, but
were later driven by the attitude of the hierarchy to form
break-away sects. Northern Italy formed in the thirteenth
century part of a broader zone which contained many
heretics and stretched from the south of France through
Piedmont and Lombardy to Friuli and the Balkans,
extending southwards on the way into Tuscany, the Papal
States and beyond. Here, in northern and central Italy, the
heresies of the Waldensians and the Cathars mingled with
more distinctively Italian movements like that of the

Umiliati, creating a spectrum of heterodoxy which ranged from puritanical Catholicism to the non-Christian and dualistic creed of the Manichee.

At one extreme, Catharism, derived from the sect of the Bogomils of Bulgaria, of the eleventh and twelfth centuries, was a body of non-Christian belief which postulated a dualism of the spiritual and the material. The spirit was wholly good and derived from God, whilst matter was utterly evil and stemmed from the Devil. Escape from the tyranny of matter was possible only through the rigorous denial of satisfaction to physical needs, and the practice of an asceticism in striking contrast to the laxity of many of the Catholic clergy. Lombard cities, including Cremona and Piacenza, offered shelter to refugees flushed out of the south of France by the crusade launched against its Cathars in the first half of the thirteenth century, and Catharism was to survive in parts of Lombardy and the Piedmontese valleys until the fifteenth century.

On the other hand the creed of the Waldensians did exist within the framework of Christianity. Their founder was Peter Valdes, a merchant of Lyons, whose doctrines were formally condemned by the ecclesiastical Council of Verona in 1184. The Waldensians, who soon spread into Lombardy, claimed to be the only true successors of Christ and the apostles; they held that laymen were fully empowered to administer the sacraments; and they laid heavy stress on the literal observance of the New Testament at the expense of the Old and of the precepts of the Doctors of the Church. Valdes had caused several books of the Bible to be translated into the vernacular. The persecution suffered by the Waldensians caused them to reject the structure, laws and rituals of the official Church, which they regarded as damned from the time Pope Silvester had accepted the Donation of Constantine – a mythical gift of terrestrial power at the hands of the first Christian Emperor. They also swung towards the Cathars, and abandoned all belief in purgatory and in those works of piety which were popularly supposed to speed the soul's passage through purgatory. In the late fourteenth century Waldensians near Turin were accused of holding 'that God did not create or make anything visible; but that this world and all others had been created by the Devil who fell from heaven'. Save in this last belief, the Waldensians, with their biblicism, their evangelism and their rejection of purgatory, anticipated many features of the Protestant Reformation of the sixteenth century: although they developed no fully-fledged doctrine of justification by faith alone, without works.

The Umiliati of Lombardy consisted of men and women determined to lead strict lives, with a rigorous ban on lying and swearing, and a thirst for moralistic rather than dogmatic preaching. It should be the preacher's business to urge men to righteous conduct, rather than to discuss theological niceties. They shared with the Waldensians a fervent belief in the importance of hard work, whether as a means of subduing the flesh or as one of accumulating money to give alms. Hence the Umiliati made a vital contribution to the textile industries of Lombardy, especially as some of them lived in communities, and helped to concentrate cloth production under one roof – making this, in a small way, into a factory rather than a cottage industry. Unlike the Waldensians and Cathars the Umiliati, or some of them, did obtain recognition by the Church. Pope Innocent III, who recognized the need to fight heresy by its own weapons and by allying with puritans and ascetics, formed a brotherhood of the Umiliati, which consisted first of a cloistered order, then of a second lay order of pious men and women living and working in their own segregated communities, and finally of a third order whose members did not live as a community, but led pious lives under supervision. Not all the Umiliati, however, consented to being thus gathered into the fold of respectability, and some preferred to remain outside the law.

In the second half of the thirteenth century other sects of more limited range and more strongly anarchistic tendencies sprang up – in the Pseudo-Apostolici, followers of Gherardo Segarelli of Parma, and in the disciples of Fra Dolcino. The Pseudo-Apostolici spread through Emilia and the Marches, and a hostile chronicler, Friar Salimbene, complained that they were more listened to than the Mendicant Friars, the Church's official evangelists, although they did not hear confessions, help the poor or do any work. Dolcino's movement flourished in mountainous regions, in the Trentino and Valsesia; it recognized no Church and no form of organization, and Dolcino prophesied the rise of a new Emperor, in Frederick III, King of Sicily from 1296 to 1337, who would establish new kings in Italy and put Boniface VIII to death.

Many Italian heretics were artisans – which may equally well have been a cause or a consequence of the importance they attached to manual labour. Humble birth might well mean exclusion from the upper levels of the hierarchy, and the humble were liable to be detached and alienated from the official Church. Their lack of formal education threatened to make the rituals and laws of the Church incomprehensible and seemingly irrelevant. In the mid-thirteenth century an Inquisitor said of the Waldensians or Poor Lombards that 'they live by their work alone, like artisans, and even their doctors are cobblers.' Heretics brought to trial in Piedmont in the fourteenth century were leather-workers, bakers, hosiers, fruiterers, weavers, dyers and inn-keepers. Moreover, by about 1280, even Catharism in Italy was losing its more socially exalted adherents and was found chiefly among butchers, innkeepers, barbers, manual workers, shepherds, wandering artisans and prostitutes. The sect of Dolcino wore a markedly subversive air, since it began to attract run-away peasants, particularly from the estates of the Bishops of Vercelli and Novara. Partly for this reason, the main body of Dolcino's supporters was crushed by a localized crusade, conducted with papal blessing, in 1307.

But heresy would not have proved so tenacious in Italy had support for it been confined to the poor and insignificant. Within the communes, heretics sometimes became pawns in factional struggles – if faction A wished to suppress heresy, faction B defended it, and so on. Heretics certainly had protectors in high places, whether or not these patrons and defenders personally subscribed to their views. The persecution of heretics in Milan by the Inquisition in the mid-thirteenth century drove them out to shelter under the wings of lay lords, who were often the disillusioned vassals of churches and sworn enemies of the clergy: among them were the castellans of Sirmione and Lazise, on the shores of Lake Garda. It was perhaps out of enmity for the communes and Bishops of Vercelli and Novara that the Counts of Biandrate defended the disciples of Dolcino. Many communes, which had only come into existence in the first place by a diminution of episcopal power, proved reluctant to demonstrate their piety by obediently enforcing decrees against heresy.

However, the religious life of Italy in the thirteenth century experienced not only a proto-Reformation but also a largely successful Counter-Reformation which halted the advance of heresy without entirely eliminating it. Innocent III had drawn into the Church not only the Umiliati but also the disciples of Dominic de Guzman and Francis of Assisi, who formed the nuclei of the Dominican and Franciscan orders. In their asceticism and in their cult of poverty they closely resembled the heretics, and helped to disarm criticism of the official Church, which they had joined; they became, not the enemies of Catholicism, but the heralds of orthodoxy, and the heterogeneous Church proved elastic enough to contain both the worldly curia of Rome and the new begging friars.

In the first years of the century Francesco di Pietro Bernardone, son of a merchant of Assisi in Umbria, renounced all the goods of his earthly father, sold his cloth and his horse in the market of Foligno, and went forth to gather a small band of companions and follow the naked Christ in absolute poverty. His story somewhat resembled that of Peter Valdes, and like so many of the heretics the first Franciscans were or became artisans and labourers. They came to be known as a mendicant order, and later generations of friars were to acquire an unsavoury reputation for importunate begging: but at first the friars learnt or carried on trades, did casual agricultural work, helped with olive- and grape-harvests, or took jobs as menial servants. On his travels Brother Giles carried water in the streets of Brindisi and sold baskets in the port of Ancona in exchange for food. Where necessary the friars were prepared to beg their bread, though not to handle money, and this helped them to identify with the poorest, the rejected of the world, even with the lepers to whom this world could offer no hope and whose only physical future lay in squalid suffering. As the first Rule decreed, 'Let the friars be happy to associate with humble and insignificant people, the poor and the weak, the sick, the lepers, and the beggars on the roads . . .'

It was the aim of the Franciscans to supplement and assist the parish clergy in caring for their flocks, and they introduced a new style of preaching and practical Christianity. 'He had not the manner of a preacher, his ways were rather those of conversation; the substance of his discourse bore especially upon the abolition of enmities and the necessity of making peaceful alliances' – thus Tommaso, archdeacon of Spalato, recalling how in his student days he had seen St Francis at Bologna about the year 1220.

But the assimilation of the Franciscans by the ecclesiastical Establishment proved an extremely complicated process which divided the order and at last drove splinter groups of radical Franciscans into the ranks of heresy. After Francis's death in 1226 the order showed signs of departing from his ideals and neglecting the precepts of his Testament, which the Papacy declared in 1230 to be not legally binding upon his disciples. Franciscans were employed in positions of great trust, and delicate missions were confided to them; Leone da Perego, promoted to the see of Milan in 1244, became the first Franciscan bishop in Italy, and many such appointments were to follow. Friars were also used as Inquisitors to hunt down heretics, and by the 1230s mendicants were enjoying spells of almost dictatorial authority in some northern Italian towns, where they amended city statutes, recalled exiles or outlaws, and helped to restore usurped rights of the Church. In such circumstances it was difficult to maintain that degree of humility and simplicity which St Francis had strictly enjoined upon his followers. St Francis, 'God's fool', had distrusted learning partly on the grounds that study interfered with humility and that the student could no longer identify with the illiterate. But his friars were now becoming theologians and setting up houses of study within the precincts of university towns, at Bologna, Padua and Naples. In the days of the Minister-General Bonaventura (1257–74) the work of the friars was no longer manual labour in the world outside the convent – but study, reciting the divine office, collecting alms and domestic chores. Although the friars set out to aid the parish clergy, there were times when they seemed to be obtruding on their preserves (especially by hearing confessions), and it was by no means always easy to keep up amicable relations.

Most seriously, the Franciscans abandoned the strict poverty which had been one of their most essential tenets, and this change of policy became the gravest cause of dissension among them. Their career was much more hazardous than that of the other great mendicant order, the Dominicans. At first the Franciscans had made the most radical attempt on the part of any medieval religious order to renounce all property, all regular income and all forms of worldly wealth and security. It was not enough that individuals should renounce personal possessions: even communities were not to be allowed to hold them. Dominic, on the other hand, seems to have regarded the pursuit of poverty as a means whereby the preacher could win influence over his audience, and not in any way as an end in itself.

When the Franciscans began to devote themselves to theology, they inevitably needed a greater degree of peace and economic certainty; convents had to be built with facilities for study, and they needed books and libraries. The Papacy showed its complicity by introducing legal devices whose effect was to enable the brethren to receive alms in the form of money and to make use of property without incurring the stigma of actually owning it. Indeed, during the 1240s the Pope obligingly declared himself to be the official owner of all Franciscan property, save in cases where the donors of goods presented to the order had expressly reserved rights of ownership therein. To purists, it might well seem that the Franciscans were being permitted on a technicality to sidestep or at least to modify their vows of poverty.

They were now in a position to share the fate of most fashionable religious orders, and gifts and bequests were heaped upon them. Increasingly popular was the arrangement whereby members of the laity could, by leaving some form of wealth to be administered on behalf of the friars by a third party, acquire the coveted privilege of being buried in a Franciscan habit and being prayed for by the friars. Franciscans were sometimes ordered to take over important

city convents whose occupants had been found wanting –
as in Rome about 1250, when they displaced the Benedictines of Santa Maria in Ara Coeli, the church which
crowns the cliff-like flight of steps on the Capitoline hill. A
building boom set in after 1245, and papal grants of indulgences were used to stimulate the generosity of the faithful.
Already the splendid basilica raised at Assisi to house the
body of the promptly canonized Francis appeared to sym-
bolize a departure from the saint's ideals, for he and his
companions had done no more than restore neglected and
abandoned churches or occupy the most remote of her-
mitages. Paradoxically, Chiara, the woman of Assisi who had
founded an order of sisters (the Poor Clares) in imitation of
the friars, could only defend Franciscan ideals by obtaining
for her own convent of San Damiano a special 'privilege of
poverty' – by which it could not, like other houses of Clares,
be forced to accept endowments to guarantee financial
security.

These compromises, the onset of fame and material prosperity, bred great discontent, and raised up among Franciscan ranks a group of rigorists, who were in time to acquire
the names of Spirituals or Fraticelli. They sought to return
to the strict and literal observance of all St Francis's
precepts, and to appeal to his supreme authority against
that of their own superiors and (ultimately) that of the
Papacy. Their defiance of living authority in the name of
the dead founder brought on them persecution and accusations of heresy. A small group of persecuted radicals
appeared in the March of Ancona during the 1270s. After
a few years' respite and even an unwonted spell of official
recognition from the unworldly Pope Celestine V, they
found themselves once more hunted during the pontificate
of Boniface VIII. The radicals derived further inspiration
from the writings of a Provençal, Jean-Pierre Olivi, who
stressed the obligation on all Franciscans – bishops included

– to be moderate in the use of goods. To the orthodox the radicals, quite apart from their disobedience, seemed to be making a fetish out of poverty, indulging in self-righteousness and transforming a means into an ultimate end.

Though outlawed by Boniface, the Spirituals survived well into the fourteenth century and acquired powerful protectors – in Robert of Anjou, in the King of Sicily, in members of the college of cardinals; others took refuge with the imperial claimant Ludwig of Bavaria, and it was from them that he recruited his antiPope, Pietro Rainalucci of Corbara in the Abruzzi, whom he set up against John XXII, the Pope in Avignon and the sternest enemy of Franciscan irregularity. In 1309–12 the Spirituals had managed to achieve some practical success, by persuading Clement V to investigate abuses within the Franciscan order – but extremists then helped to discredit the movement and undo its gains by resorting to premature 'direct action'. Groups of friars in Tuscany chose to secede from the order and deserted their convents in Florence, Arezzo and Siena to occupy neighbouring religious houses. The authoritarian John XXII became their deadliest enemy, and in 1317-18 issued Bulls condemning the so-called Fraticelli – a comprehensive term used to denote friars who formed rival associations outside the parent body. He declared that unity and obedience were far more important than the apostolic poverty which the Franciscans were transforming into an idol. In later years certain movements which strove to return to the ideals of St Francis – the Observants, then the Capuchins – were to achieve respectability and recognition by the highest authority within the Church. But this was denied to the Fraticelli.

Despite this division and despite the compromise of the majority with a wealthy and powerful Church, the Franciscans did with the other mendicants achieve great success in drawing the laity back into active involvement with the

Church: through their sermons, through their inquisitorial activities, and through their own 'third orders' of men and women who undertook to follow a strict rule of life and conduct whilst continuing to live in their own homes. Furthermore, in the second half of the century there was a great increase in the number of lay religious fraternities, many of which met on the premises of mendicant convents.

The prolonged and violent conflicts of the thirteenth century helped to create an atmosphere of uncertainty and distrust in the value of life on earth and an unusually vivid sense of standing on the frontiers of eternity, for which the fraternities strove to prepare. Many people were attracted by the prophecies of the Cistercian Joachim, sometime abbot of the monastery of Curazzo in Calabria and founder of the monastic order of Fiore – especially when these writings were reissued in popularized versions or interpreted over-literally. Joachim divided the whole course of the human past and future into three ages, of which the second was the age of the flesh and the spirit, and the third would be the age of the spirit. Having a flair for mathematical calculations, he estimated that the second age would last for forty-two generations of thirty years from the birth of Christ, and hence would end about 1260. He saw the years 1200 to 1260 as years of great tribulation, which would, however, bring the first signs of a true spiritual understanding of the Old and New Testaments, together with the conversion of the Jews and the reunion of the Latin and Greek Churches. The new age would be marked by the triumph of a new order of spiritual monks over the forces of antiChrist – and the Franciscans, especially their radical Spiritual wing, hastened to identify themselves with the spiritual monks.

As it happened, the year 1260, if it did not inaugurate the age of the spirit, did witness a strange, dramatic and wide-spread religious movement: that of the flagellants. A pious recluse in Perugia, Ranieri Fasani, had for several years in private used a scourge or discipline on himself, as a form of penance and self-mortification. He now inspired a movement in which men walked half-naked through the streets, savagely beating themselves in public. This movement began to spread from Perugia in October 1260, soon after Manfred's partisans triumphed at the battle of Monte Aperti, and it may have been seen as some form of protest against Ghibelline domination of Italy – for Manfred's henchman in Lombardy, the Marquess Pellavicino, instantly recognized it as subversive to his authority. The flagellants spread beyond Perugia into Emilia, the Romagna and Lombardy, and in the new year invaded the Marches of Treviso and crossed the Alps into Germany and France. Some Joachites took the flagellant movements as clear evidence that the age of the spirit was indeed beginning, though it is unlikely that Joachism provided direct inspiration for the movement. This may, instead, have derived from the Franciscan cult of the Passion of Christ, which the flagellants were visualizing and repeating in their own self-imposed bodily sufferings. This was a spontaneous movement of orthodoxy among the laity – 'it originated with the simple, in whose footsteps both learned and ignorant instantly followed' – but bishops and other clergy recognized it to the extent of walking in front of the processions. Although the movement died down in 1261 it left many permanent memorials in the shape of the confraternities of the Disciplinati or Battuti, which were widely established in the peninsula.

Lay fraternities of a religious character had long existed in Italy, but in the second half of the thirteenth century they almost certainly spread much wider, as part of the general process whereby the laity again became more closely identified with the official Church. From the late Middle Ages to the Counter-Reformation of the sixteenth century they remained deeply characteristic of the orthodox religious life of ordinary Italians. They were societies of persons who set out to do, in common, all the things believed to contribute to their salvation, to prepare for death, to maintain communion with the dead in purgatory, and to store up a common fund of merit on which all the brothers or sisters could draw. This fund was accumulated by the clerical members of the fraternity saying Mass or reciting the psalter, by the laity praying and performing ritual acts of devotion such as self-flagellation, and by the general performance of good works – especially acts of charity and almsgiving. The reconciliation of enemies and the composition of feuds had been a striking feature of the movement of 1260 – as a Friulian chronicler wrote, 'all quarrels were settled, even between the lord Patriarch of Aquileia and the Count of Gorizia, and the innocent and blameless did penance together with the guilty.' The fraternities in general continued to attach importance to peacemaking, which was of great social importance in a country so disturbed by factional quarrels and personal vendettas. It had been urged by St Francis himself in his sermons. Moreover, the fraternities sought to preserve morality, contriving their own disciplinary procedures to proscribe such sins as usurious moneylending, blasphemy, lying, adultery, fornication, gambling, drunkenness, slander, idle gossip and keeping lewd company. These and similar preoccupations, already found to some extent in the eleventh-century fraternity of Sant' Appiano in the *contado* of Florence, reappeared in the constitutions of fraternities as widely scattered geographically as the Scuole Grandi of Venice, the fraternity of Sant' Egidio in Florence, or the Neapolitan company of the Disciplinati dei Maddaloni. Some of these brotherhoods acquired considerable wealth and power in their native cities – indeed, the Compagnia della Madonna di Or San Michele of Florence had to be stripped of its property by the government in the mid-fourteenth century in order to restrain its excessive influence. The Venetians inherited from the flagellant movement their fraternities of Disciplinati, the so-called Scuole Grandi dei Battuti. These were successfully contained within the Venetian state, grew into a vital part of the structure of the dominating city, and developed into important mutual aid societies which dispensed alms, almshouses and small marriage portions to their less fortunate members.

Hard by San Pancrazio there used to live, as I have heard tell, a worthy man and wealthy, Puccio di Rinieri by name, who in later life, under an overpowering sense of religion, became a tertiary of the order of St Francis, and was thus known as Fra Puccio. In which spiritual life he was the better able to persevere that his household consisted but of a wife and a maid, and having no need to occupy himself with any craft, he spent no small part of his time at church; where, being a simple soul and slow of wit, he said his paternosters, heard sermons, assisted at the Mass, never missed lauds (when chanted by the seculars), fasted and mortified his flesh; nay – so 'twas whispered – he was of the Flagellants.

Fra Puccio was one of the innumerable deceived husbands who thronged the stories of Boccaccio; no doubt other pious laymen enjoyed better fortune and commanded more respect.

But the thirteenth-century Counter-Reformation did not proceed only through the spontaneous desire of the laity to return into the fold of the official Catholic Church. To some extent it was furthered by terrorism and repression, through the conquest of heresy by the Inquisition. As early as 1184 the ecclesiastical council of Verona had tried to set up an episcopal Inquisition, imposing on bishops the duty of actively seeking out heretics by holding inquiries in particular districts, rather than merely waiting for accusations to be brought by informers. Bishops were empowered to prosecute for heresy on the basis of 'common report' (the general opinion of the locality), as well as on the initiative of an official or private accuser. But the decree was not properly enforced and at a later stage, in the 1220s, the Popes began to issue more effective commissions of their own, drawing on the services of Dominicans and Franciscans to ferret out heresy with the collaboration of local authorities and usually of bishops. The mendicant orders soon became closely identified with the Inquisition, though some Dominicans at any rate regarded it as a hindrance to their proper business of preaching, and their Inquisitors tended to form an élite outside the central framework of the order. At the same time, between 1220 and 1239, the Emperor Frederick II, despite his own personal detachment and his enmity towards the Papacy, issued several savage edicts against heresy (perhaps to discredit charges of heresy against himself), and the Popes took great pains to get these edicts incorporated in the statutes of individual towns.

The new, papally authorized Inquisition sometimes encountered tough local obstructionism from authorities jealous of their own jurisdiction – whether secular, like the Venetian government, or clerical, like the Franciscan Bishop of Treviso, Alberto Ricco, who obstinately resisted the advance of the Franciscan Inquisition into his diocese during the 1260s. But in general the Inquisition cut deeply into the ranks of the heretics: it was no longer restrained by jurisdictional limitations, and could pursue its quarry across the boundaries of bishoprics, provinces and Kingdoms. From the 1260s onwards Cardinal Gian Gaetano Orsini, the future Pope Nicholas III, served as Inquisitor-General, coordinating the work of individual tribunals. In dealing with heresy, which was thought-crime and not a physical offence, the Inquisitors recognized no procedural limitations and none of the rules of evidence normally observed in dealing with common criminals. Torture, prolonged imprisonment and solitary confinement were used to obtain confessions, and the testimony of other heretics was admitted as evidence in trials conducted in secret. The confiscation of the property of heretics furnished a strong material incentive to secular authorities to support and encourage the Inquisition, Charles of Anjou displaying almost indecent eagerness to lay hands on the goods of the suspected and condemned. By the end of the century it was usual, throughout the peninsula, to make a tripartite division of confiscated property, between local authorities, the Inquisition itself and the papal treasury. The Inquisitors certainly proved able to muster lay support for the military operations frequently necessary for exterminating heresy. In the 1270s, for example, Fra Timidio, the Dominican Inquisitor who rose to become Bishop of Verona, secured the cooperation of the city's emergent seigneurs for an attack on Cathar settlements on the southern shores of Lake Garda, from Desenzano through Sirmione to Peschiera.

Violence, however, was not the monopoly of one side, and the Inquisition itself suffered spectacular losses – especially in the Dominican Peter of Verona, who was murdered by heretical conspirators on the road from Como to Milan in 1252. He was canonized by Innocent IV and became known to the world as St Peter Martyr. He and other zealots had organized bodies of lay vigilantes, from the 1230s onwards, for the purpose of defending the Dominicans themselves and of championing the Catholic faith and the liberties of the Church. The most famous of these organizations, which gave the opportunity for lay cooperation with the Inquisition, arose in Bologna in 1261, and bore the name of Ordo Militiae Beatae Verginis. Later, it became better known as the Cavalieri Gaudenti, or Jovial Knights. Its lay members remained in the world, and formed a species of 'third order' rigidly bound to obey its superiors. Members of this body were entitled to bear arms for the defence of the faith, and were encouraged to act as conciliators of factional strife – though, as their loyalties inevitably strayed towards Guelfism, they found it difficult to attain the necessary impartiality. The service of the Papacy must take precedence over any form of local patriotism, and the Gaudenti were therefore forbidden to accept magisterial office or party posts.

The campaigns of Inquisitors and the activities of Catholic militias formed one of the starkest features of the Catholic reaction of the thirteenth century. Less spectacular, but perhaps equally significant, was a recovery of authority on the part of some bishops, making up ground lost through the rise of the communes. Bishops occasionally became governors, *Podestà* or *Capitani*, of their cathedral cities, or else were authorized to nominate these high officials. Bishops, Inquisitors and papal legates were sometimes permitted to revise municipal statutes, and often took the opportunity of inserting anti-heretical legislation and decrees which barred persons suspected of heresy from occupying high office in the town. In Piedmont this happened in some degree at Ivrea, Turin, Asti and Vercelli; in Tuscany at Arezzo, Volterra and Pisa; in Lombardy at Parma, Mantua, Vicenza and Brescia.

An essential prelude to any effective Counter-Reformation was that the bishop should conduct pastoral visitations and establish his rights to exercise authority over the clergy resident within the diocese – for without such local supervision there might be little independent check on the deterioration of monastic discipline or the inefficiency and ignorance of parochial clergy. From Bari in the Kingdom of Sicily to Vercelli in Piedmont, some thirteenth-century bishops did undoubtedly prove capable of conducting pastoral visitations and of contesting with various degrees of success the claims of important monasteries to be exempted by special privilege from their jurisdiction. One central Italian diocese, Città di Castello, seems to have been visited by its bishops with exceptional regularity and thoroughness.

Some bishops, too, were sincere admirers of St Francis and drew strength from his inspiration. Federico Visconti, Archbishop of Pisa, declared with moving pride: 'Truly blessed are those who actually saw the blessed Francis himself, as I did, through God's grace. I saw him, and with my own hand I touched him, in a heavy press of people in the great piazza at Bologna.'

Legend described how Pope Innocent III, before he approved the first Franciscan Rule, had seen in a dream the Lateran palace tottering and upheld by the diminutive figure of Francis. It was a strange paradox that if the Franciscans did uphold the Church they were able to do so only at the cost of what many saw as a betrayal of the founder's ideals, and at the cost of driving some of their number into the ranks of the Church's enemies.

PART TWO

Italian City-States
c.1250–*c*.1350

Introduction

5

Italian history can be presented in a very different perspective from that which we have used so far. It can be viewed in terms of the inner developments of the cities of central and northern Italy: of their relations with each other, with the surrounding country districts they subjected to their rule, and with neighbouring feudal lords. The cities and their changing economic, social and political structures can now be portrayed in the foreground, with the Pope, the Angevin kings and the Emperors as colossi in the middle distance. The interventions of these super-powers may now seem important chiefly for their impact on the course of civic politics, deriving their force and significance chiefly from the eagerness of factions within the towns to invoke their aid in the hope of gaining the advantage in local struggles for power, wealth and prestige. Different themes come to the fore, different forms of conflict – between and within factions and clans, or between established patricians and 'new men', or between government by narrow oligarchies and government on a relatively broad basis. Among the most vital developments is the movement of some communes from corporate and constitutional government to the absolute if precarious seigneury of one man, and the assertion of communal control over turbulent families and rival corporations within the city walls. Between 1257 and 1381 the conflicts of the maritime powers of Venice and Genoa on the sea routes to their eastern markets formed a system of international relations in the Mediterranean world parallel to the contest within the peninsula between the Church and its enemies. Their friends and foes ranged from the lords in Lombardy to the Catalans and the King of Hungary, and the Venetians and Genoese were heavily implicated in the politics of Constantinople. In Tuscany attitudes to the expanding power of Florence helped to polarize opinion in Pisa and Pistoia at least as much as the old Guelf-Ghibelline division. In Pisa the party of the Bergolini were pro-Florentine, whilst their opponents, known as the Raspanti, demanded the imposition of heavy tariffs on Florentine goods.

In Italy the majority of the people did not live in towns, and were engaged in agriculture rather than in industry or commerce: but civilization developed to its highest pitch in the cities, and the cities were the real pacemakers of Italian history, the units which commanded the most intense and articulate loyalty and patriotism. A few pages of introduction, ranging very briefly over past centuries, are needed in order to explain how these dwarf-republics had arisen, and how they had come to occupy so important a place in the many-celled bodies politic of the Empire and the Papal States.

*

Some forty of the most prominent city communes of the north and centre could trace their origins to Roman or pre-Roman foundations. South of the Alps, Roman civilization had exhausted most of the natural possibilities for the formation of cities, and after the year 1000, when population began to grow in Italy as in a large part of Europe, it was usual for established towns to expand rather than for colonists to go forth and create new ones on a large scale. There were significant exceptions to this rule, in Ferrara, or Venice, or Alessandria, which had no Roman origins: but in general it holds good. These Roman administrative centres had become diocesan towns – the seats of bishops, who frequently became the administrative officers of the Holy Roman Emperors of the Middle Ages and in doing so sometimes acquired the powers of counts. When royal authority decayed during the tenth century and Hungarian and Saracen raiders invaded the peninsula, cities and bishops were left to defend themselves and hence to develop the habit of acting independently. Even before the year 1000 the rulers of northern Italy sometimes communicated directly with the inhabitants of episcopal cities, and bestowed privileges on them or officially confirmed their customs without using the bishop as intermediary. This implied that they could exist as a corporation in their own right. It was natural that the bishop should associate prominent local men – worthies, *boni homines*, respectable men of substance and probity – with him in the work of government. This category would include proprietors of lands inside and outside the city, who might well be vassals holding land of the bishop himself, of a local monastery, or of one of the great imperial feudatories in the region. Judges and notaries, businessmen and merchants, might also be found among the *boni homines*. Such men formed the nuclei of the associations – bound together by the swearing of oaths – which became known as 'communes'.

It is natural to connect the idea of the city with merchants and industrialists and with commercial and financial activity, and many cities did undoubtedly enhance their wealth and power through the great economic boom of the high Middle Ages. But even in a city of traders as famous as Genoa, the commune grew up round the so-called 'viscounts', who were vassal tenants of the Marquesses Obertenghi, and round the Bishop's subordinates (who were frequently the same people). These lesser officials and smaller landowners tended to gather within the city walls whilst the Obertenghi dwelt outside them. At a later stage in the development of Genoa, descendants of these lesser men often chose to sell their lands and invest the proceeds in commercial enterprises, though they might afterwards move some of their capital back into land, and reinvest in different estates, so that there was a repeated movement of wealth from land to commerce and vice versa. The same was roughly true of Genoa's greatest rival, for in the twelfth century (as in the ninth) Venetian magnates still owned extensive properties and employed some of their revenues in commercial enterprises in such a way as to establish a balance between trade and land-ownership. As Dr Philip Jones has written:

> The towns, for all their growth in size and economic complexity, retained the character, in varying degrees, of communities of landowners. The urban communes and *universitates*, founded in the eleventh and twelfth centuries, were the creation, not of merchants, but of landlords; many urban immigrants were or became land-holders; and land-ownership was the first ambition of all urban classes.

In Italy there was no sharp line of demarcation to cut off urban from rural history.

From the eleventh century onwards Emperors and Popes in conflict began to appreciate the desirability of winning the support of communes, for they recognized them as a third force capable of acting independently of feudatories and bishops: a new element in the social and political structure which could profitably be courted by the issue of privileges and by the official confirmation of their cherished customs, institutions and property. The urban communes were associations designed for the maintenance of peace, for the defence of the city, and for the promotion of common interests in general. They were also collective lordships, pieced together from the jurisdictional rights exercised by the small lords who formed part of them; they took over judicial and fiscal authority both from their bishops and from the feudatories of the surrounding countryside who gravitated towards them or were forced to join them. Slowly they consolidated their authority within the boundaries of the diocese and county – the *comitatus* or *contado* – in which they stood: though it would be a mistake to see this as a smooth process of expanding outwards from the centre to the periphery of the *contado*. Some quite important communes, indeed, took over their authority not from bishops but from lay counts – as the Tuscan town of Prato originated as the fortress headquarters of the feudal family of Alberti, who were called Counts of Prato in 1103.

In the late eleventh and early twelfth centuries communes in Tuscany, Lombardy, Piedmont and Liguria began to elect their own chief magistrates, who were known as consuls. Consular office could be retained only for limited periods of time, not usually for more than one year at a stretch, and was rotated among a restricted group of leading citizens. These were the chief executives, who might be empowered to negotiate treaties, to lead the city's forces in battle, and to preside over the supreme municipal courts. Effective legislative authority normally rested with councils of moderate size, small enough to be susceptible to oligarchic control – though most cities retained, at the bottom of the pyramid of the politically active, a large and unwieldy popular assembly.

A further constitutional development, common to many cities of the north and centre, occurred about a century after the establishment of colleges of consuls. Ultimately the consuls proved unable to provide the degree of administrative coordination which was vital when the complexity of social relations within the city so greatly increased in the course of the twelfth century. A growing population supplied the town with immigrants, enlarged the market, and stimulated commercial and manufacturing activity. There were several forms of free, sworn association within each

city besides the commune – guilds of merchants; guilds of
artisans; extended groups of noblemen bound together by
ties of kinship and holding property in common; and recent
immigrants to the city who found themselves excluded from
the inner circles of the city's Establishment and began in
consequence to develop a sense of corporate identity. The
commune had to embark on a prolonged struggle to come
to terms with these competing associations and to establish
a degree of supremacy over them. Bodies so large as the
colleges of consuls were divided by personal enmities and
sectional interests, and found it difficult to act in concert.
Hence, in their need for coordination, most cities began to
experiment with a form of limited constitutional monarchy
by creating a single supreme paid executive, known as a
Podestà. Frequently but by no means invariably it was
stipulated that the *Podestà* must be a 'foreigner' – that is
an outsider, from some other city or from somewhere outside the commune's jurisdiction. This was supposed to
ensure that he possessed the necessary impartiality and, since
his term of office was usually limited like that of the consuls
to a period of not more than one year, there seemed to be
little risk that any personal and lasting dictatorship might
be established. Widespread introduction of the foreign
Podestà helped to create a new gentlemanly profession for
men of high social standing in central and northern Italy.
Some cities, including Milan, acquired a reputation for
supplying *Podestà*s to other communes. Milanese *Podestà*s
served in Lombardy, Emilia, the March of Ancona, the
Romagna, and Genoa; between 1200 and 1250 more than
twenty Milanese held the office of *Podestà* in Bologna. Such
exchanges of officials between cities helped to promote a
certain uniformity in their political and constitutional
development.

Confident generalization, attempts to visualize a 'model'
city undergoing all the most broadly characteristic forms

of social and constitutional evolution: these are difficult and fraught with danger. There were always major exceptions to these broad rules, and innumerable variations upon them or differences in the timing of the processes of development. Certainly Venice formed something of a world on its own, and needs separate discussion – especially at this point, because its main constitutional tendency in the twelfth and early thirteenth centuries was to increase corporate control over a monarchical office which had been established for centuries. It was not, like other communes, specially introducing one-man government to coordinate and discipline the city's political life at this late stage.

Venice was not, as were many of the independent communes, a Roman foundation. The barbarian invasions of Italy from the fifth century onwards, and the spread of the Lombard tribesmen across the north Italian mainland, had driven refugees to retreat on to the lagoon islands in the north Adriatic formed by deposits of sand and mud from the rivers Po, Adige, Brenta, Piave and Livenza. Here the city of Venice, an impregnable water fortress, grew up round the island of Rialto from the ninth century. For a long time Venice retained its allegiance to Byzantium, the new Rome in the East, the site of the surviving imperial government; and until soon after 1400 it was to remain essentially an extra-peninsular power. Its ambitions, driven by commercial motives and sometimes realized by its naval forces, led it to expand eastwards down the coastlines of the Adriatic; and it formed no part of the imperial or papal dominions within which other cities of the north and centre were loosely comprised. Even when still subject to Byzantine rule the Venetians had been in the habit of electing Dukes (otherwise Doges) from among their countrymen. Though chosen by the people's vote, these dignitaries not only held their posts for life but also tended to form dynasties which controlled the office for several generations

– the Partecipazio, the Candiano, the Orseolo. But during the twelfth century Venice swung away from autocratic ducal government and towards a form of aristocratic constitutionalism. About 1143 the Venetians established a new council known as the *Consiglio dei Savi*, which was probably the preserve of families whose members had been associated as judges in the Doge's government and were now aspiring to impose more formal limitations on the Doge's authority. In the early thirteenth century the *Consiglio dei Savi* had thirty-five members, and a smaller body of six ducal councillors was also making its appearance. In Venice the end-product (a form of constitutional monarchy subject to control by oligarchic councils) was broadly similar to that in other cities, but the process of arriving at it had been very different; and the Doge, unlike the foreign *Podestà*, was a native of the city, holding office for life.

On the mainland the cities existed in a highly competitive environment. They fought against the country lords, against each other, and at times even against the Emperors themselves, and the motives and consequences of these struggles must now briefly be examined.

The expansion of the cities into the surrounding *contado* inevitably brought them into collision with feudal lords – though some counts, including the Alberti of Prato, were happy enough to see a prosperous market town developing within their fortress and to increase their own revenue from tolls and market-dues. On overcoming a feudal lord, the cities would often cause him to swear allegiance to the commune, or – as at Florence – to the cathedral church and its patron saint. In 1168 when Count Ranieri of Montorio swore allegiance to the commune of Orvieto he promised to submit his lands to the commune, to declare war and make peace at the commune's request (save against Pope or Emperor or his own tenants), and to reside in Orvieto for part of the year. The communes quite frequently saw the solution in the urbanization of the nobility – though there were exceptions to this, and the Romans and the people of Anagni and Tivoli showed more anxiety to drive out the turbulent nobles who had settled in their midst, transforming the classical ruins of Rome into stout baronial fortresses.

On the one hand it was possible for a German visitor to Lombardy, Otto of Freising, to form the impression as early as the middle of the twelfth century that 'it is almost impossible to find any noble or magnate, in the whole of so wide an area, who does not obey the orders of his city.' On the other, the struggle in some regions was very prolonged indeed, and the people of Siena were still in conflict with the powerful family of Aldobrandeschi in the course of the fourteenth century. In Piedmont and Friuli the feudatories rather than the cities were still dominant, and such potentates as the Marquesses of Monferrato and the Counts of Biandrate did not choose to dwell in any of the surrounding cities. In Friuli one of the principal gateways to Italy was still controlled by a great ecclesiastical lord, the Patriarch of Aquileia, and he was to retain his extensive temporal power until the early fifteenth century.

Certainly there was no straightforward triumph of the progressive forces of urbanization over those of feudalism and reaction. Noblemen were able to carry on their rivalries and vendettas within the towns, and several generations had to pass before the commune was effective enough to impose discipline on its most turbulent families. Even in Florence they built tall towers as symbols of feudal dominion and as strongholds into which their allies and henchmen could retreat during factional strife. At Pisa the Gherardesca, a family of counts, and the Visconti (who, as their name suggests, were viscounts) discovered a new outlet for their rivalry in the shape of competition for municipal office. Furthermore, the interpenetration of the city and the

contado could result, not in the cities bringing the feudatories
to heel, but in feudal landlords with armed vassal followings
setting up authoritarian régimes in the cities. This was
especially liable to occur in the Romagna, which was
primarily dependent on agriculture and did not lie in the
main path of the medieval commercial boom or possess any
vigorous socio-economic group of merchants or manufacturers. Seigneurial government was to become increasingly
common by the late thirteenth and early fourteenth centuries. Even in the more highly developed regions of
Lombardy and Tuscany the condition of almost perpetual
warfare in which the cities lived compelled them to rely
on feudal captains to raise mercenary troops to supplement
the civic militias. By the second half of the thirteenth century these still powerful lords were being invited to assume
quasi-dictatorial powers for limited periods of time over
cities as proud as Milan.

The towns contributed in another sense to the remoulding
of rural society and the break-up of feudalism – though
here again they did compromise with it for a time. One
of the most important processes in the social and economic history of Italy was the disintegration in north and
centre of the large manorial estates, whose serf tenants had
been bound to render their lords labour services and had
been subject to their jurisdiction. On the manor the relationship of tenant to lord and of farmer to farmworker was
not a purely economic one, and not based primarily on
payments in money or kind or on rents and leases. Between
the ninth and the late thirteenth centuries many of the
great manorial estates were broken down into smaller units
– although the Church, at least in Tuscany, continued to
amass land, and its gains did include some manorial rights
over serfs. Within the towns' range of influence, landlords
had many incentives to do away with the cumbersome
system of labour services, and to exchange these for cash

payments. In so far as urban markets functioned by means of cash sales rather than by barter transactions, the inducement to get hold of money became greater. As the great lords leased their estates, landholders with middle-sized tenures came into existence, and fewer peasants were serfs. Instead they tended to become sharecroppers, and to make over to their lords a half-share or a still higher proportion of the yield of certain crops specified in their tenancy agreements. Alternatively they paid fixed rents in money or in the form of produce. By the late twelfth century, for example, the feudal tenure had completely disappeared from the area of La Bassa to the south of Milan, and most of the lands there were held 'in the manner of leaseholders or proprietors'.

It was proverbial that in most parts of Europe 'town air made free', and that peasants who migrated from country to city could expect to shed servile status after a certain period of time. On the one hand the Italian communes were anxious to undermine the powers of feudal lords in the *contado*, and one means of so doing was to eliminate their jurisdiction over peasants, which competed with the commune's own jurisdiction. To some extent the communes were anxious by attracting immigrants to secure a cheap labour force and increase their own military strength – though they were more eager to attract people who might be able to build houses and pay substantial taxes, than to absorb landless refugees. Since the communes were bodies of landowners they entertained mixed feelings about the emancipation of serfs through migration to towns. None the less during the thirteenth century such cities as Bologna, Assisi, Vercelli and Florence did take steps to free serfs in the areas subject to their jurisdiction. In the more advanced regions of Tuscany, manors and serfs had virtually been eliminated by 1300. It would, however, be a mistake to attribute this state of affairs entirely to the pressure applied by the cities – for even in Tuscany the lords had chosen quite freely to emancipate many peasants, both individually and in groups, and had sometimes done so in return for cash payments which enabled the lords to purchase more land.

Among the cities war was not so much an extraordinary event as a chronic condition or a seasonal occurrence, and one of the most formidable symbols of local patriotism was the ox-drawn waggon, known as the *carroccio*, which served as a battle standard. Cities struggled, not only against feudatories, but also against each other – sometimes with feudal support. Boundary disputes were sure to arise when neighbouring cities expanded into the countryside. To further their own economic ends the most ambitious cities such as Genoa, Pisa and Venice fought naval campaigns for islands and colonial outposts abroad. On land, cities struggled for access to communications: to the great rivers of the Po and Arno, the Alpine passes, the pilgrim highway called the Via Francigena which ran southwards from France to Rome. In Tuscany the cities of Florence, Pisa, Lucca and Siena entered into fierce competition; in the Adriatic the Venetians were involved in a centuries-long rivalry with Ferrara, in consequence of their determination to control traffic up the Po, which gave them access to the interior of northern Italy. Already in the first half of the twelfth century Milan was beginning to absorb other cities into its dominion and taking Como to secure the route to the Alps, Lodi to obtain access to the Po.

Periodically, too, the communes became embroiled in war with the imperial government: especially when the Staufen attempted to make their power in Italy a reality, and to reassert crown prerogatives. The Popes saw the possibility of finding in the communes allies capable of helping them to contain imperial ambition, though some pontiffs were much more conciliatory than others. There was no

question of all the cities forming a solid phalanx against
the Emperor, for their internecine rivalries were too intense,
and he was always able to play upon them and divide the
opposition. Nor did the cities seek to break loose from the
framework of imperial government entirely: what they
wanted most was a high degree of autonomy within it,
whilst at the same time they recognized the Emperor as the
ultimate source of legal authority. When the Emperor
Frederick I of Staufen negotiated with them in 1183, he was
not compelled to acknowledge that the cities were his
equals, or to conclude a bilateral treaty with them – he
could still regard them as formerly rebellious but fundamentally loyal subjects, who could now be forgiven. Nevertheless the communes achieved great things: they inflicted
a major defeat on German troops at Legnano in 1176, and
this went unavenged for sixty years; they also obtained
some recognition of their right to form leagues in defence
of their privileges – though the Emperor Frederick II was
certainly not inclined to let such claims go unchallenged.
The prolonged absence of Emperors from Italy after 1250
was to help the communes to extend their *de facto* power and
independence. However, as the story of Henry VII's
descent has shown, there were still many opportunists in
the early fourteenth century eager to profit by the Emperor's
authority to cloak with legitimacy gains achieved by no
title other than force and cunning.

In many respects the city and its *contado* had become the
most vital and the most viable units of government in
northern and central Italy by the middle of the thirteenth
century. The power of Pope and Emperor often seems like
a flimsy superstructure erected upon the shifting foundations of urban partisanship. To describe the cities as having
triumphed over feudalism would be an exaggeration; in the
realms of theory, it would still take some time for the idea
of the small corporate republican state to challenge the

traditional notion of an all-embracing hierarchical society which culminated in the supreme authority of Pope and Emperor. But the cities had become a largely independent social and political force which could not be ignored or subdued. Their development after 1250 will now be analysed.

Urban   6
Economies

The range of influence and the economic foundations of cities in northern and central Italy varied enormously. At one end of the scale were small country towns like those of the Romagna, whose economic life revolved round the markets in corn, meat and fish where local produce from the *contado* was sold. Here, most of the inhabitants were peasants and labourers who went out into the countryside to work during the day and returned within the walls at night. At the other extreme were the great maritime and inland cities – Venice, Genoa, Pisa and Florence, which possessed elaborate networks of colonies and business connections or shipping lines extending from the Black Sea throughout the Mediterranean to the northern markets of Bruges and London. Somewhere between these two poles were such medium-sized towns as Padua, whose ruling élite consisted not of merchant potentates but of urbanized landowners and part-time moneylenders. Padua lived chiefly by the exploitation of a fertile *contado* within a radius of one day's journey from the city centre. The wealth of Milan, outstripped in the sphere of international commerce and banking by the Tuscans, derived from its capacity to distribute goods and supply services across a region much vaster than its own *contado*. It also stemmed from the city's high industrial potential, particularly in the metallurgical industries and to some extent in fustians and woollen cloth. Rome itself, and other cities in the Papal States (for the Papacy did not reside continuously in Rome), depended for their prosperity on the presence of a court, which attracted litigants and spent revenues collected from within a huge area of Europe. Even the comparatively small Tuscan city of San Gimignano could send far afield into the Mediterranean countries merchants who dreamed of making a fortune abroad and returning in triumph to make a figure in their home town. For San Gimignano happened to possess lucrative supplies of saffron, a crop extensively used in cooking, dyeing and medicine, and hence widely sought after.

The coastal cities – first Venice, then Genoa and Pisa – rose swiftly to prominence when international commerce was redeveloped on a much greater scale after the year 1000. Even during the Dark Ages the Venetians had maintained trading connections between western Europe and the Byzantine Empire. The rise of Genoa and Pisa was associated with their counter-offensive against the Muslims. This gathered impetus during the eleventh century and antedated the Crusades, to which all the great maritime powers came to supply transport and naval assistance.

Venice and Genoa differed from Pisa in that their lack of natural resources forced them to concentrate more exclusively on maritime trade and expansion seawards. Genoa was compressed in a natural amphitheatre between the Apennines and her excellent deep-sea harbour, and failed to develop her own hinterland or acquire a large territorial state. The only natural resources of the Venetian lagoons were salt and fish, and the island settlers were forced into commerce in order to guarantee adequate supplies of victuals from abroad. Trade in salt and grain remained vital to the Venetian economy even in the thirteenth and fourteenth centuries, when it was outshone by the more spectacular and distinctive commerce in oriental goods and western metals and manufactures. Thirteenth-century Pisa, on the other hand, possessed both an exploitable *contado* and the islands of Sardinia and Elba, which could guarantee supplies of industrial raw materials. Hence Pisa was more equably poised between land and sea than was either Venice or Genoa, and could industrialize more fully. Indeed, the Pisans began in the mid-thirteenth century to retreat from the Levant in the face of Venetian and Genoese competition. They began to concentrate their trade in Sardinia and Africa, and later to move in the direction of southern France and Catalonia, using overseas trade chiefly as a means of supplementing the wealth of their mainland territory. In 1284 they were defeated by the Genoese at sea in the battle of Meloria, and forty years later lost Sardinia to the expanding naval power of the King of Aragon. Hence, Pisa declined to the status of a large regional port which served Tuscany and traded only in the west Mediterranean, no longer ranging as widely as Genoa or Venice with their outposts in the Levant and Black Sea and their penetration into the Atlantic.

Commercial privileges won by the Venetians from the Byzantine government in the tenth and eleventh centuries were a first step towards the economic conquest of the Levant by Italian merchants. Later, all three of the great maritime powers enjoyed the opportunity of establishing self-contained and self-governing mercantile colonies in the newly established crusader states of the Levant. In 1204 came the conquest of the Greek Empire of Constantinople by the armies which had joined the Fourth Crusade, abetted by the Venetian fleet under Doge Enrico Dandolo. Italians did not fail to profit from the eastward advance of Catholic or 'Latin' Christendom, and to extract commercial advantage from its triumphs. The Fourth Crusade enabled western merchants to penetrate in person into the Black Sea and beyond, instead of having to depend on subjects of the Byzantine Empire to bring goods to them in Constantinople, Asia Minor and elsewhere in the Middle East. Further

advances into Asia were strongly encouraged by the conquest and unification of Asia and southern Russia by Mongolian Khans prepared to be friendly towards Italian
merchants. Middlemen were eliminated, direct contacts
established, and the horizons of Italian traders vastly
extended.

Imports from the east included spices, especially pepper,
which was vital to the preservation as well as to the flavouring
of food; luxury fabrics and raw silk; dyestuffs and alum, a
speciality of Genoa; drugs, slaves, fruit and wine. Egypt
and the Black Sea supplied the Venetians with victuals, as
well as with precious commodities for resale in northern
Italy and in Europe north of the Alps. Naturally east-west
trade was stimulated by the development of manufacturing
in the west, especially in Flanders and Artois, and Flemish
woollens, often purchased at the fairs of Champagne, supplemented the timber, metals and African gold exported
from Italy to the east. Italian cities – Genoa, Lucca and
especially Florence – began to use oriental dyestuffs for the
purpose of improving or 'refinishing' cloth from Flanders,
even before the Italians developed large-scale woollen
industries of their own in the second half of the thirteenth
century. In the fourteenth century, cotton became an
increasingly valuable import from the Levant, and the
Venetians organized special fleets to convey it from Cyprus
and Cilicia, aiming it at the manufacturing towns of Lombardy and Germany.

Venice and Genoa established populous merchant
colonies in the Levant and Black Sea. Indeed, the Venetians
theoretically acquired dominion over three-eighths of the
dismembered Byzantine Empire and settled the island of
Crete after the Fourth Crusade. They also attracted to
themselves colonies of foreign merchants, who brought
goods to their harbours to be shipped abroad and carried
merchandise away along the main overland routes into

northern Italy, France, Germany, Switzerland and central
Europe. The Venetians, though not themselves personally
involved to any great extent in the transport of goods
beyond the Alps, were determined to exploit to their own
advantage the trade routes which they straddled at the
head of the Adriatic. 'Germans' – a generic term which
included Bohemians and Hungarians as well as natives of
Germany and Austria – could bring their wares to Venice,
but were forced to sell them there, and they could be shipped
abroad only by Venetian citizens or on Venetian ships.
Venetian citizenship could only be acquired after a long
period of residence. It was also a cardinal principle of
Venetian commercial policy, asserted through naval command of the Adriatic, that all goods arriving by sea and
destined for the east Lombard hinterland must be brought
to Venice and sent on from there – a contention which
caused bitter conflict with neighbouring towns, and
especially with Ferrara, Padua and Treviso.

On the other hand, the development of Genoa did contribute to the prosperity of inland towns whose citizens
worked in collaboration with the Genoese. Men of Asti,
Chieri and Novara used their knowledge of the Alpine passes
to become commercial intermediaries between Genoa,
northern Italy and the fairs of Champagne. Merchants of
Piacenza, in particular, bought textiles from the Champagne fairs to sell in Genoa and elsewhere in Lombardy.
They also handled some Genoese financial operations,
helping them (for example) to secure repayment of a loan
to Louis IX of France in 1254 by cashing promissory notes
drawn on the Paris treasury. Milan, which overtook Piacenza in the mid-thirteenth century, was also a major distributor of goods imported and exported via Genoa, serving
Lombardy, Piedmont and the Po valley. Its anxiety to
secure access to such Alpine passes as the Splügen and St
Gotthard suggests that it must have had substantial trade

with Switzerland and Germany. Indeed, the importance of Genoa to the Milanese economy eventually provoked the expanding state to embark on the direct conquest of the city, which passed briefly under Milanese lordship from 1353 to 1356 – for it lacked the stable government and the natural defences which made Venice impregnable.

But towards the end of the thirteenth century, the Genoese ceased to rely so heavily on overland routes and on alien merchants in order to communicate with north-western Europe. They chose, instead, to organize their own regular sailings beyond Gibraltar and across the Bay of Biscay to Bruges and Southampton, for they were beginning to specialize in cheap and bulky products, such as grain, salt, wines, oil, soap and especially alum, which would not support the comparatively high costs of overland transport and still leave a reasonable margin for profit. Regular voyages to Flanders began as early as 1278, and in this the Genoese ran far ahead of the Venetians, who followed them some forty years afterwards. In the late fourteenth century the Genoese took a still bolder step by abandoning the relatively small, heavily armed galleys in favour of much larger merchant ships or 'cogs', whose carrying capacity was vastly greater and which could travel much longer distances without putting into harbour.

The Venetians, Genoese and Pisans certainly owed much of their prosperity to the development of a form of commercial contract or partnership, known as the *commenda* or *colleganza*, which enabled a large part of the population to engage in trade, whether as active or as sleeping partners. An inactive partner, or *socius stans*, could put up all or some of the capital for a commercial enterprise, and a merchant would then make use of it and the profits would be divided in determinate proportions after the voyage. This could enable rich proprietors like the Venetian Ziani, who had invested heavily in land and real estate, to amplify their fortunes through indirect participation in trade. It could also afford plenty of opportunities for small investors, since some merchants were prepared to accumulate their capital from small contributors and arm themselves with more than ten such contracts before putting forth. Similar contracts may have enabled the lords of Genoa to employ in commercial activity the proceeds of plundering expeditions against the Muslims and so contribute to their own enrichment and the city's economic expansion. There was no rigid division into categories of 'sleeping partners' and 'active merchants', since the same man might be the sleeping partner in one contract and the active partner in another – but these arrangements did, for example, enable Venetian nobles with heavy political and administrative commitments at home to continue to invest in commerce abroad. Other forms of partnership included the sea-loan, and the loan '*ad negotiandum*' for business activity in general which was not confined to maritime commerce.

In the thirteenth and fourteenth centuries Genoese enterprises were usually more individualistic than Venetian, which were often conducted under closer state supervision. The Venetians organized many state-controlled convoys or *mude* of armed merchant galleys to Constantinople, Cyprus, Cilicia and Alexandria in the east; and, in the west, to Flanders and England, Aigues-Mortes in the south of France, and the north African coast. The state supplied the galleys, which it auctioned for the duration of the enterprise to individual patricians, and regulated the voyage. The greater part of Venetian trade, in bulk cargoes such as grain, salt, wine or sugar, was carried on by free navigation. But the galleys enjoyed a monopoly of certain precious goods such as spices, perfumes, dyestuffs, drugs, silk and jewels, and of the exports and specie necessary to pay for them. Wealth was distributed fairly evenly among the Venetian ruling class, which proved at the fiscal survey of

1379–1380 to include only a small number of outstandingly rich men. Venetian control over colonies was comparatively tight. Separatist tendencies on the part of the great Venetian colony at Constantinople were successfully put down in the early thirteenth century, and control from the mother country firmly established – though Venice did later have to contend with a serious revolt of her Cretan colonists in the 1360s.

By contrast, the community sense of the Genoese was less highly developed – the first crusading squadrons had been raised by private entrepreneurs, and the family of Embriaco had organized the Genoese trading colonies in Syria. The great figures in Genoese history were individualists rather than representatives of the state; among them was Benedetto Zaccaria, a merchant and naval contractor of the second half of the thirteenth century, who was rewarded for his services with great fiefs (including Phocaea in Asia Minor, the main source of Genoese alum) by the Emperor Michael Palaeologos and by the King of Castile. In the fourteenth century Genoa was torn by Guelf-Ghibelline divisions of a depth unknown in Venice, and this caused many Genoese to live abroad – some took service with the Kings of France and England, others retreated to such near-by towns as Monaco to watch for the opportunity to return, and others migrated to the colonies of the Levant and Black Sea, which, as the havens of exiles, inclined to independence. Some of these colonies were, in the fourteenth century, handling a volume of trade which yielded nearly as much customs revenue as Genoa itself: the trade of Pera, the Genoese suburb of Constantinople, yielded 1·6 million Genoese pounds in 1334, whereas trade through Genoa itself yielded only 1·8 million pounds in the same year.

By contrast with Venice and Genoa, the inland cities of Tuscany and Lombardy were pioneers in the development of merchant-banking, international finance and industry,

and in the organization of businesses based on long-term
family partnerships with permanent branches in foreign
cities. Merchants of Piacenza, as a result of frequent jour-
neys to the fairs in Champagne, established permanent
branches in Paris in the late thirteenth century. Florentines,
dealing in a wide variety of products – victuals and wines,
cloth, weapons and metals – accumulated capital which
equipped them to engage in banking activities. The capital
of the great Florentine concerns was derived partly from the
sums invested by partners in the firm, and partly from
deposits. These they were able to attract by paying interest
at rates of between 6 and 10 per cent, giving a higher return
than investment in real property, and they could in turn
invest the capital in the acquisition of merchandise or in
loans to other persons at higher rates of interest. Holding
accounts in all the principal European currencies and
maintaining branches abroad, they were able to transfer
money from one place to another on behalf of clients without
the actual transport of cash, and to charge commissions, of
perhaps 1 to 5 per cent, for these operations. Family capital
was augmented by the admission of outsiders to partnership
in the firm. The inland cities led the way in the important
process whereby, especially between about 1275 and 1325,
merchants ceased to accompany their goods or to attend
fairs, and became 'sedentary' businessmen rather than
travelling adventurers. The development of insurance
permitted the transport of merchandise without constant
surveillance from its owner, and the establishment of permanent branches in Paris, Bruges or London enabled
'sedentary' merchants to direct operations by correspondence from their home bases. Admittedly their staffs of
clerks or 'factors' were very small by modern standards, but
the geographical range of their operations could be impres-
sively wide. Within the peninsula, all the great Florentine
firms were represented in the centres of Barletta, Bologna,

Genoa, Naples, Perugia and Venice, and beyond the Alps they maintained branches in Avignon, Bruges, London and Paris. Lesser centres outside Italy, where some but not all of the companies were represented, included Barcelona, Majorca and Seville, Tunis, and to the east the Morea, Famagusta and Rhodes. In 1336 the Peruzzi company (then the second largest Florentine firm) had eighty to ninety-five factors in its employment; the Acciaiuoli employed forty-two factors in the sixteen branches they maintained outside Florence.

During the thirteenth century Tuscan bankers were venturing into the field of royal finance, lending large sums to princes (sometimes in return for commercial concessions rather than for interest payments) and handling the collection and transfer of papal revenues. Tuscan finance was the economic mainstay of the Guelf alliance, and the Florentines moved into first place at the courts of the Pope and the Angevin after the bankruptcies of the Bonsignori of Siena in 1298, of the Ricciardi of Lucca in 1300, and of the Ammanati and Chiarenti of Pistoia. The Kings of England did not pay interest on loans, but were prepared to exempt merchant bankers from the obligation to pay duties on the wool which they exported from the country, and to free them from imposts on their goods within the Kingdom. The Angevins pledged revenues as security to Florentine companies, and allowed them to export cereals freely. However, lending to princes was a risky undertaking, for the bankers disposed of no sanctions which could force a king to honour his obligations, and they were in some danger of being expropriated or otherwise persecuted in a country which had decided to dispense with their services. In the 1290s two Tuscans of the firm of Franzesi, known as Biche (for Albizzo) and Mouche (for Musciatto), were bankers to Philip the Fair of France: for him they floated loans or provided them from their own resources, and they acted as

receivers-general and for a time treasurers of the King. But
Philip, distrustful of international organizations that could
not be subjected to his full authority, came to treat the
Italian bankers as he had treated the Italian Pope Boniface:
from 1305 he was in no way dependent on Italian financiers
and in 1311 he ordered a general seizure of Italian goods
and repudiation of debts. A generation later Edward III of
England repudiated debts to the tune of 800,000 florins
owed to the Peruzzi and Bardi of Florence, and so contributed heavily to the bankruptcy which overtook them in
the early 1340s.

Moneylending in Italy, above the level of mere pawn-
broking, was by no means confined to the merchant bankers
of Tuscany and elsewhere. In small or medium-sized towns,
such as San Gimignano and Padua, the profits of moneylending supplemented gains made from agriculture, trade
and other economic activities. In San Gimignano high
interest rates were augmented by the penalties exacted if
the principal was not promptly repaid, and by the possibility of taking possession of the debtor's property and
enjoying its revenues. The official ceiling might be fixed at
20 per cent, but it was in practice possible to place capital
at 30 per cent. Religious corporations and ecclesiastical
authorities, including the local Bishop of Volterra, frequently involved in war and embarrassed by heavy papal
and imperial taxation, were prepared to borrow heavily at
high rates of interest, and to contract loans they would
surely be unable to repay. Rich Paduans, likewise, made
extensive loans to individual persons and to communes,
especially to their own subject town of Vicenza: their personal loans were for the purpose of consumption or were
designed to help others with purchases of land, rather than
to finance commerce or manufacturing. The Venetians, not
themselves great moneylenders, sometimes drew on the
services of lenders from the mainland, and the Paduan

usurer, Enrico da Scrovegni, eventually took Venetian citizenship.

The mercantile-banking activities of Tuscans and Lombards drew them, naturally enough, into the development of high quality textile industries producing for the export-market. There was a strong incentive to encourage home manufacturing to pay for the goods they imported from abroad, and their commercial and financial operations afforded the opportunity of securing high-quality wool from England, Scotland, France, Spain and north Africa, rather than inferior Italian materials. At first the Italians dealing in Flemish cloth had developed a refinishing industry for the improvement of the goods, which reached its peak in the Florentine *Arte della Calimala*, a manufacturers' guild known by the name of the street in which its headquarters stood. But the development of a fully-fledged native woollen industry was encouraged by crises in Flanders. From 1269 onwards the Anglo-Flemish wool trade was increasingly disrupted by embargoes and confiscations, Flemish towns were suffering from acute labour troubles, and a number of skilled artisans from Flanders migrated to the south. Moreover at least one city, Pisa, seems to have adopted policies favourable to industrial development by controlling rents and food prices so as to reduce overheads and permit the payment of relatively low wages. By 1308, according to the chronicler Giovanni Villani, there were as many as 300 manufacturers in Florence, producing between them a total output of about 100,000 cloths. By 1338 total output had apparently sunk to 80,000, but the quality of the goods and their value had, it seems, been improved. Cloth production was also very widely developed in Lombard cities, though not in the great maritime centres of Venice and Genoa. Something of a woollen industry did appear in Venice, but it received only inter-mittent protection against Lombard and German imports from a government more anxious to favour the transit-trade, and was in any case handicapped by the lack of fresh water in Venice – which made the Venetians dependent for fulling-processes on such competing mainland centres as Padua and Treviso.

It would, of course, be wrong to think of Italy's industrial history entirely in terms of woollens and clothing. To the middle of the thirteenth century, Pisa's chief industry was the tanning of leather, not the production of woollen goods. The people of Lucca developed for export the manufacture of silken cloth of high quality; an expatriate Lucchese community developed this industry in Venice, and a silk entrepreneur, Bandino Garzoni, was one of the four richest men in Venice according to the fiscal survey of 1379–80. Milan's chief economic distinction lay in its metallurgical industries. It had its own silver and iron mines in Valtorta, an ancient estate of the Archbishop, and purchased iron – either in its crude state or else half worked – in the markets of Brescia and Bergamo, and also in Germany. Smiths in Milan itself and its *contado* made weapons, knives and domestic utensils, together with nails and iron work for horses and carts and for use in building. The famous glass industry of Murano was developing on the Venetian lagoon from the thirteenth century onwards. Moreover, maritime commerce could not be sustained without the development of shipbuilding, whether in private yards or in the great publicly owned industrial concentration of the Venetian Arsenal. Again, the general expansion of population and the growth of towns, which was probably still continuing during the thirteenth century, must have acted as a constant stimulus to the building industry.

Some cities remained primarily centres of consumption rather than of production, and were the seats of courts rather than the springboards of business enterprise. In the cities where they resided, the Pope, his cardinals and the

curial bureaucracy consumed revenues derived from taxation and from ecclesiastical benefices all over Europe,
offering the chance of substantial profit to local tradesmen,
victuallers and innkeepers – for the presence of the most
international law court in Europe was certain to attract a
large number of litigants with business to put before it.
From the late twelfth and early thirteenth centuries Roman
banking firms, including the Boboni, were lending money
both to the Apostolic Treasury and to ecclesiastics who
needed it to transact business at the curia. Some moneylenders, who were probably Romans, followed papal tax-
collectors on their travels abroad, and eased their task by
advancing ready cash at extortionate rates to embarrassed
taxpayers. In the later thirteenth century, however, Roman
banking firms were overshadowed by their Tuscan counterparts, and did not contribute heavily to financing the
expedition of Charles of Anjou. Many religious houses sent
their own 'proctors' or agents to represent them at the
curia, but there were also professional proctors, resident at
the Pope's court and ready to perform the task for a fee.

Apart from rendering these services Rome had little
industry of its own, and in the thirteenth century one of its
most important guilds was that of the Bobacterii, who earned
their living by agricultural pursuits. The Romans did a
lucrative trade in marble and other valuable stones quarried
in the region, but the presence of the curia and the opportunities for catering for pilgrims were their greatest sources
of potential profit. The flow of pilgrims was greatly stimulated by Boniface VIII's institution of a Jubilee year in
1300 – not a frequently recurring event, but a splendid
windfall for the Romans while it lasted. As his Bull of 22
February 1300 declared:

The trustworthy tradition of our ancestors affirms that great
remissions and indulgences for sins are granted to those who visit
in this city the venerable basilica of the Prince of the Apostles . . .

wherefore we . . . in the plenitude of Apostolic Authority grant to all who, being truly penitent, visit these basilicas in this present year, and in each succeeding hundredth year, not only a full and copious, but the most full pardon of all their sins.

The Romans maintained an equivocal attitude to the papal court, on the one hand welcoming the prestige and profit it conferred on their city, but on the other yearning for communal independence of the Pope and of the local barons who were strongly represented in the college of cardinals. The court's frequent and prolonged absences were resented – hence, in 1253, the Romans aggressively demanded the return of Innocent IV and even claimed compensation for financial losses suffered through the absence of his court in Lyons and elsewhere. But even before the court settled at Avignon the Pope's presence in Rome was only intermittent – it has been calculated that between 1100 and 1304 the Popes spent 122 years away from Rome and only eighty-two in it – and the court frequently resided in other towns in the Papal States. In Viterbo, where the Popes frequently lived until it disgraced itself in 1281 by risings against the Orsini cardinals, it was customary to double the rents when the Papacy was in residence.

There is a natural temptation to think of the history of the great cities chiefly in terms of the development of international commerce, industry and banking – the most spectacular sources of profit. But the possession of land, and the investment of capital in improving it, were also essential features of urban life, and urban and rural developments were not divorced from each other. Most towns were residential centres for landowners. This situation arose partly because the typical immigrant, at any rate to the expanding Tuscan towns of the thirteenth century, was not a landless sharecropper or labourer in flight from the oppression of a country landowner. Rather, he was a small proprietor, merchant or notary who was already a prominent man in his own village or township, and held on to his rural property after removing to the big city. Such immigrants frequently established themselves – at least to begin with – in town houses near the gates leading out to their country possessions. About 1243, for example, the 'rural, nearly suburban' commune of Piuvica, near Pistoia, had a fairly substantial rural middle class, and most migrants from Piuvica to Pistoia were of above average wealth.

Apart from this, merchant capitalists usually proved eager to invest a substantial part of their wealth in land, partly as a reasonable investment and partly as an insurance, a means of diversifying the sources of their wealth to save themselves from total dependence on risky enterprises abroad. The acquisition of lands and fiefs was also a method of social climbing, and of acquiring 'noble' status. In 1274 the Salimbeni, merchant-bankers of Siena, invested 44,000 florins in purchasing the rural fortress-township of Tintinnano, with 200 'hearths' or households. In 1318–20 many of Siena's mercantile oligarchy or their close relatives were landowners, and usually owned much more property outside than within the city. Many Sienese bankers ploughed their capital into farms, vineyards and orchards. In 1314, in the region surrounding San Gimignano, 639 landed proprietors resident in the city represented 61·8 per cent of the property-owning population, and owned 84 per cent of taxable rural wealth.

An account of one reasonably typical small Tuscan capitalist, Muzzo di Boninsegna of San Gimignano, can usefully be added to the more spectacular stories of the great Florentine firms and of the entrepreneurs of Genoa. Muzzo moved about 1310 from the village of Montignoso to settle in the urban parish of San Matteo. He lent money in the countryside and bought farms and vineyards, usurious activities forming his greatest source of profit. He entered into contracts of *soccida*, by which he would supply two-thirds of a flock or herd and the farmer who actually looked after the beasts the remaining third: the farmer would care for the sheep and cattle and feed them at his own expense, and the two contracting parties would split between them the wool and cheese that they produced. Flocks and herds would be divided, half and half, when the contract had run its appointed term of one to six years. Muzzo di Boninsegna would either lease the lands he acquired or entrust them to sharecroppers who would work the land for him and hand over to him a proportion of the crops it yielded; there were about 800 families of sharecroppers in the region of San Gimignano in 1314, most of them possessing no land of their own. Two of Muzzo's sons, Corso and Vanni, entered the business with him, whilst two others, Michele and Pietro, became notaries.

The determination to acquire more land as an outlet for capital accumulated in commerce or banking may help to account for the aggressive territorial policy of big cities, since the statutes of communes sometimes opposed the sale of land in their *contadi* to outsiders. Hence the Peruzzi bankers of Florence ran into serious legal difficulties when they tried to purchase land in the jurisdiction of San Gimignano in the 1330s. But after San Gimignano renounced its independence to Florence in 1353, the proportion of land owned by Florentines in the *contado* rose rapidly from almost nothing in 1336 to 11·2 per cent in 1375.

In some Lombard towns, such as Padua, the relationship between landowning and residence in the city was probably similar. In the Padovano of the late thirteenth and early fourteenth centuries, the only major landowners not belonging to the city were religious houses of the *contado*, together with a few monasteries or convents situated outside it altogether, chiefly in Venice. To a certain extent, Venetians too found an outlet for their capital outside the lagoon islands, which by the first half of the thirteenth century were largely occupied by ecclesiastical institutions and very fragmented private properties. Already in the twelfth century steps were being taken towards the acquisition of a large number of fiefs in the region of Ferrara, one of Venice's chief zones of influence on account of its interest in river traffic on the Po. Several Venetian families were invested with these tenures by the Bishops of Ferrara. Venetians were certainly acquiring land in the regions of Padua and Treviso during the thirteenth century. Admittedly these were subject to alien rule. But a number of Venetians held the office of *Podestà* (entrusted, as usual, to an outsider) in the mainland towns, and there was probably a party within the governing patriciate which favoured closer involvement with the mainland rather than exclusive concentration on eastward expansion.

Government policy did, however, vary: sometimes the right of Venetians to acquire land to the west of Venice was expressly recognized; at other times they were officially forbidden to do this, or to seek podestariates. Income from these sources, so long as the Venetians did not exercise direct dominion over the mainland towns, was bound to be erratic. Venetian landowners probably regarded their investments not as a major source of revenue but as an insurance, and as a means of supplementing food supplies for their families. Hence, they probably did not invest large sums in the improvement of cultivation. Much Venetian food was imported from more distant fields, from Apulia and the western shores of the Adriatic, or from the Middle East and Black Sea.

The connection between the cities and the land also owed a great deal to the enforced or voluntary migration of feudal lords to become partially resident in the towns. Some of them, such as the Gherardesca of Pisa or the da Romano, Estensi and da Carrara of the March of Treviso, became deeply involved in city affairs and for a time acquired dictatorial powers within their chosen towns. However, a significant proportion of the landed nobility and gentry did not become urbanized or show much interest in commerce except as a means of supplementing declining fortunes. In the region of Pisa the great feudal families of Visconti, Upezzinghi and Gherardesca seem to have been little committed to commerce, and it was nobles of the second rank who engaged in maritime trade. Of forty-eight noble families in Orvieto in 1322 perhaps twenty-seven resided in the city, the remainder being nobles of the *contado*. A fourteenth-century Florentine, Lapo da Castiglionchio, could write of his own ancestors, feudatories at Volognano and Quona, that

when they came to live in Florence, many years ago, they did not gain much influence among the citizens, because they never sunk to engaging in trade or industry, but spent more time on their estates in the *contado*, hunting and hawking and keeping up their style of life, down to the time of our own grandfathers. Likewise the Ricasoli are nobles of ancient lineage and have been very great men in the *contado* of Florence, but have never stood high among the townspeople, and have never cared to have residences in the town, but have been content with their country mansions.

For all the interpenetration of town and countryside, for all the interplay between mercantile activity and landed investment, there were still great tracts of Italy untamed and little touched by the towns.

Patriciate
and Popolo

The economic expansion of Italy (indeed, that of Europe as a whole) in the three centuries from the year 1000 to about 1300 was closely related to the growth of population. It depended heavily on the ability of landowners and the labour force to respond to the challenge of population pressure by extending the cultivated area, and by adopting more efficient methods of land management through the concentration of holdings. In Italy the towns had to absorb a large part of the increase, and it was natural that one of the chief problems in their internal development should arise out of the migration of new men to the city, the growth of new trades and industries, and their assimilation into the social and political structures. During the thirteenth century the process of urban expansion was still continuing, though it was probably doing so at a steady, rather than a really spectacular rate – for the well-to-do, rather than the propertyless, were encouraged to settle in towns.

In the course of this century the population curve may have begun to flatten out, as the economy approached a kind of saturation point, and it was to drop disastrously as a result of the famines and attendant plagues of the mid-fourteenth century. Urban growth and concentration were inevitably limited by the severe problems of growing and transporting foodstuffs; cramped hill-towns found expansion difficult; a form of natural limitation was probably imposed on the low-lying city of Pisa by its ill-drained swamps and its consequent liability to malaria. None the less the largest Italian cities, Florence, Milan and Venice, had probably attained populations (very high by medieval standards) of approximately 100,000 at the beginning of the fourteenth century, whilst the populations of Pisa and Siena then stood each at 40-50,000. The population of Padua seems to have stood at about 15,000 in 1174, rising to some 35,000 by 1320, when it was as large as almost any city north of the Alps. However, to establish general trends towards growth or decline is usually easier than to establish aggregates. Total population can sometimes only be guessed from fragmentary evidence, relating to the number of men of military age or the number of adult males who signed treaties, or the number of households paying taxes based chiefly on real property.

Certainly the mid-thirteenth century saw the rise to power of the Popolo. This was a form of state-within-a-state probably manned chiefly by families who had settled in the city comparatively recently, and who now began in many places to challenge the old-established 'patriciates'. These patriciates consisted partly of feudal families who had been regarded as noble before the formation of the commune, and who had come to live in the city; and partly of other families, townsmen by origin and ennobled by the commune, who had made their fortunes through trade, usury, banking, law, administration or other means, and had held civic office in the days of the colleges of consuls. These groups had assimilated one another, forming a fairly homogeneous and exclusive ruling class. More recently arrived citizens needed some form of organization to protect their own interests, and in certain towns the organs of the Popolo were able to force their way into communal government and even to take it over entirely, so that the Popolo assimilated the commune. A characteristic and widespread organ of the Popolo was a council consisting partly of representatives of professional associations (guilds of artisans, manufacturers, merchants and bankers, colleges of judges and notaries) and partly of representatives of particular districts within the city. It was often known as the *Anzianato* or Council of Elders, and the system of representation was thus both occupational and topographical. Also, the Popolo from the mid-thirteenth century onwards would sometimes appoint a *Capitano del Popolo*, as a counterpart to the commune's long-established *Podestà*. Like the *Podestà* he was sometimes a foreigner, and sometimes a native of the city. His principal task was to defend the interests of the Popolo.

The first great wave of 'popular government' immediately followed the death of the Emperor Frederick II, when 'popular' régimes were established at Florence, Lucca and Orvieto in 1250, at Rome in 1252, at Volterra and Siena in 1253, at Pisa in 1254, at Bologna in 1255, at Faenza in 1256 and at Genoa in 1257. There seems to have been some connection between the triumph of Manfred in 1260 and the restoration of 'patrician' government, and again between the victory of Charles of Anjou and the restoration of 'popular' régimes. In Florence, government by the partisan régime of the Guelfs from 1267 to 1280 was succeeded in 1282, after Cardinal Malabranca's short-lived attempt to reconcile the factions, by a new government based on specifically 'popular' institutions. Its supreme organ was a college of priors recruited from the guilds.

There was, in effect, a hierarchy among the guilds and corporations, and the most powerful of these were liable to enjoy much heavier representation in the chief organs of the miniature city state than were their humbler peers. 'Popular' government was not in essence democratic. In the large cities it tended to fall into the hands of plutocrats who felt much more in common with the patricians they were theoretically displacing than with the lesser people. Italian civic republicanism was associated with oligarchy rather than with democracy, though there could occur moments of crisis when the basis of government was forcibly broadened, through failures of confidence in the established circle of governors. The rise of the Popolo in Pisa, for example, was connected with the foundation of new guilds: a corporation of woollen-manufacturers emerged between 1267 and 1277 to rank beside the old-established organs of the inland merchants and the sea-going merchants; the vintners escaped from the merchants' control and formed a guild of their own; the shoemakers broke loose from the tanners' guild, and the notaries from the college of judges. But in most cities there were some workers, or even some small masters and retailers, who were not allowed to form their own professional associations, and were subjected to control by other merchants or manufacturers anxious to regulate auxiliary trades to their own advantage. The great wool-guild of Florence, the *Arte della Lana*, was a corporation run by the manufacturers in their own interests, with its own tribunals and prison – so that the bosses became judges in their own cases in industrial disputes. In Florence, as in Bologna and Siena, the workers in the industry – weavers, beaters, combers, carders and so on – were forbidden to form their own associations. So, for that matter, were the dyers, who were not proletarian and propertyless wage-earners, but small masters. The woollen-workers and dyers broke the surface briefly during the short-lived revolt of the Ciompi in Florence in 1378, though even then their demands were mild: for union recognition, for production to be kept up to a certain minimum level, for a more equable system of taxation. Even in San Gimignano bakers, innkeepers, vintners and millers were prevented from forming guilds. They were under surveillance from officials of the commune, who were charged to regulate victualling so as to protect the interests of the consumer. These tradesmen were not allowed to form any kind of corporation which might aspire to independence.

Hence, really humble artisans seldom took any effective part in the government of their cities, and the triumph of government by guilds did not imply any genuine form of workers' control. Membership of a professional association did not invariably mean that a person actually exercised that trade or profession. Some men of leisure, rentiers or *scioperati*, certainly entered Florentine guilds to enfranchise themselves politically and obtain access to the Priorate. To take two illustrious examples: the poet Dante, who lived as a young man on the income from his property, qualified for civic office by enrolling in the guild of physicians and apothecaries; from 1295 onwards he took part on several occasions in the city's councils and magistracies and eventually, in the summer of 1300, became one of the priors. Although the novelist Boccaccio had shown no enthusiasm for business or law and had long devoted his time to literature, he was inscribed on the guild of judges and notaries in 1351.

In the medium-sized town of Padua, whose trade was mainly local and whose industry could scarcely compare with that of Florence, the affairs of the commune were most strongly influenced by judges and notaries rather than by either merchants or manual workers. Here the Popolo, known as the Comunanza, had by the last quarter of the thirteenth century become virtually identical with the commune. Notaries and judges proliferated, their numbers rising from fourteen judges and eighty-six notaries in 1254 to at least 100 judges and some 500 notaries forty years later. The judges were mostly the sons of well-to-do rentiers, and certainly needed private means, since a judge could only hope to hold office for a four-month period every three or four years. Notaries, concerned with drafting commercial and other contracts, were often tradesmen or artisans who exercised this profession as a part-time occupation. They enjoyed some modest power: eight guilds were chosen every year to send representatives to the *Anzianato*, and the guild of notaries was the only one invariably represented. The remaining thirty-four guilds took comparatively little part in local politics.

In theory, city statutes might provide for the rapid rotation of office, and for the principal elective offices of the commune to be held only for very short periods – even for as little as two months at a stretch – after which the retiring officeholder would be barred from competing again for a certain prescribed period. Such measures were designed to resist the tendency towards oligarchy. In practice certain economic interests and certain families who had probably reached tacit agreements to share out office between them were disproportionately represented. At Florence in the first ten years of the new Guild Priorate, 1282–92, the *Arte della Calimala* (refinishers of woollen cloth) and the *Arte del Cambio* (bankers) predominated in the Priorate, and were followed by the wool and silk guilds. In some of the districts or *sestieri* one quarter of all the places in the Priorate were monopolized by only two families, more than a third by three families, and over a half by five or six families. Later, in 1328–42, 71 per cent of those who sat in the Priorate were inscribed on only three out of the twenty-one legally recognized guilds, the *Lana, Calimala* and *Cambio*. There was also a strong connection in Florence between enjoying political authority and making substantial loans to the state – the public debt was growing to impressive dimensions during the fourteenth century.

The situation was rather similar in Siena and Pisa. Between 1287 and 1355 Siena was governed by a régime of the moderately rich and well-to-do, centring on the Board of Nine Governors and Defenders of the Commune and People of Siena. This Board was re-elected every two months, but could influence the succession and procure continuity by compiling lists of persons eligible for office among the Nine, and by nominating city councillors and the principal financial officers. Members of the merchant guild predominated among those officeholders whose occupation can now be ascertained, and the same person quite commonly held office several times over a period of fifteen years or more. Likewise, in Pisa in the early fourteenth century, the *Anzianato* was dominated by the great corporations of merchants and manufacturers, and by professional men – physicians, lawyers and judges – rather than by craftsmen or manual workers. Membership of the council was again restricted in practice to a small group of families, and many *Anziani* were re-elected as soon as the prescribed interval had elapsed, or very soon after.

This tendency towards oligarchy and towards the formation of a new élite within the Popolo probably resulted partly from the fact that only a small fragment of the population possessed the leisure, the education or the interest to devote time to politics, which became a matter of more general concern only at times of severe financial or military crisis. The creation of these in-groups, which were in effect new patriciates, was sometimes balanced by the coming of further waves of new men to assert their influence and perhaps to press a distinctive point of view. When the government of Florence was broadened out after a political and financial crisis in 1342–3, the chronicler Matteo Villani superciliously observed:

The government of the city has come, in no small part, into the hands of men recently arrived from the *contado* and the district of Florence and beyond. These men, little experienced in civil affairs, had settled in the city and, with the wealth accumulated from trade and usury, in the course of time became very rich. They were able to conclude any marriage which they desired, and by means of gifts, banquets and persuasion, both open and hidden, they won such influence that they were chosen for office.

To some extent it is possible to connect 'popular' régimes and parties with distinctive policies and even with specific economic interests. Milan had two organizations, in the *Motta* (consisting of lesser nobles and merchants) and the *Credenza di Sant' Ambrogio*, of retailers, craftsmen and lesser guildsmen. These periodically opposed the nobility of feudal origins, the *capitanei* and *valvassores*. In the mid-thirteenth century, they were clearly concerned with two outstanding issues – with making positions in the cathedral chapter open to people who were not *capitanei* or *valvassores*; and (in 1240) with introducing a new system of taxation of chattels and real property, which would distribute the fiscal burden more evenly both between different orders of citizenry and between the citizenry and the *contado*. The military nobility and clergy were no longer to escape. The popular movement succeeded partly because the papal legate, Gregorio da Montelongo, who was directing the campaign against the Emperor, was himself disinclined to respect clerical immunities at times when the demand for money to further the Church's purposes was so urgent and great. Some other 'popular' régimes or parties – at Bologna in 1245–50, at Florence in 1259 – also sought to equalize taxation between the city and the *contado*: perhaps out of concern for their own properties in the countryside.

In 1252 the Romans sought a foreign leader in Branca-leone degli Andalò, Count of Casalecchio, who came of a family of professional *Podestà* in Bologna, and voted him the office of Senator for the unusually long period of three years. By 1254 he was also styling himself *Capitano del Popolo*. He vigorously promoted the expansionist policy of the Roman commune into its surrounding district, for the purpose of securing food supplies, making roads safer for pilgrims, and reducing baronial brigandage. Occasionally denying the Pope his cooperation he enforced the law harshly against the Roman nobility, some of whom had built strongholds in the city among its classical ruins – the Frangipane in the Colosseum, the Orsini in the Theatre of Marcellus, the

Annibaldi da Militia in the Markets of Trajan. In a second term of office, in 1257-8, Brancaleone hanged two of the Annibaldi, despite their relationship to one of the cardinals. According to one chronicler he razed to the ground no less than 140 towers built by the feuding nobility of Rome, in an attempt to guarantee peace and order for the lesser people of the city. When he died in the summer of 1258 his head was encased in a precious reliquary and set up in his honour on a marble column. Later, however, the office of Senator fell into the hands of claimants to the imperial title, to whom it could offer a convenient pretext for appearing in Rome without waiting for a summons from the Pope. For many years the position was held by Charles of Anjou, who governed Rome through vicars and other functionaries recruited mainly from the bureaucracy of his Kingdom of Sicily, and allowed the Romans little part in the administration of their city. The office of *Capitano del Popolo* did, however, reappear at intervals in Rome and was held for brief periods by natives rather than aliens – by Angelo Capocci in 1267, and in 1284 by Giovanni di Cencio Malabranca, who was chosen during a revolt – sparked off by famine – against the Senatorship of Charles of Anjou.

The policies of the Popolo in Pisa in the second half of the thirteenth century were closely connected with the introduction of the woollen industry to the city, and were probably designed to break the control of the established 'patricians' on the urban property market. The high rents they charged threatened to hinder economic development since labour costs and manufacturers' overheads were naturally related to the level of rent. The Popolo reduced the metallic content of the coinage whilst increasing the quantity of coins in circulation – the effect of this would normally have been inflationary, but controls were imposed both on rents and on grain prices to prevent them from following the upward curve to their natural extent. Very heavy taxation seems to have been imposed on city rents at the close of the thirteenth century. The strength of the Popolo probably lay in small-time merchants from the *contado* who had originally lived by bringing its products to the city merchants, and who were now developing the manufacture of textiles. Price controls on breadstuffs – if they were at all effective – may have encouraged the balance to shift away from arable farming, where profits were restricted, and towards the rearing of sheep and cattle.

In some cities, however, the rise of the Popolo had no such influence on the course of action and affairs. Milan certainly had its 'popular' organs, and these could be vociferous and could clash head-on with the families of sometime military vassals. But they could recruit leaders only among families of opportunists among the *capitanei* and *valvassores* who were prepared to break away from the main body, in search of personal power based on the headship of the *Credenza*. Hence the interests of the *Credenza* were subordinated to the personal ambitions of the family of the Torriani, and the *Credenza* failed to become an autonomous power – all the more, perhaps, because in the late 1250s the other Milanese 'popular' association, the *Motta*, was drifting towards the *capitanei* and *valvassores*.

Venice in particular was largely untroubled by the rise of a Popolo in the normal sense of the term, and again (as a very important special case) it needs separate treatment. Venice knew no *Anzianato*, Guild Priorate, Union of Guilds or *Capitano del Popolo*, though there were waves of 'new men' whose first appearances in influential positions can be roughly dated. If the ancient families which had once provided Doges and tribunes, such as the Morosini, Falier and Michiel, formed the bottom layer of the Venetian patriciate, another storey was added in the more recently rich and powerful families, including the Dandolo, Ziani and Mastropiero, who were judges and members of the

Consiglio dei Savi which restricted the Doge's authority in the mid-twelfth century. Some of these, typified by the Ziani, were big landed proprietors who also supplemented their wealth through commercial investments and activities. After them came another group of merchant families which depended to a certain extent on these great houses for financial support, and were not initially great owners of land or house property. Such new clans began to appear in the college of electors of the Doge before the end of the twelfth century and, during the 1220s, obtained access to the small council surrounding the Doge.

Their ascent was relatively smooth, and the assimilation of new families to old was certainly more apparent than were any fierce outbreaks of class conflict. There was evidently room for more manpower in the government, at least to fill the more arduous posts and those most likely to run their occupants into expense: for laws had to be introduced in the late twelfth and early thirteenth centuries making it compulsory to accept offices to which one had been elected. In the early thirteenth century pressure on the available supplies of office was certainly relieved by the migration of many families to Venice's new possessions in the Aegean and eastern Mediterranean, and this may well have increased the opportunities for 'new men' at home. Though the Venetian government concentrated in general on holding islands and strategic coastal points rather than on penetrating into the interior of its new Balkan possessions, Venetian emigrés did settle Crete very extensively. Also, the size of the resident colony in Constantinople increased, and several Venetian families were enfeoffed with islands in the east where they took the titles of Duke or Count – among them the Sanuto, Giustinian, Venier, Michiel and Querini. Constitutional developments in Venice itself created further opportunities for new men to enter the circles of the governing class: for a new legislative council, the *Quarantia*, was set up in Venice between 1207 and 1220, and the council of the *Rogati* or *Pregadi* – later known as the Senate – was added between 1229 and 1255. Indeed, a new man rose to become Doge in 1229–49, when Giacomo Tiepolo defeated in the election Marino Dandolo, one of the families of judges. Tiepolo was a former merchant and his greatest achievement had been to keep Crete loyal to Venice in 1212–13, thereby resisting the designs of an enfeoffed adventurer, Marco Sanuto, Duke of Naxos. But the Tiepolo sought to be like the older families, rather than to challenge their way of life and the socio-political order they had established.

At the end of the century old and new families merged to form a homogeneous ruling class. Those families, such as the Dandolo and Gradenigo, which had already been prominent in the *Consiglio dei Savi* in the mid-twelfth century, continued to carry great weight in the thirteenth and early fourteenth centuries. By the late thirteenth century ultimate sovereignty was concentrated in the Great Council of all adult patricians, which enjoyed the prerogative of determining its own membership and electing members of smaller councils and salaried officials of magisterial rank. The total strength of the Great Council was reduced from 400–500 in the 1260s to 260 in 1295–6. But shortly afterwards its membership was greatly enlarged, chiefly by the restoration of established families which had recently dropped out, rather than by the admission of new ones – but entrance then became very carefully restricted, so that it is usual to speak of a 'closing' or *serrata* of the Great Council from 1297 onwards. This manoeuvre has been interpreted as an attempt by the great and long-established families, the *Grandi* and *Monsignori*, to purchase the support of lesser men by allowing them to share the monopoly of political power; or as an attempt to frustrate the formation of large clientèles. The hangers-on of the Tiepolo, for example, would henceforth be excluded from the Council and disenfranchised. Closure of the Great Council was not however complete until the last quarter of the fourteenth century. Fifteen new houses were admitted for their loyalty to the régime during the Tiepolo-Querini conspiracy of 1310, and the very heavy fiscal demands of the state during the last war with the Genoese in 1379–81 necessitated the admission of thirty new families. In 1311 the strength of the Great Council stood at 1,017 members; by the early sixteenth century it had reached over 2,500. The period of almost total closure of the Great Council stretched from 1381 to 1646.

In Venice, moreover, the guilds were not autonomous bodies. They were not, like the Florentine guilds, the foundations of the state. Rather, they were the organs through which the state, dominated by merchant-land-owning administrators and naval officers, imposed on the artisans a discipline which extended to prescribing regulations about techniques of production, methods of sale, the acquisition of primary materials, prices, and the wages of dependent employees. Many were under the supervision of a government magistracy, the *Giustizia*, and were not empowered to make their own ordinances or rules without its approval. The Venetians imposed restrictions on the employment of large numbers of journeymen and apprentices by guildsmen, on guild masters acquiring control of chains of workshops, and on their working in partnership with other masters. This may have been a cause, or it may have been a consequence, of the failure of large-scale industry to develop in Venice. In general the Venetians maintained firmer control over all corporate institutions than did most other communes, and successfully ensured their strict subordination to the state. Artisans formed religious societies for the purposes of devotion to a chosen saint and to aid each other in times of distress – these, too, were placed under state supervision. For a time the larger religious bodies or Scuole Grandi, the legacy of the movement of the flagellants in 1260, escaped such close observation; but in the early fourteenth century they too were subjected to the surveillance of the formidable Council of Ten. This was a committee of public safety which grew up after the Tiepolo-Querini conspiracy of 1310, and, by means of procedures recalling those of the Inquisition, worked to forestall conspiracies against the state and to maintain the corporate rule of the patricians.

Such conspiracies against the mercantile régime as did occur during the fourteenth century were for the most part the work of secessionist noblemen rather than of Popolani, and were often the product of crises caused by the unsuccessful conduct of wars. Venice had no outstanding large-scale industry comparable to the Florentine or Pisan woollen industries, and hence the patriciate was not challenged by any homogeneous group of industrial capitalists outside it. At the fiscal survey of 1379–80 the largest identifiable professional groups among non-nobles consisted – apart from merchants – of druggists or grocers, of butchers, and of weavers. A considerable number of well-to-do Popolani proved to be richer than the poorest noblemen, but on the whole the balance of wealth lay with the patriciate. Twenty-five nobles and only six others had apparently accumulated taxable fortunes of over 20,000 lire, whilst 780 noblemen and 376 non-nobles owned to taxable fortunes of between 1,000 and 60,000 lire.

Venice was the most tightly organized republican state in Italy. But other governments in the thirteenth and fourteenth centuries were beginning to extend their competence. They were aiming at the more rigorous discipline of the most powerful and turbulent families in their midst. They showed themselves capable of imposing heavier taxation to support war, defence, municipal amenities and buildings, expanding bureaucracy and the relief of famine. They were still striving to achieve more perfect control of their own *contadi*.

The dominating cities used to be portrayed by historians as ruthlessly exploiting their surrounding country districts in order to secure their own interests. But since townsmen owned so great a proportion of the land in the *contado* they were unlikely in their capacity of citizens to oppress themselves in their character of landed proprietors, or deliberately to cripple their peasants with fiscal exactions so that they could no longer pay them any rents. The Sienese government of the Nine undoubtedly made some attempt to develop the *contado* by improving communications and reclaiming land. It showed a particular interest in regions to the south-west of Siena, and tried (for example) to launch new towns, such as Paganico in the Maremma, as a means of colonizing an unhealthy area. It also dreamed, though without success, of developing the harbour of Talamone and transforming it into a major seaport. There is nothing to suggest that the Sienese *contado* was taxed unduly heavily in the early fourteenth century. Certainly Florentine rule permitted prosperous market towns – Empoli, Figline, Borgo San Lorenzo, Poggibonsi – to flourish in the shadow of the dominating city.

On the other hand all or most communes had a strong interest in securing cheap supplies of food, which may have cut the landowners' profits. They could, for example, impose prohibitions on the export of grain from the *contado*, especially in emergencies caused by famine or war, and some of these embargoes were reasonably effective. They might stipulate that producers must bring their grain directly to the city, thus depriving middlemen of their profits. Some cities, including Florence and Siena, were prepared to sustain heavy financial losses by purchasing grain in famine years and selling it at low prices in order to frustrate speculation and forestall riots. The Pisans insisted that grain from the subject island of Sardinia be brought to Pisa; they made large purchases from Catalan importers and from the Bardi and Peruzzi of Florence; they established a large grain deposit or *canova* of their own to control the market; and they forced subject rural communes to sell to them at the Pisan price. As Professor Cipolla has put it:

The greatest concern of modern governments, in the field of economic policy, has been, in the last half-century, the 'business-cycle'. The greatest bogey has been unemployment. Throughout the whole of the Middle Ages the greatest concern of governments was the 'crop-cycle'. The greatest bogey was famine.

Control over the grain supply was often extended to other commodities vital to everyday life – wine, oil, meat, fish, vegetables, straw, candles, wax, firewood, timber or building materials.

Communal finance depended chiefly on direct and indirect taxation, and on raising substantial loans. It could also be supplemented by revenue from communal property in the city and *contado* (as the commune of Padua raised money from hot springs, mills, and rents from market stalls), or from judicial fines, including the composition of death penalties for money payments. Some governments enjoyed a monopoly of salt extraction, and passed laws obliging all subjects over a certain age to purchase a determinate quantity of salt every year, at prices fixed by the state. Systems of direct taxation were usually based chiefly on assessments of land and real estate, the most easily traceable and identifiable forms of wealth. In the late thirteenth and early fourteenth centuries, however, systems of indirect taxation began to be developed, and came to occupy the chief place in the revenues of such towns as Florence, Venice, Milan, Genoa, Siena, Pisa and Reggio Emilia. They included excises on wines and foodstuffs, gate-tolls, sales taxes, and the proceeds of the sale of salt, and were known by the generic name of 'gabelles'. They were frequently used to meet interest payments due to creditors of the state.

Systems of communal finance based on loans and indirect taxation were clearly advantageous to the rich and hard on the poor, since the foodstuffs on which some of these taxes were imposed obviously bulked much larger in the poor man's budget than in the expenses of the rich. Hence the demand of the Ciompi and the lesser people in Florence in 1378 for the abolition of interest payments on the public debt, for the eventual amortization of the capital, and for the restoration of a system based chiefly on direct taxes related to the wealth of the taxpayers. In this respect the humbler inhabitants of the towns were probably worse off than their counterparts in the *contado*: both in Florence and in Lucca, in the first half of the fourteenth century, the urban fiscal system rested chiefly on indirect taxes, whilst direct taxation was retained in the *contado*. In Florence the chief direct tax was abolished in the city in 1317. It was reintroduced only for brief periods during financial crises, by foreign seigneurs temporarily imported to take responsibility for unpopular measures. On the other hand, gabelles did not completely displace direct taxation in the communal budget of Siena, and the most equitable of the direct taxes (the *lira* or *dazio*) was levied on at least eighteen occasions between 1287 and 1355.

In the thirteenth and fourteenth centuries, huge public debts were amassed at least by the states of Venice and Florence through extensive borrowing from their own citizens. Some loans were compulsory or 'forced', and others were voluntary, but both paid interest, and there was a strong connection between wielding political authority and having large holdings in the public debt. Members of the ruling oligarchies literally enjoyed a financial stake in their city, and investments in government bonds were among the favourite securities held by Venetian patricians.

In Venice, forced loans were in existence by 1167, and quotas were assessed according to the patrimony or revenue declared by the taxpayer himself. The funded debt stood at approximately 1·5 million lire in 1299, at 6 million in 1373, and at 12·8 million in 1386. The golden age of the Venetian public debt, or *Monte*, lasted from the mid-thirteenth century to the 1370s. Interest at 5 per cent was regularly and punctually paid, and the ruling class, in its own interests, was able to pursue policies which kept up the value of government bonds almost to par, especially between the 1320s and 1370s. People with very modest resources usually had to get rid of their holdings quickly, sustaining a loss of at best 10 to 20 per cent on the transaction, and selling them to others who could afford to wait to realize their assets and continue to enjoy the interest. This encouraged a certain concentration of the bonds in the hands of relatively few big lenders. However, rocketing taxation in 1377–81 and the desperate efforts called for by war against Genoa forced a general sale of these holdings, whose value tumbled catastrophically by as much as 70–80 per cent. This disaster set in train something of a social revolution and was probably a potent cause of impoverishment among certain families of the patriciate. However, the policy of 'defending' the value of government bonds, which might entail substantial repayments of the capital in order to maintain confidence, was subsequently resumed.

The accumulation of a massive public debt was also a prominent feature of Florentine history in the fourteenth century. In 1303 the state debt was still relatively modest, and stood at less than 50,000 florins, but by 1338 it had expanded to 450,000. Before 1345 the interest officially payable on government bonds was in the region of 10–15 per cent, but that year saw the establishment of a consolidated debt fund – with irredeemable titles paying only 5 per cent interest. Private individuals could sell or otherwise alienate state bonds to one another, but could not cash them with the government. By 1380 the state debt, in the aftermath of the War of the Eight Saints, had reached $2\frac{1}{2}$ million florins. A modern historian, Professor Marvin Becker, has compared the Florentine state of the mid-fourteenth century to 'a giant corporation in which the 8,000 most affluent men in the community were the principal shareholders', and has argued that the existence and popularity of this method of finance provided the economic foundation for the civic patriotism of the well-to-do. In the first half of the fourteenth century the ambitious foreign policy of Florence and its efforts to conquer or purchase Lucca contributed heavily to the expenditure which sent up the state debt. The cost of war was rising. Since the late thirteenth century the Florentines had supplemented their own forces by the employment of mercenary troops. Even the civic cavalry, composed as it was of the richer citizens, was paid for in the late thirteenth century.

Likewise, the government of Siena raised funds by forced or voluntary loans, not only for the purpose of conducting military campaigns, but also to subsidize the relief of famine. Voluntary loans were clearly more important here than in Venice, where the forced loan was paramount; and the Sienese public debt, unlike the Florentine, actually diminished during the first half of the fourteenth century. Voluntary loans were attractive to rich Sienese, partly because they were short-term undertakings. As Professor Bowsky has suggested, they offered a way of employing funds when banking and trade were slack, without tying up one's capital for undesirably long periods. In Siena, too, lending to the state was a means to power and prosperity for such families as the Piccolomini and the Bonsignori, for the commune would often pledge rural properties and fortresses as security for the loan: and, though these were frequently redeemed, there was some possibility that the lender might be able to keep them in perpetuity.

Most 'popular' governments, determined to preserve the corporate, oligarchical government of the moderately rich and to carry out their duty of maintaining peace and order, introduced by the late thirteenth century laws designed to curb the violent behaviour of certain powerful families addicted to blood-feuds and vendettas. A term commonly applied to these overmighty subjects and citizens was 'magnates', though several other epithets might officially be used to describe them. They were, for example, known in Padua as *potentiores*, *magni homines*, or *male ablati* ('the ill-conducted'). Such terms were not essentially connected with nobility of blood or with membership of a great feudal house, although – as at Pisa in 1286 – such an association, or the presence in one's family of somebody who had been dubbed a knight, could mean that one qualified as a magnate. Certainly, as at Florence or Siena, merchant-banking families could be stigmatized as magnates. Of seventy-two families listed as magnates in Florence between 1293 and 1295 only eight had actually started out as feudatories, though there were others which had accumulated wealth through commerce, industry or banking and subsequently invested in landed estates and fiefs. In Florence, as the historian Nicola Ottokar pointed out, the status of magnate was associated with the concepts of 'greatness', 'power' and 'tyranny', but not necessarily with noble lineage. In Padua, nine families were called *male ablati* in 1256–66, and these included both the feudal family of da Carrara and the non-noble Dalesmanini, who had climbed to wealth up the dishonourable ladder of usurious money-lending.

The general principles, found in some degree in most towns that adopted such legislation, were that magnates

should be required to put down securities for good behaviour (instead of merely being subject to the imposition
of fines after they had committed offences); that magnate
families should be held liable collectively for the misbe-
haviour of one of their members; and that they should be
excluded from certain principal offices of state. Arbitrary
procedures, apparently at odds with the rules of natural
justice, could be set in motion against magnates – hence, in
Padua in 1281, the *Podestà* was ordered to proceed against
magnates disturbing the citizenry on the strength of a sworn
statement by one single complainant and without further
proof. However, not all these restrictions were imposed
simultaneously – the anti-magnate legislation which
appeared in Florence in 1281 may have been designed to
protect the magnates against each other rather than as a
general act of revenge aimed at all magnates. Until 1293
and the introduction of the Florentine Ordinances of Justice
there seems to have been no question of reducing their
political rights or juridical standing.

Public loyalty to the commune had to struggle against
private allegiance to the extensive family, public peace and
order against the vendetta and the blood-feud. Public legislation was doubtless aided by the peace-making activities of
preachers and religious confraternities. Leaders of the
Roman people, from Brancaleone in the 1250s to Cola di
Rienzo in the 1340s, were deeply concerned with the problem of order and with containing a turbulent nobility. At
least in Tuscany, there seems to have been a struggle for
order rather than a conflict between distinct classes or
social groups – this was not a contest between the 'feudalism'
of the magnates and the bourgeois ethic of the Popolo.
However, there was some risk that the struggle to achieve
order might itself degenerate into a factional contest, and
that designation as a magnate, like any process of purging
or proscribing, might be used as a means of working off

personal scores against opponents. The Falconieri, a Florentine clan much addicted to feuding, escaped being pro-
scribed when the Ordinances of Justice were issued in 1293.
In the fourteenth century such Popolano families as the
Strozzi and the Medici imitated the violent style of life
associated with the magnates. Magnate status could not in
practice be objectively applied; nor was it indelible, and it
could certainly be shed at Florence and Pisa by consistently
proving loyal to the institutions of the Popolo. In Florence
530 of the most law-abiding magnates were rewarded with
the status of Popolani in 1343.

There was not invariably a great deal of difference in
wealth between magnates and the richer Popolani. Apparently there was a considerable disparity at Orvieto, but
less of a contrast between the two groups either in the
metropolis of Florence or in the small Tuscan town of Prato.
In Prato there were nineteen magnate families in 1319, and
these accounted for approximately 25 per cent of the taxable
wealth of the city and *contado*; but it has proved possible for
a historian, Professor Fiumi, to select nineteen Popolano
families of Prato which were nearly as prosperous, and controlled more than 20 per cent of taxable wealth. Likewise,
there was little social or economic difference between the
Rossi, Bardi or Scali of Florence, who were magnates,
and the Magalotti, Peruzzi, Alberti, Antellesi, Strozzi,
Acciaiuoli, Bacherelli and Capponi, who were Popolani.
In the early fourteenth century the magnate families of
Bardi, Cerchi, Frescobaldi, Pazzi, Pulci and Scali were
heavily involved in commerce and banking – though after
1343 they did show a strong tendency to withdraw from
business, and after that date few magnates were enrolled
in the great guilds of the *Lana, Cambio* and *Calimala*.

Similarly, there was no question of total war between
magnates and Popolani, of enmities being carried over into
all branches of private life. Both in Florence and in Siena

they were quite capable of forming business associations and entering into partnership with each other. In Siena, persons eligible for membership of the Nine became partners in the magnate companies of the Tolomei and Bonsignori, and some inter-marriage took place between magnate families and others. However, certain restrictions on marriage alliances were imposed in 1350, soon after the Black Death. Non-noble orphans, especially female, were forbidden to marry nobles without the prior consent of their Popolani kinsmen. This may have been an attempt to prevent the many legacies of deceased Popolani from falling into the clutches of magnates eager to recoup damaged fortunes or add to existing wealth.

Furthermore, the exclusion of magnates or great nobles from civic office was by no means absolute in the Tuscan communes. In Siena after 1287 noble houses regarded as a public menace were not the only excluded group. Professional men – judges, notaries and physicians – suffered the same fate, and the ban was in practice more rigorously imposed on them. A few members of theoretically excluded houses – such as the Squarcialupi and Bonsignori – were allowed to sit on the Board of Nine. Magnates in Pisa could penetrate into most of the organs of the Popolo, which needed their military aid and support – even, on occasion, into the *Anzianato*. Even the feudal family of the Upezzinghi were reconciled with the commune in 1296 after making war on the town from fortresses in the *contado*, and were expressly permitted to hold communal office, provided they paid taxation and were prepared to carry out other duties. Magnates in Florence might be barred from the Priorate and its advisory colleges, but they were well entrenched in the Guelf party, over which communal control was somewhat uncertain; they enjoyed a generous share of fiscal, diplomatic and military office; and they could participate in the *Balìe*, *ad hoc* commissions with very extensive authority, which in practice transacted much government business.

In general it was very difficult for communes heavily involved in warfare not to resort for aid to their more powerful families, which often had extensive military experience. In any case the economic power of the magnates – whether founded chiefly on land or on other economic activities – had seldom if ever been destroyed. At Orvieto in 1292, of 205 persons with taxable property of over 2,000 lire, only three were members of the guilds associated with the government of the Popolo. The proscription of certain families as Ghibellines in the early fourteenth century resulted in the further concentration of landed wealth in the hands of such families as the Monaldeschi, whose estates were scattered throughout the *contado*, and the Counts of Montemarte, the Ranieri, Alberici, della Terza and Avveduti, some of whom were regularly named in anti-magnate laws. In the Romagna anti-magnate laws were ineffective, partly because of the ease with which landed noblemen could infiltrate the guilds, including those of butchers, smiths, ploughmen and flaxworkers, and so shed their disabilities. This certainly happened at Imola and Ravenna in the late thirteenth and early fourteenth centuries.

In any case, the laws for the repression of crime and violence on the part of magnate families were not always applied with consistent rigour. The Florentine Ordinances of Justice of 1293 were the product of a revolutionary situation rather than a norm to be strictly followed in more peaceful times. Although, in the 1330s, about two-thirds of the magnate families in Florence were convicted of serious offences against communal law, an extensive traffic in pardons usually enabled them to buy their way off. But the régime became generally stricter after 1343, when the government was more open to influence from 'new men'.

Siena's law enforcement against the magnates was far from totally effective, despite the large force of policemen (mostly foreign infantry) employed for this purpose. Sienese and Florentine law did not completely deny the legality of the vendetta, but did seek to narrow down the circle of persons against whom it could be practised. When general amnesties were granted in Siena, some nobles had to be released from four or more death sentences, all of which had proved to be theoretical, and the government often had to content itself with persuading hostile clans or alliances to conclude private truces with one another – the Tolomei with the Salimbeni, the Malavolti with the Piccolomini, and so on. It did, however, sometimes prove possible to enforce sanctions against the powerful – to execute delinquents from the great families, including certain Piccolomini, or to destroy the houses and palaces of the Tolomei.

In general, the conflicts between old-established régimes and the Popolo, or between Popolani and magnates, were probably not class conflicts so much as struggles between generations, with relative newcomers to the city striving for a place beside or within the entrenched oligarchy; or else they were struggles to assert public order against private violence, and to preserve corporate rule against the threat from ill-disciplined and overmighty subjects. The desire of newcomers to assimilate to established families was frequently more in evidence than was any attempt to erect an entirely new social and political order, to create a genuinely democratic society, or to promote fiscal policies favourable to the poor. None the less, some city-states were greatly extending their competence and were building the more elaborate fiscal machinery which would enable them to handle greater responsibility.

The Coming of 8
the *Signori*

The existence of a state of chronic warfare in most parts of
Italy; the recurrence of financial crises and military defeats;
persistent internal conflict between factions or between
different orders of citizenry; the survival, despite the rise
of the communes, of a powerful landed aristocracy: none
of these things was favourable to preserving republican or
corporate government. In the thirteenth and fourteenth centuries many cities and their *contadi* became at least intermittently subject to the rule of dictators or seigneurs, some
of whom succeeded in building up for their families a personal lordship which lasted for several generations.

In eastern Lombardy, for example, the first of the ruthless
opportunists was Ezzelino III da Romano (1194–1259), a
feudal lord of German descent, who intervened repeatedly
in the factional quarrels of Verona and at last managed, in
1236–7, to secure a comparatively stable multiple lordship
over Verona, Vicenza and Padua. The presence of the
Emperor Frederick II in Italy was originally responsible
for Ezzelino's triumph, and he came to power as Frederick's
henchman. But he was no mere puppet of the Staufen, and
his personal empire (though diminished when Padua broke
free in 1256) survived Frederick for several years. Although
vigorous communal government was restored in Padua, a
new and talented family, the della Scala or Scaligeri, rose
to supremacy in Verona after Ezzelino's death, and
gradually established a dynasty of seigneurs which survived
for a century and a half. Near by, Pinamonte Bonacolsi and

his descendants governed the city of Mantua from 1272 to 1328, until their designing Scaligeri neighbours helped to engineer the conspiracy which overthrew them and another resilient family, the Gonzaga, took their place. Already the Marquesses of Este had established what proved to be a very enduring seigneurie over Ferrara, which was to be interrupted only briefly by the attempts of the Papacy to secure direct dominion over the city. A princely dynasty, the Carraresi, came at last to power in Padua in 1328.

Resort to seigneurial government was more general in Lombardy and the Romagna than in Tuscany, where corporate republican rule continued in Florence and Siena, and the Florentines were to develop into staunch and self-conscious champions of republican 'liberty' – though even they were known to put themselves for brief periods of time under lords armed with extensive authority. Grave external threats – from an aggressive neighbouring city, from an imperial overlord reasserting rights over the *contado*, from the Papacy seeking to consolidate its authority in the Romagna – often created the incentive to seek a powerful protector, or to concentrate authority in the hands of one man. This might well be the best means of securing continuity of policy, secrecy, and rapid decision-making, such as could not be achieved in large open councils or in communes in which municipal office was rapidly rotated. On the other hand Pinamonte Bonacolsi probably succeeded in Mantua because he could offer peace to a community weary of repeated wars and incessant factional struggles. In principle the cities had already taken steps towards the erection of a kind of monarchical government through the institution of the *Podestà*. A much longer-term and more absolute form of government might now be required – though it was true that many seigneurial families began by holding the office of *Podestà*, in their own cities or abroad in the region.

Some cities found their lords among the leaders (in their own area, or throughout the whole of Italy) of the Guelf or Ghibelline factions to which the most influential families belonged: in the Pope, in the Angevins and their relatives and servants, in the Estensi of Ferrara, in the Emperor's henchmen, or in the great Ghibelline feudatories of Piedmont, Lombardy and the Romagna who were able to raise armies from among their dependents. Such were the Marquess Uberto Pellavicino, the Marquess Manfredi Lancia, the Marquess William VII of Monferrato, Uguccione della Fagiola and the Counts of Montefeltro. Under siege in 1318 from the exiled Ghibelline clans of Doria and Spinola, the Genoese Guelfs appealed to Robert of Anjou to intervene with his fleet, and voted him the lordship which he held for seventeen years. Dreading the power of Asti, several neighbouring communes – Cuneo, Alba, Cherasco, Savigliano and Mondovì – put themselves under the lordship of Charles I of Anjou, who wielded great influence in Piedmont. In Lombardy there was a first generation of potentates who, like Ezzelino da Romano, owed their position partly to imperial might, and a later generation which maintained power independently of imperial backing, but still found it worthwhile to bolster it up by purchasing imperial recognition.

Lasting lordships, even principalities, were sometimes established by feudatories or ennobled landowners from the *contado* or region in which the city stood, or by families of feudal origin which owned town houses and had come to regard themselves as citizens. Such seigneurs included the competing Milanese families of the Torriani and Visconti; the Gherardesca at Pisa; Ermanno Monaldeschi at Orvieto; the Estensi and the Carraresi in the March of Treviso.

The Estensi, for example, were marquesses descended from an ancient clan of imperial feudatories, the Obertenghi, which had ramifications in Tuscany, Liguria and Lombardy. Their particular branch had begun to amass possessions in the Basso Padovano and the Po valley about the year 1000, and these estates included the township of Este from which the family took its name. During the twelfth century they had begun to expand their possessions in the direction of Ferrara, and to acquire town houses and fiefs in the *contado*. At intervals from the turn of the century they held the office of *Podestà* in the city, alternating with their bitter rivals, the Salinguerra. In the early thirteenth century Azzone VI of Este enjoyed the impressive but ephemeral honour of being enfeoffed with the March of Ancona by Pope Innocent III. At last, with the collaboration of the Venetians, who were interested in promoting their own commercial advantage, the Estensi triumphed over their rivals in Ferrara in 1240. They managed to secure the succession for themselves some years later in 1264, partly because their Guelf allies in other towns were eager to ensure that a reliable collaborator remained in command in Ferrara.

The origins of the Carraresi and the economic basis of their power were rather similar. Reputedly, the Carraresi were descended from German immigrants who had built up authority based on concentrations of estates in the *contado*. At the time when they were listed as magnates at Padua, between 1256 and 1266, they held large estates round Carrara (hence their name); a secondary centre round the castle of Agna, near the Adige; and several town mansions in Padua itself. They intermarried with other great families, with the Torriani of Milan, the Fieschi of Genoa, the Gradenighi of Venice. At last in the early fourteenth century the threat to Padua from Verona brought the magnates to the fore, and Marsiglio da Carrara took power in 1328 as a satellite of Cangrande della Scala.

Landed possessions were the key to political strength as well as to social prestige and economic power. The link between landed lordship and urban seigneurie was certainly not restricted to Padua and Ferrara. Both the Bonacolsi and the Gonzaga had built up great estates outside Mantua and accumulated house property within it before coming to power. The urban acquisitions of Pinamonte Bonacolsi had included several stout and well placed towers. The landed possessions of the Gonzaga, formed by systematic purchases and judicious marriages, were particularly extensive and could be found as far afield as Ivrea in Piedmont. Likewise the Visconti, who established a lasting command over the Milanese state, were a family of *capitanei* – greater vassals of the Archbishop, holding of him fiefs which conferred the right to receive tithes and to exercise seigneurial powers over the inhabitants of the parishes from which they were collected.

But not all seigneurial families could claim such aristocratic antecedents. Mastino della Scala, who climbed to power in Verona in and after 1259, probably came of a fairly modest family, and the della Scala seemed surprisingly disinclined to have distinguished origins fabricated for them by imaginative genealogists. It was rumoured in the fourteenth century that the family could be traced to 'a low fellow called Jacopo Fico, who, it was said, made steps (*scale*) and sold them'. Taddeo Pepoli, lord of Bologna from 1337 to 1347, was the son of a banker, Romeo, who had won great influence by advancing large sums of money to the commune.

The power of the seigneurs spread and multiple lordships began to be established when some lesser towns, in search of protection, turned to the ruling families already entrenched in formidable neighbouring cities. Towards the end of the thirteenth century both Modena and Reggio Emilia subjected themselves for the time being to the Marquess Obizzo d'Este, lord of Ferrara. In the Romagna, from the middle of the fourteenth century, members of the family of Malatesta ruled, not only over Rimini, but also over

Pesaro, Fano and Fossombrone; and the union between these communes was of an essentially personal character, based upon family ties rather than on any amalgamation of institutions, in no way superseding the traditional rivalries between cities. Milan had established in Lombardy a hegemony which rested, not only on military force, but also on the great prestige of its metropolitan see, and on the city's capacity for supplying goods and services (including those of the *Podestà*) throughout much of the region. Its authority derived, too, from its diplomatic initiatives in organizing leagues of cities to negotiate with representatives of the Emperor or the Pope. It was natural enough that, when the Visconti had been reestablished in Milan in the wake of the Emperor Henry VII, they should become 'general lords' of many other Lombard cities, some of which they governed through deputies or 'vicars'.

Certain constitutional devices, though not ubiquitous, were common to many *Signorie*. These lordships were often established by capturing control of the offices of *Podestà* or *Capitano del Popolo*, or by acquiring some such title as Captain-General or Perpetual Rector. The *Signore* might assume the offices of *Podestà* or *Capitano del Popolo* himself, or he might merely influence appointments to them; and, owing to the persistent respect for traditional forms, it was often difficult to say at what precise point the *Signoria* had actually begun and a drastic break with the old constitution had been made. For example, a Veronese annalist could write, under the year 1259: 'Note that at this point the lord Mastino della Scala began to make himself lord of the city of Verona', and later add:

1260: after the death of the lord Ezzelino da Romano, the lord Mastino della Scala became *Podestà* of Verona.

1261: in the month of September, when the lord Mastino della Scala had completed his year of office as *Podestà*, by his wishes the lord Andrea Zeno of Venice became *Podestà*.

1262: the lord Mastino della Scala was appointed and created Captain of all the people of the city of Verona by the common will and consent of the people of that city.

Some years later, it was provided in the city statutes that the then head of the ruling family, Alberto della Scala, must be present when representatives of the guilds elected the *Podestà*, and that the election must be carried out 'with the assent and approval of the lord Alberto'. The early della Scala also used the title of Head of the Merchants, *Podestà dei Mercanti*, and Alberto della Scala rejoiced in the title of 'Captain and Rector of the Heads of the Guilds and *Capitano del Popolo* of Verona'.

There were parallels elsewhere for these claims to an authority based on the leadership of the Popolo. The authority of the Torriani in Milan was based partly on their position as Heads of the *Credenza di Sant' Ambrogio*; and in the last quarter of the thirteenth century Matteo Visconti, a relative of the reigning lord Archbishop, repeatedly held the office of *Capitano del Popolo*. In 1285 at Pisa Ugolino della Gherardesca was named both *Podestà* and *Capitano del Popolo* for a ten-year spell. Similar titles, which seemed to draw together the two bodies politic of the city under a single head, were subsequently held by Federico da Montefeltro in 1310 and by Uguccione della Fagiola in 1314–16. At Bologna Taddeo Pepoli preferred to use the title of Defender of the Peace, undertaking to preserve it both against violence within the commune and against the Pope who claimed sovereignty over Bologna.

Formal grants of authority by commune or Popolo were often used to give an appearance of legality and constitutionalism to *Signorie*. But they were seldom if ever spontaneous and voluntary, and had usually been preceded by a *coup d'état* on the part of the *Signore* and his allies and clients, or by their gradual penetration into the chief organs of state and accumulation of office. The assembly at Ferrara which formally established Obizzo d'Este as lord in 1264 had been very carefully rigged by Aldighieri Fontana, an Estense supporter, and was influenced by strong external pressure. Guelf leaders from Bologna, Padua, Mantua and Modena were present, together with the Archbishop of Ravenna. The Estensi managed to disarm the people in general, but at the same time they allowed their own vassals to carry weapons, and were careful to keep citizens of suspected loyalties at a distance.

Moreover, when the opportunity presented itself, the *Signori* were eager to legitimate their authority by seeking approval from above, so that they should no longer be dependent on power voted to them by their subjects. In Lombardy Henry VII's shortage of money proved a godsend to local lords, for it forced him after a time to sell the position of imperial vicar to potentates with deep local roots, rather than install his own followers from outside. Beneficiaries of this new policy included the da Camino of Treviso, the della Scala of Verona, the Bonacolsi of Mantua and the Visconti of Milan. Even the Papacy, despite the vigorous centralizing policy it pursued in the days of the legate du Poujet, was forced to recognize local lords – such as the Estensi of Ferrara – as its vicars for a term of years, and thus to confirm in office those it would have liked to dislodge.

In theory, authority devolved from above and power voted from below met together in the *Signore*. But genuine constitutional monarchy was probably unknown outside Venice. There the Doge was chosen from and by the ruling oligarchy, and – at least after 1268 – there was virtually no popular participation, even of a formal character, in this complicated process. Although he held office for life, he was bound by an oath or 'ducal promise'. The text of this undertaking was reviewed by a commission of Correttori, during the periods when the office was vacant, and it could be suitably amended in the light of any acts of misconduct which the late Doge had committed. One Doge, Marino Falier, was convicted of treason against the Republic and executed in 1355. Few of the long-established *Signori* were dispatched by so formal a process, though several of them were assassinated.

None the less it was still true that many *Signori*, even though they did not really share power with commune or Popolo, chose to preserve the old communal structures of government and administration – though they were quite capable of packing the communal councils with persons acceptable to themselves, or of grafting on to the body politic new, small and manoeuvrable organs which were emanations of their own authority. Certainly the Bonacolsi of Mantua were slow to come out into the open. In 1285, thirteen years after Pinamonte's *coup d'état*, the communal councils were still making their decisions according to the traditional forms, and had only just begun to append to their resolutions the significant rider 'with the approval of the lord *Capitano*'. By the early fourteenth century the Bonacolsi were empowered to summon the communal council at will and to use it to sanction their acts of government; to determine Mantua's relationship with other communes; to wield judicial and executive power; to change ordinances, statutes and decrees; and to dispose of public money without having to account for it. Bardellone Bonacolsi (1291–9) had begun to select from reliable citizens his own small *Consiglio del Signore*, which was destined to supersede the larger communal councils as an effective organ of business. But it was characteristic, if illogical, of the reigning Bonacolsi that he should take the trouble in 1311 to get his imperial vicariate officially recognized by the communal council. It may be, as a distinguished Italian medievalist remarked, that changes of legal form were much more feared than were changes of substance in government.

Many *Signorie* arose in the Romagna – those of the Alidosi

of Imola, the Manfredi of Faenza, the Ordelaffi of Forlì, the Malatesta of Rimini, the da Polenta of Ravenna. Some of them, with their armed followings, were much in demand as military contractors elsewhere. Uguccione della Fagiola, at one time Henry VII's vicar in Genoa, lord of Arezzo and later of Pisa, hailed from the mountainous regions on the borders between Tuscany, the Romagna and the March of Ancona. In the Romagna urban expansion into the *contado* and the interest of the lords in the cities meant that the towns came to be dominated by the country, and not the other way about. The noble landlords were eager to control the city administration in order to free themselves to market their produce independently of restrictions imposed by the commune. Also, the towns wanted defenders against the papal government, which was seeking to establish effective mastery over the province which had been formally acquired from Rudolf of Habsburg in 1278. Hence the Romagnol lords won control of their cities either as leaders against papal oppression, or as allies of the Papacy against others in the province. After about 1317 factional rivalries tended to be replaced by a union of almost all the feuda-tories in the commune behind the leading family. At approximately the same time the communes began to acknowledge their lords by voting them the office of *Capitano*. Acknowledgement from below was followed, rather later, by recognition from above. Like the Emperors, the Popes sometimes found it advisable to allow some local potentate to govern in their name, realizing that they could not dislodge him and that he was the man who would be obeyed in the district. If the Pope made his rule legiti-mate, tribute could be demanded from him. In the Romagna, the office of papal vicar was first granted to the Alidosi of Imola in the 1340s, and the process was completed some thirty years later when Sinibaldo Ordelaffi was made vicar of Forlì and its subject region.

But papal vicariates were slower than imperial to develop into independent and hereditary offices, and several *Signori* – having failed to meet their obligations to pay tribute – were eventually dispossessed by the restoration of direct pontifical authority. Hereditary and perpetual vicariates began to appear only when the Papacy was weakened by the Great Schism of 1378–1417. Indeed, the Malatesta of Rimini were never granted full hereditary succession, though succession for two generations was granted in 1391. The Pope's vicars wielded far-reaching judicial power, and were frequently authorized to punish rebels and to appoint all officials, though in these matters a right of appeal to the Pope might be reserved. Again, a vicar would be empowered to impose all taxation and collect revenues pertaining to the Church. In return the Popes would require the payment of annual tribute, the swearing of an oath of fealty to the reigning pontiff and his successors, the performance of military service, and the duty of attending parliaments.

Of a very different character were the short-term *Signorie* conferred in moments of military and financial crisis by the city of Florence. Not unnaturally, the Florentines then resorted for aid to the Guelf connection. In 1325, after sustaining a grave military defeat at Altopascio in the course of a struggle against Lucca, they voted the *Signoria* for a ten-year period, by a proper two-thirds vote of the communal councils, to Charles, Duke of Calabria, son of Robert of Anjou. This lordship in fact lasted only three years, and was ended by the almost simultaneous deaths of Charles himself and of the Lucchese warlord, Castruccio Castracani. In the late 1330s an exceptionally severe and complex crisis arose. Florence's greatest banking firms suffered embarrassment and then failure; outbreaks of plague and famine reduced the commune's income; the expensive decision was made to purchase Lucca from its current lord, and at the same time the Florentines faced the prospect of having to fight the Pisans and their allies in order to make the purchase good. The Florentine oligarchy then conferred the *Signoria* on Walter of Brienne, who had acted as vicar to Charles of Calabria in 1326 and was a kinsman of Robert of Anjou and a marshal of the French royal armies. His aid was invoked in the hope that he might protect the tottering firms of merchant bankers from the claims of their creditors; reduce military expenditure so as to end the current moratorium which had had to be imposed on interest payments on the public debt; and overhaul the system of taxation.

Both Charles of Calabria and Walter of Brienne took the unpopular but necessary step of reintroducing for brief periods direct taxation based on a general survey of the property and goods of the citizens, in order to supplement communal income from gabelles. The strong hand of an extraordinary government was required to carry such drastic measures through. Walter of Brienne did in fact succeed in concluding peace with Pisa, and in asserting much more rigorous control over communal finance. This entailed the recovery of tax-arrears, the strict exaction of obligations due to the city on the part of the *contado*, and measures against persons who had illegally usurped the public property of the Florentine commune. Brienne certainly obliged his summoners by granting protection to near-bankrupt firms, but he also proceeded to investigate their corrupt activities and to try to reduce his own dependence on them by seeking wider popular support. He kept down the level of the excises on wine and meat, and began to permit greater autonomy to small masters and workers in the woollen industry who had previously been denied any form of union recognition. The dyers received permission to form their own guild in November 1342, and workers in the wool-guild generally were allowed to form their own military companies. But popular support proved too unreliable to sustain Walter of Brienne against a general revolt on the part of the more well-to-do citizens in the summer of 1343. These short-lived dictatorships in Florence were the products of military and financial crises, and were not deeply embedded in the structure of society and the state.

Walter of Brienne was not the only lord to seek wider support among artisans in order to be free of oligarchic control. Some parallels can, for example, be found in Pisa – where both the Gherardesca (1284–8) and Uguccione della Fagiola (1314–16) favoured guildsmen against their social superiors. Uguccione, indeed, beheaded two of the merchant family of Bonconti, who were almost certainly members of the Ghibelline faction which had called him in. Earlier still, in the mid-thirteenth century, Ezzelino da Romano had increased the size of the communal council in Verona from 525 to 1,285 members in 1252–4; and of 665 members of the largest communal council in Padua in 1254 nearly 150 were recognizably of the guildsman-artisan class.

However, *Signorie* which had consolidated their rule did not usually prove, in the long run, eager to govern either demagogically or democratically. Here, as in the republics of Florence, Siena and Venice, the tendency was towards a return to oligarchy. In Verona the independence of the guilds waned some time during the reign of Alberto della Scala, who provided in 1298 that guild representatives were not to assemble without his consent. At Padua, under the Carraresi, a statute of 1338 made the largest communal council into a closed body, whose members held their positions for life, and could dispose of them as if they were private property to others who had the necessary residence qualifications, and whose tax liabilities reached the requisite minimum level. In any case, in the second half of the century, Francesco da Carrara the Elder took many of his most important decisions with the aid of a *Consiglio del Signore* of his own. On momentous occasions – as in 1372, when the question of the boundary between the Venetian and Paduan states was under discussion – he consulted with an assembly of notables summoned and selected by himself for the purpose. He did not deal with any constitutional body whose composition was determined by rules and procedures beyond his control. Nor was the commune, in any genuine sense, consulted about the succession of one Carrarese lord to another, though it might be called upon to ratify a decision already made. Hence, there was little question of a 'dyarchy', of a division of rule between the *Signore* and the commune which had in theory established him or his ancestors in power. In any case the surviving communal councils were not the organs of a democracy, but of a restricted, property-owning and self-perpetuating oligarchy.

In view of the great regional importance of the Milanese lordship, and in view of the role which it came to assume in the later fourteenth century as a pacemaker in a new system of inter-state relations, it is worth examining its story in slightly greater detail. It cannot be presented, however, as a typical case, for it had one fairly distinctive feature: the importance in thirteenth-century Milan of the battle for control of the Archbishopric, and of the fusion of civic lordship and ecclesiastical authority in the person of Archbishop Ottone Visconti. Bishop-seigneurs were not unknown elsewhere – for example, in Arezzo – but there was none so great as the Visconti. The estates of the Arch-bishop supported many noble families which held lands from him in fee, attended his court in the city and kept houses there. Hence, there was a strong tendency for the Archbishop to ally with the greater vassal-families of the *capitanei* and the lesser vassals who were called *valvassores*. It was these families that normally controlled elections to the see, through their monopoly of places in the cathedral chapter. But the social and political structures of Milan

were complicated, as in other Italian cities, by the formation of organizations which rivalled the Establishment of
capitanei and *valvassores*. The first of these, called the
Motta, may have consisted partly of *valvassores* who, chafing
under oppression at the hands of their superiors the
capitanei, had renounced their fiefs in order to enter Milan
as free citizens. But it may also have included prominent
citizens whose wealth had originated in the city, through
commerce or manufacturing. Some of them had doubtless
acquired feudal rights in the countryside, but this did not
enable them to enter the ranks of the *capitanei* and *valvassores*, who had come to form something of a closed caste.
The other association, the *Credenza di Sant' Ambrogio*, was
more plebeian, and consisted of artisans and shopkeepers,
of small masters rather than labourers or journeymen. The
first of the native *Signorie* of Milan was formed by ambitious
families breaking away from the *capitanei* and *valvassores*
and putting themselves at the head of the *Credenza di Sant'
Ambrogio*.

By the mid-thirteenth century Milan was the fulcrum of
the Guelf alliance against the Emperor Frederick II, and
this stimulated a move towards monarchical government.
Authority was concentrated in the hands of the Papal
Legate, Gregorio da Montelongo, and of his protégé, the
Archbishop Leone da Perego. On the other hand the *Motta*
and *Credenza* were creating a multiple authority by electing
their own chieftains, thus violating a pact of 1225 which had
forbidden them to do so and had theoretically subjected
them to the commune's *Podestà*. They were demanding a
more equable system of taxation and trying to insist that
the cathedral chapter should be thrown open to persons
who were not *capitanei* or *valvassores*. After the Emperor's
death the Milanese at first tried to restore order with foreign
aid. In 1252, as though forgetting their Guelf affiliations,
they resorted to the Marquess Manfredi Lancia, a feudal

lord and a former imperial partisan. He now became lord
of the city for a period of three years, with a paid force of
1,000 soldiers recruited from various parts of Italy. At the
same time, the unenviable task of allotting the tax burden
and finding new sources of revenue had also to be entrusted
to a supposedly impartial foreigner, Beno de' Gozzadini of
Bologna.

But Milan was on its way towards the foundation of a
Signoria based on the rule of a native aristocratic family, the
della Torre or Torriani, whose heads were now out of
personal ambition offering leadership to the *Credenza di
Sant' Ambrogio*. At first Martino della Torre needed an
ally from outside Milan, in the shape of Manfred's henchman, the Marquess Uberto Pellavicino, whom he succeeded
in introducing to Milan as Captain-General in 1259. Their
relationship was not an easy one, because although the
Marquess's functions were supposed to be essentially military, he did intrude into the political field and get relatives
appointed as *Podestà*. But local support for Martino della
Torre did prove strong enough within a few years for him
to lever Pellavicino out of his post as Captain-General in
1264. The Marquess's prestige had already been badly
tarnished by his excommunication as an enemy of the
Church and as a protector of heretics. He was left to take
his revenge by seizing the goods of Milanese merchants at
Cremona and by offering his protection to Milanese exiles,
victimized by the régime of Martino della Torre. From
November 1263 Martino had become 'perpetual lord of the
people of Milan', and the regional influence of the great city
helped him to build up a multiple personal lordship in
neighbouring towns, to become '*Podestà* and lord of the
communes of Bergamo, Como, Novara and Lodi'. In 1265
a relative, Napo or Napoleone della Torre, succeeded him
as lord in Milan, with titles which included that of *anziano
perpetuo del Popolo*, and by 1272 the formal responsibility of

the *Podestà* was to secure obedience, not to the statutes of the commune, but to Napoleone della Torre and the *Credenza di Sant' Ambrogio.*

But in one respect the Torriani had failed. They had not secured the Archbishopric, although Martino's cousin, Raimondo della Torre, had been a candidate for the dignity in 1262. In view of a prolonged vacancy in the see, the Pope had intervened and appointed the archdeacon Ottone Visconti, a member of a rival Milanese family of *capitanei.* But Martino della Torre and his ally Pellavicino then retaliated by forcibly occupying most of the lands of the Archbishopric, so as to prevent Visconti from taking possession. Furthermore, the pro-Angevin and Guelf foreign policy which the Torriani subsequently adopted did successfully confuse the issue, in that it inhibited the Pope from wholeheartedly backing his own candidate and insisting that he be installed. Indeed, Raimondo della Torre, who was already Bishop of Como, was compensated by being appointed by Gregory X in 1273 to the immensely rich Patriarchate of Aquileia, another ecclesiastical dignity which was still a great territorial power. This was a means to further honour for the Torriani. Desire for the sympathy of the Patriarch, who controlled the gateway to Italy through Friuli, helps to account for the decision of Rudolf of Habsburg to bestow the office of imperial vicar on Napoleone della Torre.

But Ottone Visconti did not abandon hope. Although his exile lasted for fifteen years, he was able to conduct operations from outlying fortresses belonging to the diocese and to commit his agents to collect his revenues from various parts of it. In 1276 he became the leader of the Milanese exiles. Meanwhile, the Torriani unwisely narrowed the basis of their support by quarrelling with, and driving abroad, a number of families which had followed them when they took over the leadership of the *Credenza.*

The Visconti and their fellow exiles proved able to enlist self-seeking military support from great landlords in the countryside, from the Marquesses of Monferrato and the Counts of Langosco, and to inflict defeat on the Torriani at the battle of Desio in 1277. Ottone Visconti was at last able to occupy the Archbishopric and to assert effective rule over the city. However, until a further and more decisive victory over the Torriani on the banks of the river Adda four years later, he was compelled, like Martino della Torre before him, to rely on the services of an outsider, (this time the Marquess of Monferrato) as Captain-General. Once again it proved possible to ditch this external support when the régime was soundly established. The wealth of the Archbishopric sustained Ottone's personal lordship over Milan, and he was able to import many vassals from the *contado* to the city and to set up gate-companies to give him military support. To coordinate the city's government, he erected a *Consiglio delle Provvisioni*, a commission of twelve deputies which was still to be the most effective instrument of Visconti rule in Milan itself throughout the fourteenth century. He exploited the office of Archbishop to bring up his family with him, practising on a smaller scale the kind of nepotism associated with the Orsini Pope, Nicholas III. His young relative, Matteo Visconti, became for substantial periods *Capitano del Popolo*, not only in Milan itself, but also in Novara and Vercelli.

However, the combination of archiepiscopal authority with the lordship of the city lasted only until Ottone's death in 1295, after which Boniface VIII intervened to prevent the see from becoming effectively the hereditary preserve of the Visconti family. The Archbishop Francesco Fontana of Parma, who ruled the see from 1296 to 1308, finding that the Visconti had infiltrated the administrative machinery of the diocese, began to reach an understanding with their enemies. Matteo Visconti tried to contain the threat by

THE COMING OF THE SIGNORI 159

having his son Galeazzo associated with him as *Capitano del Popolo*, and by arranging marriage alliances with the houses of potential enemies, such as the della Scala of Verona and the Estensi of Ferrara, Modena and Reggio. But for all his precautions, in 1302 the Torriani were restored from exile by a confederation of cities fearful of the preponderance of Milan. There was a brief moment, in 1308, when the old combination of the metropolitan's throne with the lordship of the city looked like being revived, for Cassone della Torre became Archbishop in 1308. But the inner cohesion of the Torriani clan was not sufficient to keep them in power, and the appearance in Italy of the Emperor-elect created a new complication.

Henry VII's work of formal peacemaking restored the Visconti to Milan as private citizens. Guido della Torre was removed from his post of *Capitano del Popolo*, and Henry VII installed his own vicar. The communal statutes were handed over to a commission of lawyers, who were instructed to cleanse them of all marks of Torriani rule. The Torriani, who were obviously suffering from these arrangements far more than were their rivals, engineered an abortive rebellion against the Emperor in February 1311, and rejected the generous peace-terms offered to them. Henry's lack of money impelled him to fall back on local leaders of vaguely Ghibelline history who were prepared to pay him. Matteo Visconti became his vicar in July 1311 – in return for an initial payment of 50,000 florins, and on the understanding that in return for an annual tribute of 25,000 florins he should be entitled to receive and retain imperial revenues from Milan and its *contado*. He was prepared to hold on to his vicariate and maintain his power in Milan for several years in defiance of Pope John XXII's stringent demands that, with the Empire vacated by Henry's death, he should lay it down.

Meanwhile the authority of the Visconti – as in earlier

times – spilled out into neighbouring cities within Milan's zone of influence. Hence, a multiple *Signoria* on the part of several members of the Visconti family rapidly developed in the years after 1311: with Galeazzo Visconti as lord in Cremona and Piacenza, Marco in Tortona and Alessandria, Luchino in Pavia, Stefano in Lodi, Como and Bergamo. The grasp of the Visconti family on Milan and surrounding Lombard areas, expanding and contracting, was to be exerted until the line of male heirs died out in the middle of the fifteenth century. In subsequent years, the watchword of the Visconti was 'peace' – to the cities submitting to their lordship they offered the orderly conditions in which factional conflict would be stilled and the economy might flourish. Hence, when the Visconti took over Como in 1335, the former lord of the town proposed that Azzone Visconti should succeed him to bring the population 'under the authority of peace'; Vercelli submitted to the Visconti 'so that it might enjoy perpetual peace'. At Bergamo in 1333, the agreement between the Visconti and the townspeople established that all who had suffered confiscations of goods since 1296 should have their property restored; that all merchants should be allowed to pass through the territory of Bergamo without fear of reprisals; that the government should undertake to indemnify anyone who was robbed. All contracts or other agreements made under the threat of violence in the past were to be annulled.

In Milan itself, the authority of the Visconti rested on the two legal or quasi-legal pillars common to so many other seigneurial régimes – on their vicariates, and on the formal delegation to them by the communal councils of full governmental powers. These included the authority to make and enforce law; civil and criminal jurisdiction; the power of imposing taxation; and that of declaring war and concluding peace. The Visconti kept in existence a vast communal council in Milan itself – the Council of Nine Hundred – on which they relied for the legitimation of their acts. However, this body was far too cumbersome and too little capable of secrecy to enjoy very much effective authority in making decisions. The real power in Milan itself was the so-called *Consiglio delle Provvisioni*, to which, from 1313 onwards, the Visconti themselves nominated members. Since – at least from 1364 – the twelve members of this small board held office only for periods of two months at a stretch, it was clearly up to the Visconti lord to provide the thread of continuity. Moreover, the *Consiglio delle Provvisioni* was responsible for hand-picking the Council of Nine Hundred from among the 'best' and 'richest' citizens – aided only by nominations advanced by the local self-perpetuating parish councils. The lord of Milan was bound to respect the statutes of the commune he was supposed to represent. But he enjoyed full power to alter them when necessary, and at intervals throughout the century, in 1330, 1348–51 and 1395–6, the Visconti ordered commissions to prepare new bodies of statutes. Communal councils might formally bestow authority on the Visconti, but the lords of the city carefully determined the composition of those councils. Except in a formal sense, there was no divided sovereignty of lord and commune – although the Visconti, like all reasonably stable governments, obviously depended on a real measure of tacit popular approval, or at least on their ability to condition their subjects to accepting their rule.

*

By the middle and late fourteenth century it was clear that the general trend of development within Italian cities had not been towards the greater realization of liberty. All too often, liberty had most strongly implied the freedom of the powerful to engage in anarchic conflict, and had been sacrificed to the maintenance of peace and order through relatively strong and concentrated government. The triumph of the Popolo over the entrenched patriciate had not meant the establishment of democracy or manhood suffrage, but had often foreshadowed the formation of rich oligarchies which felt more in common with the old patricians or magnates than with small retailers or with craftsmen dependent on the work of their hands. The economic needs of the city could seldom be divorced from the need for vigorous military strategy to maintain commercial outlets, and even cities with a vigorous mercantile and manufacturing community as active as the Milanese could fall under the dominion of seigneurs. The rise of the communes had not meant their universal and complete triumph over the feudal lords and the great landowners of the *contado*.

PART THREE

The Beginnings of the Renaissance

The Concept of the Renaissance

9

About 1300, the Italians were the leaders of all Europe in the related spheres of commerce and law. Two hundred years later they were still the most commercially experienced people, but their economic leadership was being eclipsed by their own genius in art and architecture, and by the achievement of Italian scholars in the recovery and interpretation, indeed the re-living, of antiquity. The Italians had for a time wrested intellectual and cultural supremacy from the French. In conventional historical terms, the Italy of the Renaissance was superseding the Italy of the communes and of the medieval commercial revolution; the Italy of the native princes the Italy of the Guelfs and Ghibellines. But what was this Renaissance, which to so many historians and lovers of Italy is the very peak or apex of Italian history, and the most tangible monument to its past?

Essentially, the Renaissance was a conscious and deliberate movement of revival in certain fields of human activity, in which men believed themselves to be rejecting commonly accepted values and techniques, and reviving those of an idealized past which had been obscured by time. History cannot be reduced to algebraic formulae, but something of the idea can be grasped by postulating four ages or epochs, and calling them A, B, C and D. Age C rejects the values of age B, which immediately precedes it, and seeks to return to those of the long-distant age A, which lies hundreds of years back in the past: though age C's rejection of age B is by no means as complete as the men of age C would like to think, and they unconsciously retain many unacknowledged attitudes surviving from age B. Out of the conscious interaction between A and C, and out of the persistent influence of B upon C, there gradually emerges another age different from all three – age D. Intellectuals of the fourteenth and fifteenth centuries were formulating a view of history, or chronological scheme, in these terms: first, the ancient, pre-Christian world, which was for the first time clearly recognized as pre-Christian; then the corrupt Middle Ages, in which the ideals of the ancient world were obscured or barbarized; then, finally, the present age, the era of conscious revival, the age whose distinctive mark was the Renaissance. Hence, by contemporaries, Middle Ages and Renaissance were seen as contrasting concepts, neither of which could have part with the other; and the Renaissance has been associated not only by contemporaries but also by its students in the nineteenth and twentieth centuries, with a mentality, an outlook or a 'world view' which contrasts – more or less dramatically – with the medieval 'world view' or system of values. Many modern historians, however, have tried to show how the Renaissance was really a natural development or growth originating in the situation in which Italy found herself in the thirteenth century, or how thirteenth-century Franciscans contributed to forming some of the mental attitudes identified with the Renaissance. This does not, however, alter the fact that the men of the Renaissance believed themselves to be breaking with the Middle Ages, even if they exaggerated their own originality.

The idea that there had recently been a dramatic revival of eternally valid and permanently correct principles in literature and painting was certainly present in the mid-fourteenth century in the writings of Giovanni Boccaccio, the Florentine novelist and scholar. His collection of short stories, the *Decameron*, included an anecdote about the

Florentine painter, Giotto, in which he said that Giotto had 'brought back to light that art which had for many ages lain buried beneath the blunders of those who painted rather to delight the eyes of the ignorant than to satisfy the intelligence of the wise'. A sincere admirer of Dante, a fellow Florentine, Boccaccio described him in his biography as having 'opened the way for the return of the Muses, who had been banished from Italy', and as having revived 'dead poetry'. Some years later, in a letter to the Logothete of Sicily, he described how in Italy in his own time there were men of the same calibre as the ancients, seeking fame and immortality through poetry. Poetry had not been totally extinguished in Italy since ancient times, but its spirit had been weak and barely half alive. Not only Dante, but another great Florentine, Petrarch, had breathed life into it anew. He told how Petrarch,

neglecting the precepts of certain writers who scarcely attain to the threshold of poetry, began to take the way of antiquity with so much force of character, with such enthusiasm and perspicacity, that no obstacle would arrest him, nor could ridicule turn him from his way. Far from that, breaking through and tearing away the brambles and bushes with which by the negligence of men the road was covered, and remaking a solid road of the rocks heaped up and made impassable by inundations, he opened a passage for himself and for those who would come after him.

The germ of the concept of the Renaissance was here: the notion of abrupt revival, the role in it assigned to certain great figures, the implied belief that Florence, which had fathered them, was to Renaissance Italy as Athens had been to fifth-century Greece. Later writers were to elaborate upon this notion, seeing a coordinated movement in literature and the fine arts, which tended to flourish or decay in unison with each other; seeing the Florentine architect Brunelleschi as a reviver as great as Giotto. They were also to explain how ancient principles had come to be buried and lost – how architecture had declined as a result of repeated invasions from the north after the fall of the Roman Empire and through the introduction of 'customs and traditions from north of the Alps'; how painting and sculpture had supposedly been smothered to death by the puritanical iconoclasm of the Christian era.

The men of the Renaissance, then, believed themselves to be taking part in a kind of 'antiquarian revolution'. At this time, as in previous centuries, revolutionaries sought, not to apply principles which had never previously been tried, but to return to an idealized past: they could not formulate the notion of infinite material progress, or see the possibility that human skill and achievement might be indefinitely extended. In the twelfth and thirteenth centuries innovation had commonly been disguised as return, in many spheres of action; the Franciscans, to say nothing of many thirteenth-century heretics, had dreamed of the renewal of the Church through a return to its primitive, uncorrupted state. In a sense, therefore, the Renaissance was a movement for which there were numerous 'medieval' precedents, and it was by no means the first revival of antiquity to take place since the fall of the Roman Empire in the west.

But the Renaissance of the fourteenth and fifteenth centuries could not have acquired such significance if it had merely been seen as one of a series of revival movements. It has been associated, by many of its observers in the nineteenth and twentieth centuries, with the birth of certain attitudes or other intellectual phenomena which are held to foreshadow those of the modern world. Historians have found themselves making a kind of stylized contrast between 'the Renaissance mind' and 'the medieval mind', and assigning distinctive attributes to each of these: the 'Renaissance mind' is connected, for example, with the spirit of individualism, where the Middle Ages are said to have upheld a corporative spirit; the men of the Renaissance are believed to have attached a positive value to the things of this life (which the men of the Middle Ages could allegedly regard only as a rehearsal for the life to come), and to the physical world, which medieval people supposedly thought of as a realm of sin and corruption. There is, perhaps, no reason why one should not think in such terms, provided that in doing so one bears in mind that 'the Renaissance mind' and 'the medieval mind' are really neatly tailored models or intellectual abstractions which the historian has himself established for the sake of argument and exposition – and that they are both much tidier than the historical reality ever was. There was no one way in which all people, or even all intellectuals, thought during the Middle Ages. Still less was there any specific point in time at which a 'Renaissance' outlook replaced a 'medieval': the two mentalities were quite capable of coexisting, and they could appeal not only to different people living at the same time, but also to the same person in different moods.

As already hinted, the Renaissance is associated with the idea or spirit of 'individualism' in many fields of human action. For the writer, individualism took the form of expressing his personal feelings or reactions to a situation, in the belief that they were unique, and were worth communicating to others and recording for posterity – it opened the way to a literature of introspection, and to a greater interest in psychology. In literature there arose a greater interest in biography, and in art a greater interest in portraiture: so that people were seen as unique and individual personalities – not just as social types, as symbols of humanity at large, as allegorical figures of no particular character, or as vessels of the divine grace and instruments of God's purpose. Also, in fourteenth- and fifteenth-century Italy, significant changes began to occur in the status of sculptors or painters. They – or some of them – ceased to be regarded as just highly skilled manual workers practising traditional crafts, or as anonymous members of teams working on a façade, a pulpit or a fountain. The intellectual content of their profession was recognized, and some aspired to be creative beings following their own personal inclinations, leaving their own mark upon their work, and creating their own distinctive style. In the words of Jacob Burckhardt, the nineteenth-century historian who did most to evoke the modern concept of the Renaissance, medieval man had been

conscious of himself only as a member of a race, people, party, family, or corporation – only through some general category. In Italy this veil first melted into air . . . man became a spiritual *individual*, and recognized himself as such.

The phrasing is significant. At all times, perhaps, people have in practice thought and acted in an individual and unique manner: but they have not always known they were doing it; they have not always been aware of the differentiation of individual characteristics or of the importance of recording subjective feelings, and have not always sought to develop personality.

Individualism has not been identified solely in art and literature. It has also been seen in the general Italian political situation, although the individualism of the Renaissance has very little to do with modern liberalism or democracy: with any belief that every mature individual has a right to a say in the running of the community to which he belongs. When the Renaissance was at its height the prevailing tendency – even in those Italian states which had preserved republican forms – was towards the formation of more rigid and more exclusive ruling oligarchies. The general drift was from communal to seigneurial government, and not the other way about. But, or so Burckhardt argued, fourteenth- and fifteenth-century Italy was, in a sense, a land of opportunity within which there had been a breakdown of the old feudal-hierarchical society culminating in Emperor and Pope. To an unusual extent, the ethic of worldly success and failure was beginning to replace the conventional Christian ethic; moral restraint was disregarded in relations between states and cities, and in the pursuit of power. Social position, wealth and power came to depend on the talent and achievement of the individual person, rather than on the circumstances of his birth or the excellence of his lineage; an aristocracy of talent sprang up beside the old aristocracies of birth. This kind of individualism was embodied in the *condottiere*, the mercenary captain or soldier of fortune who might, as did Francesco Sforza in the fifteenth century, rise from undistinguished origins to become lord of a state as great as the Duchy of Milan. Other historians, seeking to extend the concept of the Renaissance into the realms of economic history, have pointed out that the opportunism and resourcefulness displayed by Italian merchants and travellers was at least as significant as that of the *condottiere* or of the self-made *Signore*. There was no democracy in fourteenth- and fifteenth-century Italy, and in the Venetian Republic, for example, the individual nobleman was completely overshadowed by the class or caste to which he belonged. But there was room for a certain kind of ruthless opportunism to be practised by a small number of people, with an unusual degree of self-awareness.

The Renaissance is also associated with a belief in the positive value of human life and in the beauty of this world – with the cultivation of values which lay stress on human dignity rather than on the utter unworthiness of man in the sight of God, and place man at the centre of the universe. This is closely connected with the Renaissance's rediscovery of the pre-Christian ancient world, which was recognized as something to be admired in its own right. It did not necessarily lead to paganism or atheism on the part of fifteenth-

century Italians. Rather, it favoured a tendency to stress
what Christianity had in common with ancient religions,
and hence to play down the sacraments and the role of the
clergy, whilst emphasizing the ethical and rational content
of Christianity. There was growing stress on man's ability
to find his own salvation through systematic and righteous
conduct rather than through the performance (regular or
otherwise) of rituals endowed by the Church with mystical
or magical power.

To some extent, the outlook associated with the Renaissance can be defined in terms of its opposite. It reversed the
sentiments which were expressed, for example, by the
brothers of a Venetian religious fraternity, the Scuola di
San Giovanni Evangelista, in the first decade of the fourteenth century, in the preamble to their Rule:

> Human frailty itself clearly teaches and shows us how profound
> are the uncertainties of this present life. For every day, man, in his
> wretchedness, is oppressed with care, overwhelmed by toil, and
> imprisoned in bondage to the Devil. He is always immersed and
> enmeshed in sin. Hence, as Scripture tells us, even a day-old child
> is not free of sin; and, as St John the Evangelist says, 'If we say
> that we have not sinned, we deceive ourselves'. Since, as St
> Augustine says, every mortal man living out this temporal life is
> dwelling in a foreign country, he should always keep before his
> eyes the end of this fleeting and transitory life, and must always
> think about receiving in future the rewards of good and evil.

The 'Renaissance mind' no longer viewed this present life
as a dreary exile in bondage to sin, or saw it merely as
preparation for death: though one must remember that
throughout the fourteenth and fifteenth centuries, even
whilst a small group of intellectuals were beginning to place
a changed value on human life and the material world, many
other people were still subscribing to the Rules of fraternities similar to that of San Giovanni Evangelista. The two
cultures or mentalities coexisted; the Renaissance was an

avant-garde movement involving an élite, rather than a 'spirit of the times' which penetrated to every social and intellectual level, and infected every branch of human activity.

More specifically, the Renaissance has been associated with a growing belief that the active life, the life of a citizen who seeks or accepts public responsibility within the world, may actually be of greater value than that of the ascetic or the solitary sage who turns his back on the world and devotes himself to a life of contemplation. It has also been connected with a changed attitude, not only to the temporal world in general, but to worldly wealth in particular: riches were no longer seen as a snare or encumbrance, or as an asset to which the virtuous man ought at best to be indifferent. Wealth was now actively praised by certain intellectuals who were prepared to declare what could be done with it, and to show what virtues could scarcely be practised without it. An open and avowed interest in material things, and in the active rather than the contemplative life, led naturally to an increased interest in the writing of history as the study of change, and to a greater readiness to see it in purely human terms – rather than as the working out of some divine purpose, guided by the hand of Providence.

*

Hitherto, the attributes of the Renaissance have been discussed in a deliberately abstract fashion. The adjectives 'medieval' and 'Renaissance' have hitherto been used to describe two contrasting systems of values which were quite capable of coexisting. They can, however, also be used to describe successive periods in history – the 'Renaissance period' succeeding the Middle Ages at some point near to 1300 and extending for anything up to three centuries thereafter. If one uses the terms to describe differing mentalities, then by definition the Renaissance seems like a revolt against the Middle Ages, a dramatic fracture with it. But the Renaissance can equally well be seen as a natural growth stemming from the situation in thirteenth-century Italy, as an evolutionary process masquerading as a revolution: emerging from the chronological Middle Ages, rather than rebelling against them. The task of the next chapter will be to describe the growth of a distinctively Italian culture from the thirteenth century to the mid-fourteenth, to try to relate it to the general political and economic situation in Italy, and to connect it where possible with the concept of the Renaissance already outlined.

Antiquity and the Vernacular

10

Italian culture was partly shaped by Italy's peculiar position as the most invaded country of Europe, as a half-way house between east and west, and as the heiress of ancient Rome. For Italians, antiquity was to become the symbol of their own past greatness, and the Latin language was always a natural literary rival to their own vernacular tongue. Italian artists were exposed in the thirteenth century to the influence of Gothic styles in sculpture, architecture and book illumination imported from the west, and also to the inspiration of early Christian and Byzantine art – kept alive by their contacts with the east. From both these sources they were to learn how to create 'picture space', so that the flat surface of a painting seemed like a window on a scene happening beyond it.

French influence on Italian writers was considerable, even before the Angevin conquest of the south, and French showed signs of rivalling Latin as the language of educated men. The Florentine Brunetto Latini, a teacher of Dante, chose after several years of political exile in France to compile a learned encyclopedia in French prose, because this was 'the most delightful tongue, which has most in common with all other languages.' As a prisoner of war in Genoa, the Venetian explorer Marco Polo dictated the story of his adventures to Rustichello of Pisa, who rendered it in the language of French chivalrous romance. In the late thirteenth and early fourteenth century, legends of Charlemagne were imported to the Veneto in italianized French.

Nearly a hundred years later, it was still necessary for Benvenuto of Imola, a commentator on the works of Dante, to protest at the admiration which some Italians still cherished for the French language, and at their rooted belief that it was superior to their own vernacular.

In the thirteenth century the forms and the sentiments of Italian poetry were strongly influenced by the lyrics of troubadours from Provence, by their songs of 'fine love', love of the heart and mind, which foreshadowed Dante's worship of Beatrice or Petrarch's of Laura. During the French crusade against the Albigensian heretics, troubadours migrated to the courts of feudal lords in northern Italy, and in parts of the north, especially in Genoa, lyric writers chose to write in Provençal rather than Italian. But in southern Italy at the court of Frederick II Provençal was less easily understood, and poets and minstrels chose to use their own version of Italian, and so to create the first substantial Italian literature. Their work was later to be recognized as the foundation for a poetic language common to all Italy.

The spoken dialects of Italy had, in past centuries, naturally separated themselves from Latin, the written language of learned men and of official communication. From the early thirteenth century, Italians were beginning to make increasingly common use of their dialects for literary purposes – as Francis of Assisi wrote his *Canticle of the Sun* in a refined or 'ennobled' form of his native Umbrian. Guido Faba, a teacher of rhetoric at the University of Bologna, compiled a treatise containing Italian 'models' or formulae for letters and public addresses towards the middle of the thirteenth century. By this time it was undoubtedly necessary for the civic authorities to take account of people who did not know Latin: hence the statutes of Bologna laid down in 1246 that notaries must be able to translate Latin documents into the vernacular for the benefit of the ignorant. Municipal or village statutes were occasionally issued only in the vernacular in the late thirteenth century, and in central Italy the translation of civic and guild statutes became increasingly common in the first half of the fourteenth century. Wills and petitions were frequently drawn up in the local version of Italian prose. Religious confraternities of flagellants composed songs or *laude* in Italian; in some of these, roles were distributed among several singers, and hence the songs began to develop into rudimentary plays.

But the development of a common poetic language for Italy, and the growing prestige of the Italian vernacular, depended heavily on a great poet and a learned man who deliberately chose to use it for the instruction of ordinary people. Dante Alighieri was a citizen of Florence, born in 1265; at the age of thirty he entered active political life, took part in the city's councils on several occasions, and rose to serve a term in the supreme magistracy, the Priorate, from June to August 1300. The Guelf party of Florence having split disastrously into the factions of the Black and of the White Guelfs, Dante was exiled in 1302 for his identification with the defeated Whites and their opposition to the schemes of Pope Boniface VIII to subject Tuscany to the temporal power of the Church. Generations later, champions of the virtues of the 'active life' were to see in Dante a modern Socrates or Cicero, who had combined literature and philosophy with the life of a responsible citizen and been martyred by his political enemies. For the rest of his life he was intermittently dependent on the hospitality of alien courts – of the Malaspina lords of Lunigiana, the lords of Verona, the lords of Ravenna, where he died in 1321. Exile made of him a citizen of Italy, rather than a citizen of Florence: he wandered, he said, 'through almost every part of the land where the Italian language extends, a pilgrim, almost a beggar', 'a vessel without sail or rudder, carried to various ports and river mouths and shores by the dry wind that wretched poverty brings forth'.

He cherished the hope of returning to Florence on honourable terms; he was anxious to justify himself, and to compose learned works that would demonstrate beyond doubt that he was not just a maker of verses. He had probably acquired an interest in popularization from the encyclopedist Brunetto Latini, and he determined to communicate his knowledge by the use of the vernacular tongue, so that it could reach as wide an audience as possible. Although he believed that Latin was ultimately a nobler and more virtuous tongue, less subject to corruptibility and change, he was still ready to proclaim with almost prophetic fervour the possibilities inherent in the development of the vernacular. 'This shall be the new light, the new sun which shall rise when the old one has set, and shall illuminate those who are in shadow and darkness because the wonted sun does not shed its beams on them.' In his treatise *De Vulgari Eloquentia*, he strove to define a 'noble' literary style in poetry distilled from the fourteen regional dialects which he had identified. This style was already found in the work of the poets of Frederick II's court, in Dante's own writings, and in that of certain other admired authors: Guido Guinizelli of Bologna, the Florentine Guido Cavalcanti, and others. To some extent, however, the effect of his work was to enhance the prestige of the Florentine dialect, and to give it a disproportionate influence on the development of a common poetic language for Italy. He was prepared to use any Florentine word that he needed, even if it was markedly plebeian. From other sources – Tuscan, other Italian dialects, Latin or French – he used only words which had already found their way into literary currency.

In this vernacular, too, he wrote the *Commedia*, the story of his visionary Easter journey into the depths of Hell, up the cornices of Mount Purgatory and into the heights of

Paradise. His was a concrete and forceful vision of eternity, peopled with figures from the recent as well as from the remote past, imagined in strangely intimate and everyday terms. The Venetian arsenal, for example, gave him inspiration for the punishment in hell of the barrators or grafters who had made money out of trafficking in public offices:

> As in the Venetian arsenal, the winter through
> there boils the sticky pitch to caulk the seams
> of the sea-battered bottoms when no crew
>
> can put to sea – instead of which, one starts
> to build its ship anew, one plugs the planks
> which have been sprung in many foreign parts;
>
> some hammer at a mast, some at a rib;
> some make new oars, some braid and coil new lines;
> one patches up the mainsail, one the jib –
>
> so, but by Art Divine and not by fire,
> a viscid pitch boiled in the fosse below
> and coated all the bank with gluey mire.

As Dante himself described it in a letter of 1319 to his former host, Cangrande della Scala, lord of Verona, the aim of the work was 'to remove those living in this life from a state of misery, and to bring them to a state of happiness' – it was conceived with this very practical objective, of conveying to ordinary people the importance of being in harmony with God at the moment of death. The subject of the poem was 'man, as by his merits or demerits in the exercise of his free will he is deserving of reward or punishment by justice'.

The influence of the *Commedia* on the development of an Italian poetic language – on style, metre and vocabulary – was enormous. Dante himself became the subject of learned commentaries, which began to appear from the 1320s onwards. The Florentines, reproved by Boccaccio, rehabilitated the memory of their most distinguished citizen, and eventually appointed Boccaccio to lecture on the *Commedia* in 1373. But although, through Dante, Italy came to possess a common poetic language, there was still no common language of Italian prose. Admittedly, Boccaccio's *Decameron*, 'written in the Florentine vernacular', did enjoy great popularity. It consisted of a hundred mercilessly irreverent stories of carnal love and trickery, of merchants, adventurers, usurers, pirates and fraudulent friars, with settings all over the peninsula as well as in the foreign capitals frequented by Italian men of business. But only at the beginning of the sixteenth century was the Venetian Pietro Bembo, the first distinguished non-Tuscan author to write in Tuscan prose, to start an effective literary movement for getting Tuscan generally accepted as the universal Italian language of prose, as well as of poetry. The absence of a common Italian language was reflected, for example, in the persistent use of Latin for diplomatic purposes in correspondence between cities or states in different regions. As late as 1453 the Florentines were to feel it necessary to explain apologetically to the Sienese why they had taken the step of replying in the vernacular to a communication. Likewise, the great fifteenth-century Franciscan, Bernardino of Siena, appears to have used Latin for the sermons he preached outside Tuscany.

The cultural achievement – in the literary field – of thirteenth- and fourteenth-century Italy did not however lie only in the triumphant creation of a vernacular literature. Italian men of letters also began to establish an entirely new relationship with the world of antiquity. In earlier centuries educated men had always to some extent looked back to a Roman past and at intervals talked of its renewal. Certain Latin authors – among them Virgil and Ovid, Cicero and Seneca – had never lost their popularity and reputation. But these earlier generations had not grasped the fact that the Roman world was fundamentally different from their own, nor realized that it subscribed to values which were independent of Christianity: they were not conscious of any fracture between the Roman world and their own time, and, showing no sense of anachronism or historical perspective, they clothed the figures of the classical past in modern dress – investing them with Christian significance, portraying them among Gothic buildings or playing chess, conceiving them as romantic and chivalrous heroes. A thirteenth-century Florentine chronicler, Ricordano Malespini, knew that Catiline had lived before Christ: but he was incapable of imagining a world without churches or Catholic Masses in which to put him. The Roman world was believed to have lived on, and the Roman Emperors of the twelfth and thirteenth centuries were held to be the heirs and successors of the Caesars. Even for Dante the ancient world was not a thing in its own right, a self-contained entity: the Roman Empire's supreme glory was that it had been chosen to prepare the world for Christ, to create the universal earthly peace into which Christ was born, and the framework within which Christianity was to spread. The peace created by the Roman Empire had been restored by Justinian and Charlemagne in their day, and Dante looked briefly to Henry VII, another honorary Roman, to restore it in his own time.

But among Italian 'humanists' of the fourteenth century a new attitude to antiquity was born. They realized that the ancient world had been buried beneath the rubble of the despised Middle Ages, and that it was quite alien to their own times: alien, but certainly not irrelevant, for its glories (contrasting with the miseries of the present time) could serve as an inspiration for the present. The ancient world must be re-created and re-lived, as a conscious and deliberate act. The concept arose of a purely literary education, which was not subordinated to philosophy, science or theology; which was based on the reading of certain ancient authors; and which involved the study of grammar, rhetoric, history, poetry and moral philosophy: the so-called 'humanities', the civilizing disciplines whose subject was man.

Although 'humanism' did in a sense involve the conscious rejection of the Middle Ages, it was an educational programme which had developed quite naturally out of the educational traditions of earlier centuries, and particularly out of the teaching of rhetoric. As Professor Kristeller has argued, the humanists were essentially rhetoricians, not just academics, antiquarians or classical scholars. They were writers of letters, orations, panegyrics, poems and history, cultivators of written and spoken eloquence. They were frequently employed to conduct the official correspondence of princes, Popes, prelates or cities, and to serve in their secretariats or chanceries or go on diplomatic missions. Such careers were eventually to afford exciting opportunities for able men of undistinguished birth or scanty inheritance. For a few people they did create a kind of social and geographical mobility which has contributed much to the idea that the Renaissance raised up a new 'aristocracy of talent' beside the older élites of birth and money. In the mid-fifteenth century Tommaso Parentucelli, who came of modest antecedents from Sarzana on the Ligurian coast and had been a tutor to certain great Florentine households, was to rise to become Bishop of Bologna, then a Cardinal, and finally (in 1447) Pope Nicholas V. Enea Silvio Piccolomini, born in 1405 of a noble Sienese family desperately impoverished by exile, served as secretary to distinguished prelates; was employed on a diplomatic mission to Scotland; was retained for a time by the Council of Basel; entered the service of the Emperor Frederick III; and at last in his middle age embarked on the ecclesiastical career which brought him to the Holy See as Pope Pius II in 1458.

Since the late eleventh century the art of composing formal letters (*ars dictaminis*) and that of composing speeches (*ars arengandi*) had been taught in Italian schools and universities. In the thirteenth century there was already a large 'speech-literature', consisting of orations designed for weddings and funerals and for academic and other solemn occasions, or speeches intended for delivery by *Podestà* and other functionaries on taking up office. Rhetoric became an important part of the training of judges, lawyers and notaries, who were prominent figures in the government and administration of their cities. The University of Bologna, in particular, acquired a high reputation for training in the art of rhetoric, and instructors educated at Bologna departed to found their own schools elsewhere – as, for example, Mino of Colle di Val d'Elsa, who studied at Bologna in the early 1280s, went to teach in the Tuscan towns of Pisa, San Miniato, Volterra and Arezzo, and compiled manuals of model letters specially adapted to the needs of the various social groups which made up the communes.

Italian university education had always been directed towards the more practical and worldly disciplines – towards law and medicine rather than theology, and towards civil as well as canon law. Students of theology gravitated, rather, to the seminaries of the mendicant orders. The concept of an essentially secular education, independent of religious preoccupations but scarcely antagonistic towards them, was therefore not strange to Italy. In the late thirteenth and fourteenth centuries the study and practice of rhetoric, which was concerned with worldly uses, became linked with classical scholarship. Rhetoricians began to acquire a new plainness and direct-ness of style, and a new and fervent interest in antiquity. Hitherto, mere proximity to the ruins of Roman civilization had not inspired any very deep appreciation of antiquity as such among Italians. Ancient objects were treasured, not because they were ancient, but because they were precious or pretty. Moreover, the ancient monuments of Rome served as a vast marble quarry – they were not preserved *in situ* but were used, for example, in building cathedrals elsewhere. Classical scholarship and the concept of a literary education based on the writings of ancient authors had flourished more conspicuously in northern Europe and in France than they ever had in Italy. But after the mid-thirteenth century, classical studies, antiquarianism and the re-creation of the ancient world began to make spectacular progress in Italy at a time when they were declining in France.

From the beginning there was a strong bond between 'humanism' and a legal training, between classical scholarship and practical administrative experience; and this occurred in cities scattered throughout the peninsula, from Naples to Venice, from Padua and Verona to Bologna and Florence. Lawyers and notaries had almost invariably been trained in rhetoric, the art of persuasion by words. Also, as the late Roberto Weiss pointed out, lawyers were used to applying to contemporary problems the great codes of Roman law drawn up in the sixth century by the Emperor Justinian, and this invited them to see Roman civilization as a living thing, and to approach the classics in a similar spirit. The first of the 'humanists' to acquire a reputation that was more than merely local was Albertino Mussato, a notary of Padua writing in the early fourteenth century. He used the tragedies of Seneca as a model for his play dramatizing the rise and fall of Ezzelino da Romano, the tyrant who had ruled Padua from 1237 to 1256. It portrayed a situation intensely relevant to the present day, since the commune of Padua was now threatened by the expanding might of Cangrande della Scala of Verona. Mussato also used concepts drawn from Roman historical writing, and especially from Sallust, to analyse the recent history of his own city; and to explain how, after the years of prosperity from 1256 to 1313, the Paduans had been infected by luxury and greed, and had sunk into an 'immoderate corruption' which accounted for their decay.

The connection between law and humanism was to persist into future generations, though not all humanists were professional men, and rich amateurs were certainly prominent in fifteenth-century Florence. Petrarch, the greatest of the early humanists, came of a family of notaries which originated in the small town of Incisa on the Arno. He read law at the universities of Montpellier and Bologna – although he never practised it, and instead derived financial support from the yield of ecclesiastical benefices. Boccaccio, who in his later career devoted himself to scholarship and to compiling encyclopedias of biography and geography based on classical literature, was originally intended by his father for a business career and was sent to Naples to prepare for it. But he was later, in 1329, allowed to transfer to the study of canon law. Subsequently he abandoned this to devote himself to literary pursuits, though these left time for the occasional holding of public office, and he was inscribed on the rolls of the Guild of Judges and Notaries in Florence in 1351. Again, in the later fourteenth and the fifteenth centuries, certain highly accomplished humanists combined classical scholarship and controversy with the office of chancellor in Florence. The chancellor, as head of the permanent civil service, conducted the Republic's foreign correspondence, and his rhetorical skill helped to make him an effective propagandist. The first of these was Coluccio Salutati (1331–1406), a native of Stignano in the Valdinievole, who was trained as a notary and followed the *ars dictaminis*. At first he served as notary in various small Tuscan towns and villages, but after 1366, perhaps because his marriage compelled him to be more ambitious, he began to seek more influential posts. Having served at Todi, Lucca and the Vatican, he eventually rose to become chancellor of Florence in 1375, and was regularly re-elected to this position until his death. His eloquent pen served the Republic in the war against the Papacy and in the later struggle with the Visconti of Milan. Of those known to have corresponded with Salutati on matters connected with classical scholarship, about forty were notaries, scattered throughout Italy north of Rome; a dozen were chancellors, usually trained as notaries; five held positions in the papal curia; and eight held doctorates in law.

In fourteenth-century classical scholarship there was always a strain of pure antiquarianism, of interest in the ancient world for its own sake – as at Verona, whose cathedral library contained one of the finest collections of ancient manuscripts in Italy. From about 1335 Oliviero Forzetta, a moneylender of Treviso, began systematically to collect ancient marbles, bronzes, coins and engraved gems. But beyond this there was a strong emphasis on re-living the classical past and using it as a spur to action, deriving practical lessons from it. For some time certain towns had been in the habit of comparing themselves to Rome, with more extravagance than accuracy – seeing themselves as colonies founded from Rome, their power and glory now in the ascendant, even while Rome's declined. The commune of Siena boldly adopted as its emblem the Roman she-wolf suckling her human cubs. Civic patriotism delighted in a town's association with some great figure of antiquity, in Mantua's link with Virgil or Padua's with Livy: commemorative statues were erected and alleged tombs discovered. Cola di Rienzo, the tribune of the Roman people and another notary, saw the ruins of ancient Rome as a reminder of past greatness and as a vivid inspiration for the present. He found a text for a forceful political oration in a bronze tablet inscribed with a law of the Emperor Vespasian, which he regarded as proof that supreme power had once belonged to the Romans themselves, who had then delegated it to their Emperor.

Cola's sympathizers included Petrarch, who was both an Italian poet of high reputation and a humanist of great accomplishment: he, above all men, lived in the past as a contemporary without deserting the present. He embodied many of the qualities and much of the outlook usually associated with the Renaissance. He was born in Arezzo in 1304, into a family exiled from Florence, though he was never as closely tied to that city as either Dante or Boccaccio. His family followed the papal court to Avignon in search of employment, but, finding the city overcrowded, settled some miles away at Carpentras. Petrarch despised and criticized the corrupt and exiled court of Avignon, but as a clerk in minor orders he depended on it for patronage and in the course of his life held several canonries, mostly in Italy. As a young man he visited Italy frequently and in his later years, from 1353, committed himself entirely to his native country, where he lived under the protection first of the Visconti of Milan and later of the Carraresi of Padua. He also had a house in Venice, and there was for a time an understanding – which later fell through – that he should bequeath his precious library to the Republic. He died in 1374, on his country estate at Arquà, in the Euganean hills near Padua.

As Petrarch himself wrote, in his autobiographical *Epistle to Posterity*:

I devoted myself, though not exclusively, to the study of ancient times, since I always disliked our own period; so that, if it hadn't been for the love of those dear to me, I should have preferred being born in any other age, forgetting this one; and I always tried to transport myself mentally to other times.

He no longer saw antiquity as a mere prelude to the Christian era, but as an epoch of supreme human achievement in relation to which subsequent ages had declined. Among Petrarch's specific achievements as a classical scholar was the discovery of Cicero's *Letters to Atticus* in the cathedral library at Verona, and he was quick to enter into an imaginary correspondence with Cicero and other ancient authors, whom he treated as friends and contemporaries rather than as remote objects of study; he did, however, maintain his awareness of the distance between ancient times and his own century. He also showed an eager interest in Greek. This was still uncharted territory for most classical scholars, although in the south Robert of Anjou had strongly encouraged translation from Greek into Latin by Calabrians, who had never forgotten Greek. Petrarch delighted in the possession of a manuscript of Homer, although he could not read him, and for a time he and Boccaccio – his friend and admirer – tolerated the eccentricities of an oafish Calabrian Greek, Leontius Pilatus, who prepared for them an erratic translation of Homer.

Petrarch's culture and learning, and his natural inclinations, gave him an intense interest in communicating and in recording for posterity his own personal and highly individual feelings, and in the pursuit of fame and recognition in his own lifetime. Himself the biographer of famous Romans and author of a Latin epic on the general Scipio Africanus, he paved the way for his own biographers, and assembled for posterity a carefully trimmed and streamlined edition of his own correspondence, adding other imaginary letters to make the collection balanced and complete. He ardently desired the honour of being crowned with laurels as a poet of sublime distinction – this somewhat garbled version of the ancient ceremony of crowning poets had been revived in 1315 for the benefit of Mussato of Padua, and Dante had longed for coronation in Florence. Petrarch was in fact 'examined' and sponsored for the laurel crown by King Robert of Naples, with whom he stayed in 1341, and was later crowned in Rome by one of the then Senators, Orso dell' Anguillara.

Despite his passion for fame Petrarch was by no means a self-confident egotist, interested only in himself, since he possessed a gift for friendship and even a disarming modesty. He later said of his coronation that 'There was more affection and encouragement to youth in it than conscientiousness.' He was not an archetypal 'Renaissance man' in any uncomplicated sense, for he was troubled by inner conflict between thoughts of salvation and thoughts of glory and love, and – his brother Gherardo being a Carthusian monk – he retained a profound respect for the religious life. Moreover, he showed no signs of acclaiming the active life of a citizen within the world as essentially superior to a life of solitude and contemplation. He did not shirk political and administrative responsibility, but he was no convinced republican. He was deeply concerned at the anarchy and conflict within the Italian peninsula, longed for the return of Pope and Emperor to restore order, and, thinking it shameful that one Italian state should make war upon another, begged Andrea Dandolo, Doge of Venice, to make peace with the Genoese. By no means indifferent to the condition of the world he still found his greatest pleasure in retreat into the country, to which his intense love of nature drew him (he had country houses at Vaucluse in Provence and at Arquà near Padua), in leisure and tranquillity rather than in the transaction of business. If Renaissance and Middle Ages are conceived as representing two contrasting mentalities, then it must be conceded that both had great appeal for Petrarch.

Art and   11
Society

The Renaissance has long been conceived as a general revival of activity, a return to correct but long-obscured principles, involving not only literature but also the visual arts – painting, sculpture and architecture. In these fields there was, initially, not a return to classical antiquity so much as a return to nature, to the realistic, vivid and often dramatic representation of the human and natural world, which was now rediscovered and portrayed with a high degree of technical skill. Ancient sculpture and architecture did admittedly exert some influence – as the sculptor Nicola Pisano drew inspiration from a Roman sarcophagus depicting Hippolytus and Phaedra, which had been used since the eleventh century to house the bones of the Countess Beatrice of Tuscany. Likewise, as Erwin Panofsky argued, painters in the first half of the fourteenth century began to find models in the tangible relics of the ancient world – in reliefs, buildings, statues, gems and coins – although inspiration was generally restricted to individual motifs, and did not permeate compositions in their entirety. As a direct inspiration for the revival in the arts, the evangelism of the Franciscans was more obviously and immediately relevant.

Most Catholic revivals have imposed their own characteristic demands on the artist and have enlisted his aid in conveying their ideals and preoccupations to a popular audience, and in celebrating the lives and acts of their saints and martyrs. The Franciscans and Dominicans set up a demand for preacher's churches, with excellent acoustics and a clear view of a dominant pulpit, to house the big congregations they were attracting in the cities; to this purpose a simplified form of Gothic was well suited. Most of the great churches raised in the thirteenth and early fourteenth centuries were mendicant churches, rather than cathedrals – though magnificent cathedrals were built in Florence and Siena, which had undergone formidable economic growth, and in Orvieto to celebrate a spectacular miracle believed to have occurred in nearby Bolsena. Despite the qualms of the rigorists some Franciscan churches were soon richly decorated, and paintings in the basilica at Assisi reflected St Francis's mysticism and his devotional tastes – his emphasis on the Passion, his love of the angels, his devotion to the apostles and especially to St Peter and St Paul. St Francis himself, as described in the official Life by St Bonaventure, became a subject for·painters. Mendicant churches soon attracted the patronage of the rich, and Santa Croce in Florence was favoured by the banking families of the Bardi, Peruzzi, Alberti and Baroncelli. In commercial societies, there was an acute tension between the Christian ideal of the renunciation of wealth and the determination of merchants, bankers and other entrepreneurs to pursue it – especially where, as at Padua or in Tuscany, they did so by means abhorrent to the official law of the Church. Particularly offensive to this were the usurious speculations which caused money to breed money without its owner doing honest work to earn it or making the effort to employ it for the benefit of the whole community. The renunciation of a portion of one's wealth to the Church, or to the poor, or to the mendicants as poor churchmen, became a means of expiation, or at least of soothing the conscience. The barn-like Arena chapel in Padua, whose walls were painted by Giotto, was probably intended by Enrico Scrovegni to atone for the sins of his moneylending father.

The religious revival created a demand for visual narrative, in sculpture and painting – for vivid scenes from the Bible, for stories from the lives of Christ, the Madonna and the saints, for dramatic episodes which had something in common with the presentation of mystery plays. These were sometimes linked in extensive cycles: on wooden panels, as in Duccio's great *Maestà* in Siena; or in elaborate decorative schemes which peopled the walls and ceiling of a whole interior, as in Padua's Arena chapel or the upper church of St Francis at Assisi; or, carved in relief, round the circumferences of the rich Pisani pulpits of Pisa and Siena. The general tendency was to accentuate the human qualities of Christ, the Madonna and the saints, and to portray them, not as the remote and majestic divinities of the Byzantine style, but as beings capable of tenderness, emotion, pain and suffering. In the conquest of reality, sculptors naturally enjoyed some initial advantage over painters, since their figures stood or moved in space, and they did not have to face the problem of creating the illusion of depth on a flat surface. But painters, too, developed by the early fourteenth century the skills which enabled them to transform the flat surface on which they worked into a window opening on a scene beyond, and to impart both weight and depth to the figures enacting it. The Renaissance has been equated with the 'discovery of the world and of man', and Franciscanism has been credited with much of this. Initially at least, this discovery of the world did not imply the evolution of any irreligious or secularized system of values, since it was designed to increase the hold of religion upon men's hearts and minds by fusing it more intimately with familiar, everyday things and people.

But religious revival was never the only source of inspiration to artists and architects, nor was the Church their sole patron or employer. Civic patriotism, municipal prosperity, the need of the commune and the Popolo to assert their supremacy over private interest and factional conflict: all played their part. *Podestà*, *Capitani* and priors needed suitably imposing – and sometimes adequately fortified – headquarters from which to transact their business. The Palazzo Pubblico in Siena was the first building in central Italy to house all the principal civic offices and council chambers under one roof. Some of these city palaces, including the Bargello and Palazzo Vecchio in Florence, were built as solid fortresses. Others had open loggias on their lower storeys, or great external stairways to the upper chambers where the city councils met, though it does not seem possible to relate preferences for the open or closed style of architecture to the degree of turbulence and struggle or democracy or authoritarianism prevailing within the city. By the beginning of the fourteenth century, however, there were signs of conscious and deliberate town planning: of an interest in making the whole city a thing of beauty, rather than merely with making it strong enough to withstand enemies, from inside or from without. Hence, for example, a proposal which came in 1316 before the Council of Nine in Siena:

It is a matter of great honour to the various communes that the officials occupy beautiful and honourable dwellings, both for the sake of the commune and because foreigners often go to their houses upon affairs. This is of great importance for the commune of Siena, according to its quality.

At Gubbio, from 1322 onwards, the architect Angelo of Orvieto was chiefly responsible for a scheme whereby the Palazzo dei Consoli, the Palazzo del Pretorio and much of the Piazza della Signoria formed a single huge construction built out from the hillside.

Nevertheless, whilst the growth and self-assertion of the commune created an architecture designed for purely secular and utilitarian purposes, civic pride could express itself with equal force in the building and decoration of cathedrals or mendicant churches. Public buildings could form a second centre for the town, complementing the union of cathedral, baptistery and belfry: as, at Siena, the black and white cathedral dominates the city from its hilltop, and, some distance away, the Torre Mangia pricks the sky above the shell-shaped Piazza del Campo where the Palazzo Pubblico stands. When, at the close of the thirteenth century, the Florentines resolved to replace the old cathedral of Santa Reparata, they financed the new buildings not only by the use of pardons and indulgences but also out of civic poll-taxes and subsidies from the treasury. The secular art of the early fourteenth century might be independent of the Church and of direct religious inspiration, but it was not antagonistic towards it.

To some extent, painting was enlisted in the service of civic pride and patriotism, and used to point moral or political lessons, and to disseminate propaganda. One of the lower and less romantic tasks of the artist might be to produce the so-called *pittura infamante*, which was often no more than a daub on the wall of a building, designed to bring crime into a proper disrepute. More dignified was the celebration of patron saints. The people of Siena believed that it was through the mediation of their sacred painting, the Great-Eyed Madonna, that they had won the battle of Monte Aperti against the Florentines, and after that victory they proclaimed the Virgin Queen of Siena. In 1308 they resolved to replace this picture, and Duccio's *Maestà*, with the great frontal panel of the Virgin Enthroned, was one of the first paintings known to have been commissioned by a commune. It excited great public interest, and on its completion in 1311 it was transported by a solemn civic procession from the master's workshop to the cathedral. The people prayed the Virgin to protect the city from evil, and to guard it against enemies and traitors. For artists an important saint was Louis of Anjou, canonized in 1317, the

elder brother of King Robert, who had renounced to him
his right of succession to the Neapolitan throne in order to
become a Franciscan friar. The honour done in paintings
to Louis, who had died Bishop of Toulouse in 1297, helped
to bolster the prestige of the Angevin dynasty, the lay
chieftains of the Guelf connections.

The acuteness of factional conflict, especially in Siena in
the early fourteenth century, created some demand for
painting which would assert the need for strong, just and
orderly government, and proclaim the supremacy of the
common good above all private and factional interest.
Simone Martini's *Maestà*, on one wall of a council chamber
in the Palazzo Pubblico, bore an inscription putting into
the mouth of the Virgin the words:

> The angelic flowers, the rose and lily,
> With which the heavenly fields are decked
> Do not delight me more than righteous counsel.
> But some I see who for their own estate
> Despise me and deceive my land
> And are most praised when they speak worst . . .

A few years later Martini expressed himself in an exclusively worldly idiom, when he portrayed the Republic's
mercenary captain, Guidoriccio da Fogliano, in the year of
his great victory over Castruccio Castracane, lord of Lucca.
Guidoriccio, a symbol of the strength of the commune
abroad, was seen riding before the little towns of Monte-
massi and Sassoforte, which he had 'liberated'. In the late
1330s Ambrogio Lorenzetti painted the allegories of Good
Government and Tyranny on the walls of the Chamber of
the Nine: Good Government showed the citizens choosing
for their ruler a figure which simultaneously represented
both the 'public personality' of the city-state and the concept
of the common good. The effects of good government, the
peace and order it could bring to town and countryside,
were depicted with a wealth of intimate detail. Here, in

Siena, a worldly moralistic art was taking its place beside religious art. The use of painting for public propaganda was not confined to Siena: in Rome Cola di Rienzo, when he erected his famous bronze tablet on a wall outside St John Lateran, employed a painter to surround it with a fresco which showed the Roman Senate bestowing sovereignty upon Vespasian.

In the course of the early fourteenth century there were signs of a marked improvement in the social standing of certain artists, so that these few ceased to be regarded merely as manual workers pursuing a traditional craft and following the instructions of those who commissioned their work. A small number asserted their independence and earned recognition in their own time as men of genius, or at least of vastly superior skill. This did not, however, overshadow such great cooperative enterprises as the cathedral façade at Orvieto, which involved craftsmen from Siena, Gubbio, Assisi and Como, several of them working together to carve a single figure. Early statutes of the Guild of Painters in Venice, spanning the years 1271 to 1301, assigned them the same subordinate status as other artisans and subjected individual workers to close supervision by the officials of the guild. The regulations envisaged that they would be concerned with the decoration of helmets and shields covered with leather, of stools, dining-tables, caskets, plates and icons; and, among other things, expressly stipulated that these objects must always be varnished before being put upon the market. Artists were forbidden to work on certain saints' days and festivals, and no member of the guild could, without special permission, employ more than one apprentice and two masters to work for him. Duccio di Boninsegna, who painted the famous *Maestà* in Siena, had first appeared in surviving records in 1278–9, receiving payment for painting twelve account-book cases and covers. Even quite eminent artists could be paid a wage for their services, like any other workmen – as, between August 1301 and February 1302, Cimabue was paid ten *soldi* a day for carrying out work on the figure of St John in a mosaic in the apse of the cathedral in Pisa.

In Florence, however, although painters were incorporated into the guild system, their standing gradually rose during the fourteenth century: in any case guild membership was a means to enfranchisement in Florence, rather than a way of being supervised by a powerful state. Painters were originally classified as men who bought, worked and sold colours, and in 1314 they were enrolled on the guild of physicians and apothecaries as dependants of the branch of apothecaries. However, in mid-century, painters of panels and frescoes were called *dipintori*, and were differentiated from those who merely decorated chests and furniture. Later the *dipintori* became dependants of the physicians, who enjoyed professional standing, and finally, in 1378, they were authorized to form a separate branch of their own.

A few major figures, great innovators who had evolved a style of their own and were later believed to have broken dramatically with the 'ignorant' traditions of their times, stood out clearly against the background. The temperamental, quarrelsome sculptor, Giovanni Pisano, son of Nicola, announced his own genius to posterity. An inscription on the pulpit of Sant' Andrea in Pistoia declared: 'Giovanni carved it, who performed no empty work. The son of Nicola, and blessed with higher skill, Pisa gave him birth, endowed with mastery greater than any before.' And on a pulpit at Pisa, ten years later in 1311, he called himself 'skilled above all in the order of the art of pure sculpture, carving splendid things in stone, wood and gold. Even if he wished he could not carve what is ugly or base. There are many sculptors, but to him remain the honours of praise.'

The notion that individual artists, as well as poets, could

pursue fame and compete for supremacy was certainly
recognized by Dante. During his journey through purgatory, on the cornice devoted to the purging of pride, he met
Oderisi, a master-illuminator from Gubbio, bowed beneath
the penitential load of a vast block of stone:

> 'Brother,' said he, 'a touch more magical
>   Smiles now from Franco of Bologna's page;
>   Some honour's mine, but his is all in all.
>
> I should have been less generous, I'll engage,
>   While yet I lived, and ardour to outshine
>   Burned in my bosom with a kind of rage.
>
> For pride like that we here must pay the fine;
>   Nor yet should I be here, but that contrition
>   Turned me to God while power to sin was mine.
>
> O empty glory of man's frail ambition,
>   How soon its topmost boughs their green must yield;
>   If no Dark Age succeed, what short fruition!
>
> Once, Cimabue thought to hold the field
>   In painting; Giotto's all the rage today;
>   The other's fame lies in the dust concealed . . .'

Cimabue had begun to depart from the rigidity of the
Byzantine tradition, but Giotto was to be acclaimed as the
supreme restorer of painting to life. He was the pride of
Florence, and was officially proclaimed as such when,
about 1334, the commune appointed him to supervise the
building operations of the city and of the cathedral. He
was no mere artisan, though there was a well-known story
of how an ignorant workman had tried to commission him
to paint a coat-of-arms upon his buckler. He became rich
enough to be a businessman in a small way, with several
notaries looking after his interests, and to own land at Colle.
Tradition portrayed him as a genial and agreeable man,
capable of holding his own with kings, and Vasari, the six-

teenth-century art historian, was to record his wit with as much affection as his artistic achievement. His skill was believed to be of so high an order that it could not be appreciated by the ignorant, as Petrarch observed when he bequeathed to the lord of Padua his treasured Giotto portrait of the Virgin. The concept of an art of such sophistication that it could only appeal to an élite of discerning viewers probably helped to raise the status of a very few artists still further, and to number them among the intellectuals and the men of genius.

*

The century from 1250 to 1350 had seen the growth of a culture distinctively Italian – though by no means independent of foreign influence – owing much to men who, like Dante and Petrarch, were citizens of all Italy and aware of its common inheritance; but also deriving great strength from a vigorous urban life and an intense local patriotism. It was a culture in which pioneers of genius could be proclaimed as giants by their fellow men, though they never lacked precursors and masters on whose work they built. By the mid-fourteenth century Italian society had begun to affirm a distinctive and familiar relationship with antiquity, to offer freedom to creative power, to applaud defiance of tradition, to link beauty with patriotism. This may have been evolution, not revolution, a development out of the thirteenth century as much as a rejection of the immediate past and of the dark age of ignorance. But by 1350 change had become sufficiently marked to be seen by contemporaries with almost religious fervour as a great renewal or rebirth.

PART FOUR

The Territorial States, *c.* 1350–*c.* 1450

Recession and Adaptation

12

From this point onwards the Renaissance will be considered as a facet of the Italian historical situation. It is of course clear that intellectual and artistic change must to a large extent be explained in intellectual and artistic terms and cannot be related in any simple sense to the political and economic environment in which it occurs – though there are some forms of intellectual activity, such as historical writing or practical political theory, which are by their very nature a commentary upon the political world observed by their authors and can only be understood by reference to it. These chapters will not be focused primarily or essentially on the task of explaining the Renaissance, because the Renaissance is best regarded as no more and no less than an *avant-garde* movement in literature and the arts, and there is no reason to suppose that its 'spirit' permeated all levels of Italian society and all branches of human activity, even though it became a great distinguishing mark of Italian civilization. But where practicable, attention will be drawn to some of the relationships which can be traced between Italian politics and society and Italian culture, in the century stretching from 1350 to 1450.

*

In all probability this century was one of general economic depression and contraction, in which short-term booms and periods of recovery were insufficient to compensate for the slumps heralded in the 1340s by the Black Death and by the collapse of Florence's greatest banking houses. It was also characterized by a prolonged struggle for power and territory in northern and central Italy – one no longer dominated by the universalist authorities of Empire and Papacy or by the loose alignments of Guelf and Ghibelline, but by a conflict between native Italian states. This contest was to be seen by contemporary propagandists not as a struggle between the Church and its enemies but as a battle between the forces of republicanism and tyranny – or between the 'peace' which the expanding Visconti state proposed to offer to its subjects, and the 'liberty' of which the Florentines and for a time the Venetians claimed to be the defenders. By the middle of the fifteenth century the political map of Italy was to become simplified through the formation of five large territorial states, maintaining among themselves a kind of equilibrium. These were the Duchy of Milan, the Republics of Florence and Venice, the Papal States and the Kingdom of Naples, which overshadowed the more modest territories of Genoa, Lucca and Siena, and of Mantua, Monferrato and Ferrara. Strange transformations had occurred, for Florence had become a sea-power with a fleet of galleys, whilst Venice had turned westward and acquired a landed dominion stretching to the banks of the Adda.

Recent interpretations of the Renaissance have not, on the whole, claimed confidently or convincingly that it was the reflection of a highly opulent society. Rather they have thrown emphasis on acute political crises and prolonged wars which demanded great self-sacrifice, and tended to heighten civic self-awareness and patriotism or to call for a sharper analysis of the threatening political situation. Such wars were scarcely conducive, at least in the short term, to material prosperity or economic advancement: nor were they undertaken entirely from economic motives, though these may have contributed to some of them. It may be that one of the starkest features of this Italian century was the high incidence of taxation on peoples reduced by famine, disease and war itself, and the compulsory investment of a large part of the country's wealth in waste and destruction.

The great economic crisis of the middle to late fourteenth century was the product of a number of unfavourable occurrences which did not all spring from the same root cause, but happened to fall upon Italy with disastrous effect at more or less the same time. To some extent the Italians were merely sharing in a depression common to all Europe, most parts of which suffered from serious depopulation and a consequent slackening in the production, distribution and exchange of goods. But the people of the north and centre of Italy probably had to face the hazard which sooner or later besets most economically advanced nations – in that other, less highly developed countries were beginning to establish their own systems of shipping and finance (dispensing with the services of Italians) and to launch competing industries. Native financiers such as the Arteveldes and Jacques Cœur arose in France and the Netherlands, and the English began to develop their own woollen industry, rather than merely export raw materials for the Italians to work. It is possible therefore – though there are no statistics that can prove it – that the Italian economy declined, not only in an absolute sense, but also in relation to Europe as a whole; although it is also true that the Italians could still find backward countries, in Spain, Portugal and Ottoman Turkey, to which they could export goods and services and from which they could obtain primary materials and foodstuffs.

In the second half of the fourteenth century there was also a serious contraction in the opportunities for trade in the Far East, when the position of Italian merchants in the Mongolian Khanates of Kipchak and Persia began to

deteriorate. This, together with the conquests of the great
Turkic warlord Tamerlane and the advance of the Osmanli
Turks into Asia Minor and the Balkans, had devastating
effects on the eastern trade routes which terminated on the
shores of the Black Sea. It made Italian trade with the Far
East perilously dependent on the Syrian and Egyptian
routes and on the will of the Soldan. The creation of this
bottleneck, however, was probably much more detrimental
to the Genoese than to the Venetians, who were firmly
entrenched in Damascus and Alexandria.

Also contributing to the economic crisis, though it was
not in any obvious sense related to the other causes, was the
Great Schism. One economic effect of the divided allegiance
and of the subsequent conciliar movement was to deprive
the Papal Curia of revenues from abroad which would
otherwise have accrued to it, and to rob the return of the
Papacy to Rome of much of its power to re-inject wealth into
Italy. Instead, there arose a growing need for the more
efficient fiscal exploitation of the Papal States themselves.

It seems probable that in certain areas the curve of
expanding population was beginning to flatten out even
before 1340. From that point onwards the numbers of the
people were liable to be drastically reduced by recurrent
epidemics of pestilence; some of these were certainly outbreaks of plague, in its bubonic, pneumonic or septicaemic
forms. The Black Death penetrated into Italy in 1347–8.
This pandemic had probably started its march in Central
Asia eight or nine years earlier, and may well have been
spread to Europe by contacts between Italian merchants
in the Crimea and the infected Tartar peoples. The infection
was probably conveyed to Genoa, Venice and Messina by
galleys from eastern ports. The Black Death was the most
dramatic of the plagues, and the one with the most distinguished literary record – for it provided the macabre
setting for the *Decameron*, for the stories told by a company

of young men and women in retreat from the stricken, mourning city of Florence to the villas of the countryside. But it is best seen as one of a prolonged series of epidemics which periodically raised the death-rate to high peaks. Milan, which had suffered comparatively little in the years of the Black Death, succumbed to later epidemics seven times between 1361 and 1485. Venice suffered no less than twenty-two outbreaks of pestilence, recurring on average every seven to eight years between 1361 and 1528 – after which the incidence of the disease significantly changed.

These plagues disrupted communications by demanding the imposition of strict quarantines and by prompting panic flights of rich men and employers from the big cities. An epidemic at Genoa in 1458 appears to have paralysed economic activity for a spell of up to five months. Moreover, plague was by no means exclusively a scourge of cities and ports, though its lethal powers may have been slightly greater in urban than in country districts. In the town of San Gimignano the total number of hearths fell from 1,687 in 1332 to 695 in 1350 – a descent of 58·7 per cent; whereas in the surrounding *contado* the corresponding figures showed a drop from 852 to 468 households, one of 45 per cent. During the 1430s the epidemics which raged in the provinces of Lombardy and Liguria seem to have inflicted demographic losses of approximately 30 per cent on the rural township of Lomello, between Pavia and Alessandria: losses occasioned both by the death of whole families and by the emigration of others. Unlike the temporary retreats from the towns, migrations from rural settlements were more permanent, and justified elaborate petitions for reductions in tax-assessments.

It has frequently been argued that before the eighteenth century European demography·was characterized not only by high death-rates but also by high birth-rates, in the absence of modern methods of contraception; and that these high birth-rates would rapidly replace the heavy losses inflicted by disease. However, depopulation persisted at least in some parts of Italy well into the fifteenth century, and is fairly well documented in certain regions of Tuscany. The population of Florence had probably reached 90,000 in 1338, but in 1380 it had sunk to about 55,000, and was no higher than 37,000 in 1427. Between 1244 and 1401 the population of the Pistoiese dropped from 31,000 to 9,000 – by over 70 per cent. In Prato and the Pratese demographic decline had already set in before the Black Death. In 1339 a victualling census had revealed the presence of 18,249 'mouths' in the city and *contado*; in 1428–9 the corresponding figure, lower by 55 per cent, was 8,240. The number of hearths or households in San Gimignano and its *contado* fell by 77 per cent between 1332 and 1428, although it is only fair to point out that in periods of economic depression people sometimes tend to congregate in larger family units, and hence the number of heads or 'mouths' may not have descended quite as steeply as the number of households. In and around Prato there were four people per hearth in 1339 and 1372, but 4·3 in 1428–9.

It is uncertain when recovery and replacement began. In the *contado* of Florence the total number of households was little more than 20,000 as late as 1470, whereas between 1350 and 1384, even after the Black Death, it had varied between 26,000 and 29,000. Here the fifteenth century was not, as a whole, one of population increase. On the other hand the admittedly fragmentary data collected by Professor Jacques Heers in his work on Genoa does suggest that in that densely settled city some of the damage was being repaired by the middle of the fifteenth century: the average testator had had 3·18 children in 1343, and the number had dropped to 1·37 in 1348, but rose again to 2·8 over the years 1451 to 1458.

High mortality in epidemics seems insufficient to explain

this prolonged stagnation or depression in the levels of population, especially as the tendency of plague seems to have been to kill the very young and the aged, and to spare persons of childbearing age. Persistent depopulation probably has to be explained in terms of a lowered birthrate, which in itself may have been a reflection of depressed economic conditions. Historical demographers are now prepared to maintain that even pre-industrial communities could sometimes – though not invariably – develop customs conducive to the limitation of families, especially when the economy was incapable of supporting new recruits to society. Always available were such indirect methods of family limitation as prolonged breast-feeding, or raising the age at which women first married – to say nothing of abortion, infanticide, or failing to take good care of sickly children. The recurrence of famine and malnutrition may have increased the risk of miscarriages or still-births. Unfortunately, however, there is little or no direct evidence about these matters in fourteenth- and fifteenth-century Italy.

In the countryside, the settled area contracted. Naturally enough, the poorer soils, the marginal lands which had only been brought under cultivation in periods of population pressure, were abandoned as the peasants retreated on to more promising territory. Italian agriculture also suffered as a result of the sedimentation of rivers, from the coasts of Sicily past the mouth of the Tiber to the Maremma; and the spread of marshland and swamp from coasts and deltas increased the risk of malaria. Depopulation seems to have been very severe in the Kingdom of Naples, in Sardinia and in Sicily. From Pisa southwards, the effects of population decline were to accentuate an existing tendency towards the formation of great barren landed estates, towards the encouragement of sheep-farming and transhumant grazing, and towards the desertion of villages. With pressure on the land reduced, the demand for grain eventually fell and there was a shortage of hands to till the soil, so that the greatest profits might well be gained from livestock-rearing. Hence the revenues of Rome and the Patrimony of St Peter in the fifteenth century were swelled by taxes levied on beasts brought down from the hills to the plain, and by the profits which the Pope's Apostolic Treasury derived from allocating pasture-ground. In the Kingdom of Naples in the mid-fifteenth century the fisc was drawing a large return from the state pasture-grounds of Apulia, which now proved capable of supporting 800–900,000 sheep a year, with a few thousand head of cattle.

In Tuscany no more than about 10 per cent of villages seem to have disappeared in the fourteenth and fifteenth centuries (despite the terrible population losses documented in certain localities). But the proportion rose to 25 per cent in the province of Rome by 1416, to 50 per cent in Sardinia. When Cardinal Oddone Colonna reigned as Pope Martin V, his kinsmen purchased thirty-five local villages between 1422 and 1428. Half of these were ruinous, and they did not bother to reconstruct more than three in the remainder of the century. They were content to be the lords of bare, unpeopled earth.

Nevertheless, depopulation was not quite universal in the peninsula, and by the mid-fifteenth century some instances did occur of new rural settlements being formed or greatly expanded – as on the Riviera and in the Lunigiana. Mountainous regions were often still too densely populated for their sparse food-supplies, and their inhabitants might seldom eat grain but depend upon chestnuts to eke out their diet: emigration might be the only solution. Indeed, in 1451 the village of Bagnone in the Lunigiana was said to be 'completely inhabited by people come from the interior', from the villages of the Apennines; and only four out of thirty-eight heads of families had lived in the place for more than one generation. Other mountaineers descended into the Arno valley, to take part in the reclamation of land round Pisa or Lucca. In the Pistoiese the mountains seem to have suffered rather less gravely from depopulation than the middle-hills, which had been most densely settled at the height of the thirteenth century. Other mountainous regions which were overpopulated in the early fifteenth century but later solved their problems by emigration were those of Piedmont, the Comasco, the Tyrol, the Trentino and the Bergamese Alps – which profited from Bergamo's absorption after 1426 into the Republic of Venice. In later generations the capacity of Bergamese immigrants for hard work and money-making was to become proverbial in the city of Venice.

Stagnation, decay and lack of enterprise did not prevail everywhere in the mid-fifteenth century. Indeed, Professor Carlo Cipolla has argued that whilst the thirteenth century was one of great prosperity based chiefly on industrial and commercial enterprise and the fourteenth one of decline, the fifteenth century experienced a great revival based on agricultural capitalism. Considerable advances were made in Lombardy and the Po valley, where the dynasties of Visconti and Sforza pursued a fairly coherent economic policy, which aimed (at least in the intervals between campaigns) at economic self-sufficiency and at increasing the population. The rulers promoted inland navigation and irrigation, and between 1356 and 1365 the newly dug canal of the Navigliaccio came to link Milan and Pavia. Excellent irrigation made it possible to develop highly productive dairy-farming, through the presence of the so-called *marcite* or permanent meadows. These yielded seven or eight cuts of grass yearly rather than the usual three. Where central and southern Italy developed sheep-farming, areas of Lombardy turned to commercial crops and particularly to the growing of dye-plants, a large part of which were exported through Genoa to serve the needs of the textile industries in England and northern Europe. The cultivation of woad, a very fast-growing plant from which four or five harvests a year could be expected, came to replace that of the much less lucrative madder. A zone of some 1,500 square kilometres between Milan and Genoa, stretching from the hinterland of Savona to the edge of the territory of Piacenza, was partially devoted to this crop, whose distribution was organized by merchants from Milan and Genoa, Pavia and Alessandria. Moreover, it seems likely that at least in the region of Pavia churches and ecclesiastical corporations began to lose control of a large fraction of their lands, and that these were more efficiently – or more ruthlessly – exploited by lay speculators bent on large profits. The total area covered by the Church's landed possessions had been enormous, but it had often consisted of innumerable small scattered holdings bequeathed or given by a great variety of benefactors. The new occupiers were able to some extent to concentrate these tenures into more viable units.

However, there is room for grave doubts as to how far these advances found parallels outside Lombardy: they were surely not common to the whole peninsula. Nor does it seem likely that the products of agriculture were sufficiently profitable or sufficiently distinctive to fill in the Italian economy anything like the same role as the industrial and commercial goods handled by the merchants of the thirteenth and early fourteenth centuries.

But were the effects of depopulation wholly depressive? They clearly resulted in an absolute reduction in the total volume of trade, industry and agricultural activity, but it is rather less clear that they reduced production and consumption per head of the surviving population or greatly lowered the standard of living among the survivors. In all probability Italy, and much of western Europe, had become overcrowded in relation to food resources in the early fourteenth century, and the growth of population, which about the year 1000 had become a major stimulus to economic expansion, now threatened to impoverish peoples threatened with exhaustion of the cultivated soil and unable to do more to reclaim land from swamp and forest. Were not the plagues a drastic and corrosive remedy, a painful exit from an intolerable situation which could not as yet be relieved by technical advances in agriculture? No generalized answer can confidently be returned to such questions – though even a cursory glance at Florence in the late fourteenth century suggests several reasons why ordinary people are unlikely to have benefited from the relief of population pressure. By the late 1370s the production of woollen cloth had been even more steeply reduced than the population of the city. Florence's population had dropped from about 90,000 in 1338 to some 55,000 forty years later. In 1338 Florentine cloth-workers had produced some 80,000 bolts of cloth. But when they rose in revolt in 1378 they demanded only that production should be kept up to a minimum level of 24,000 cloths a year, and in 1383 their output reached only 19–20,000 cloths. There is, therefore, no reason to suppose that the fall in the numbers of the labour-force had created a demand for more hands which would lead to a rise in wages. Furthermore, even though declining population ought in theory to have reduced the pressure on land, there were in practice long stretches of time when agriculture and communications were disrupted enough by war, weather and unruly mercenaries to force the price of grain to still higher levels than before the Black Death. According to M. de la Roncière, the index of Florentine grain prices rose from 100 in 1320–38 to as much as 164 over the decade 1368–78. At the same time, the Florentine people found themselves subjected to increasingly heavy taxation imposed to finance wars no longer conducted by civilian militias, but by expensive mercenary troops.

On the other hand, Professor David Herlihy has argued a rather different case with reference to two rural communes in Tuscany. Between 1340 and 1427 the population of Impruneta and its adjoining parishes, a few miles south of Florence, decreased by 42–70 per cent. But this did make it practicable to introduce a more balanced agriculture, better suited to the character of the soil: there was less emphasis on wheat, and more on vines and olives. Over this period there was also a very strong tendency towards the greater concentration of land-ownership in the hands of fewer proprietors, and for independent peasants to be replaced by sharecroppers who cultivated the lands of others in return for a share in the produce. Indeed, nearly half the 358 family heads recorded in the land registers for the district were sharecroppers. Likewise, in 1243 in the commune of Piuvica (near Pistoia) no family had been completely without taxable wealth, but in 1427 more than 30 per cent of the population had no taxable wealth at all. It cannot, however, simply be assumed that they were all poor: some of them were sharecroppers, and Professor Herlihy has maintained that the position of a sharecropper was in many ways preferable to that of an independent peasant. This drift towards landlessness was probably caused by such disasters as crop failures coupled with high taxation. These were liable to plunge the peasant into an indebtedness which eventually forced him to sell out or forfeit his land, to persons of greater resources or to local usurers. With the wider prevalence of sharecropping, peasants were to some extent relieved of the need to borrow to provide themselves with equipment, and they did not have to bear the total loss from a bad harvest themselves. However, another modern scholar, Dr Philip Jones, has argued that on the contrary the spread of sharecropping may have marked the depression of peasants into a rural proletariat owning virtually nothing but the hands with which they laboured – and that sharecropping arrangements were by no means an infallible protection against incurring debt. Landlords might provide houses, wine-presses, seed, tools or oxen – but their tenants might still be forced to borrow to raise other things, such as seed-corn, manure or vine-props. Again there must be serious doubt as to whether the decline in population resulted in any marked improvement in peasant conditions, by relieving pressure on the land and creating shortages of labour.

Economic history can never be divorced from that of politics and war. Prolonged warfare took a heavy toll of the country's wealth: the cost of war remained constant or became still further inflated even while the number of tax-payers was reduced. The return from direct rural taxation levied by the Florentines increased from about 30,000 florins in 1336–8 to approximately 35,000 after the Black Death, even though the population had dropped meanwhile by one-third to a half. In the next two decades the Florentines steeply increased the contribution levied on subject cities in the territorial state, on Pistoia, San Gimignano and Bibbiena. The territories of great feudal lords, the Counts Guidi and Ubaldini, lost their immunity from Florentine taxation during the 1380s, and between 1400 and 1420 the newly acquired territories of Arezzo, Pisa, Volterra and Cortona were compelled, as the Florentine state expanded, to take their share in servicing the public debt. Expansion annexed more tax-paying territory, and the cost of expansion ensured that taxes would have to be stepped up on newly conquered lands. Florence's funded debt had grown from about half a million florins in 1345 to $2\frac{1}{2}$ million by 1380. Between 1377 and 1406, $11\frac{1}{2}$ million florins were spent on warfare, and between 1380 and 1427 forced loans extracted from Florentine pockets sums amounting to about 19 million florins. Likewise, the Venetians suffered from crippling taxation, not only in the conflict with Genoa in 1377–81, but also after their entry into full-scale war with the Visconti by the side of their republican ally, Florence. The level of forced loans in Venice rose especially high between 1431 and 1441, when the average annual rate seems to have been no less than 26 per cent of *patrimonio imponibile*, or 'taxable estate'. Government bonds were paying reduced interest and the market-prices of government stock were falling.

Subjects of the Visconti state could not fail to suffer from the ambitions of their rulers, however strongly the Visconti might subscribe in theory to the doctrine of keeping taxes as low as possible. As a Milanese annalist wrote of Giangaleazzo Visconti, who died in 1402:

our Duke imposed such heavy and continuous taxes upon the subjects of his state that they were forced to emigrate because they could not bear such burdens. And there was an outcry from widows and orphans and other individuals, and loud laments from the lesser people, and terrible hardships.

It was small wonder that fifteenth-century commentators should look back with nostalgia on the halcyon decade from 1414 to 1423, which separated the death of Ladislao, the conquering King of Naples, from the outbreak of war in the north between Venice, Florence and the renewed Visconti state of Duke Filippo Maria. At this time, wrote the Florentine merchant Giovanni Rucellai, 'for ten years, we joined a tranquil peace, without any fear; the commune had few expenses for troops, and few taxes were levied, so that the region became wealthy'. Over the same years the Doge Tommaso Mocenigo reigned in Venice, and at the end of his life he was able to paint an idyllic but not implausible picture of the economic prosperity of Venice in his day, and of its close rapport with the flourishing industries of Tuscany and Lombardy. Under Mocenigo, no forced loans were imposed, save between January 1419 and

October 1420, when Venice was at war with the Emperor Sigismund in Friuli. But this decade stood out precisely because it was exceptional, and Mocenigo's fears for the future were at least partially realized when the Venetians chose as his successor Doge Francesco Foscari, the advocate of war in the west.

The deficiencies of surviving statistics, which make it hard to quantify the evidence, hinder the economic history of this century of depression. It is not true that fifteenth-century Italians were living in a pre-statistical era, for they were already well used to counting and measuring for the purposes of victualling and taxation. But there is a lack of the kind of all-embracing statistics which would enable the historian to determine how far, for example, the growth of the silk industries compensated for the supposed decline in woollens; or to assess the extent to which the woollen industry, having contracted in the old-established centres of Tuscany, migrated to Lombardy instead. It is rarely possible to compile statistical series stretching over long periods of time in which all the figures are drawn from the same kind of source, and therefore contain similar elements of error. It is often necessary to rely on ambiguous and puzzling circumstantial evidence.

The Tuscan woollen industry may have been a serious casualty of the depression years. Labour troubles impaired the running of the Sienese and Florentine industries, especially in the 1370s and 1380s, and although they were to some extent the product of a political situation in which patricians exploited artisan discontent, there is no reason to doubt that workers' risings were a reflection of economic depression, or that the subsequent reprisals against them caused still greater dislocation. In Siena, at intervals from 1355 onwards, woollen-workers, artisans and small shop-keepers were involved in risings instigated by richer and more powerful members of Sienese society, and visited their hatreds on the headquarters of the wool-guild, the Mercanzia and the tax-office. In 1371, when similar troubles broke out in Perugia also, 'the carders and other workers of the wool-guild in Siena had a dispute with their masters and said that they wanted to be masters too, and to have their pay regulated by the commune, and not by the guild': thus the Sienese chronicler, Neri Donato. Troops ran wild in the workers' quarter of Ovile, many of those implicated suffered banishment, and a significant number were condemned to death. Fourteen years later, after the fall of the Sienese party called the Riformatori, mass expulsions – again according to Donato – drove '4,000 good citizen artisans from the city'; though the chronicler did suggest that other parts of Italy (the Kingdom of Naples, the Marches, the Roman Patrimony and Pisa) benefited from the dispersal of these artisans. The woollen industry had suffered dislocation, if nothing worse.

Later misfortunes afflicting the Florentine industry included the economic effects of war, when wool-supplies were cut off through blockades of Pisa, or when the Visconti – alert to the possibilities of economic warfare – discomfited their enemies by forbidding the export of wire used to make instruments for carding wool. Doge Tommaso Mocenigo credited the Florentines with exporting 16,000 woollen cloths through Venice alone towards 1423. But at about that time many of the workshops which had previously been used for the manufacture of woollen fabrics were still untenanted. On the other hand the Florentines did succeed in reducing the risk of being deprived of primary materials by acquiring direct control of Pisa and its outports, and the fact remains that the most important of the voyages sailed by the Florentine galleys between the 1420s and the 1460s was the route to Flanders and England – to bring back (among other things) English wool. The needs of the woollen industry were still uppermost in public policy.

It is also true that a flourishing textile industry had developed in Lombardy by the end of the first quarter of the fifteenth century: to judge, again, by statistics propounded by the Doge Mocenigo. He described the export through Venice of approximately 50,000 bolts of cloth to a total value of 700–800,000 ducats per annum. Cloth of the highest quality came in relatively small volume from Milan itself – 4,000 cloths at thirty ducats the piece. Como was the largest producer of medium-priced goods (12,000 cloths at fifteen ducats apiece) and Bergamo of cheap cloth (10,000 cloths at seven ducats each). Alessandria, Tortona, Novara, Pavia, Monza, Brescia and Parma also contributed significantly to this export drive. Cremona, too, was manufacturing fustians on a large scale. No very strong conclusions can be drawn from such evidence, but at least it shows the folly of making simple and unqualified statements about the decline of Italy's woollen industries in the century after the Black Death.

The silk industries, aimed at the luxury markets of Italy itself, of Europe and the Levant, offered some compensation for any decline which may have occurred in the manufacture of woollens. The products of Lucca, Venice, Genoa, Bologna and Florence competed at the fairs of Geneva in the mid-fifteenth century, and the Lucchese tightly controlled the north-European market at Bruges. About 1442–3, Duke Filippo Maria Visconti was clearly eager to offer very favourable treatment to entrepreneurs willing to introduce the silk industry into Milan, and his efforts seem to have met with success – in 1459–61 there was talk of about 15,000 persons being employed (not necessarily full-time) in the various branches of the silk industry in Milan alone. The Milanese produced an elaborate form of silken cloth, shot through with silver and gold. The Genoese silk industry had eventually, by the first third of the sixteenth century, become much more important than the woollen – to judge by the fact that in 1531 the town contained 2,303 silk-weavers and only 423 weavers of woollen cloth. By 1427 there were forty-five to fifty 'silk-shops' in Florence, and the number may have risen by the 1470s to more than eighty. These shops were the premises where raw materials and finished products were stored, most of the work being given out to artisans and done in their own homes.

In the course of the fifteenth century the Mediterranean commerce in silks may well have changed direction, so that taffetas, brocades and fine silks were no longer being sent predominantly from the Levant to the west. By the end of the century the Florentines were certainly exporting these fabrics in significant quantities eastwards. Furthermore, although the growing industries were still obtaining a large part of their primary materials from beyond Italian shores (from their traditional sources near the Caspian Sea or from the Kingdom of Grenada in the west), these new enterprises did act as a powerful stimulus to the development of silk-worm rearing in various regions of Italy itself. Thus Andrea Banchi (1372–1462), a retailer and manufacturer of silks in Florence, found the highest-priced raw silk at Modigliana in the Romagnol region of Forlì, and the cheapest in Calabria. Silk also came to Florence from the Abruzzi and the Marches and to Lucca from the Valdinievole, whilst by the mid-fifteenth century attempts at sericulture were being made in the vicinity of Genoa.

The commercial scene was no less complicated than the industrial. The adaptability of the Genoese, the tenacity of the Venetians, the modest if temporary success of the Florentines in becoming a third sea-power through the revival of Pisa: these things stand out clearly from a prevailingly dark background. In the Middle East the power of the Osmanli Turks was expanding to fill Asia Minor and to penetrate with increasingly formidable thrusts into the

Balkans; Constantinople was to fall to them in 1453. None
the less, the advance of the Turks was not continuous, they
were slow to become a sea-power, and the impact of their
conquests on the colonies of the Genoese was far more
serious than the (nevertheless considerable) damage they
inflicted on Venetian commerce. The Turks first passed the
Dardanelles in 1353, and with the occupation of Salonica in
1387 they offered a direct threat to Venice's eastern trade.
But the Turks were gravely distracted by the rise of another
conqueror to stab them in the back – Tamerlane, the
warlord of Samarkand. Even after his death in 1405 the
reconstruction of the Turkish empire was still postponed
by internecine struggles over the succession to the Sultan
Bajazeth. Venice gained time by offering support to Bajazeth's eldest son, Suleiman, and it was left to Mohammed I
(1413–21) to resume hostilities. The Venetians probably
suffered their gravest losses in the Balkans during the prolonged wars of 1463–79, when they lost Scutari and Negro-
ponte, and found both their sovereignty over the Adriatic
and their chain of stepping-stones to the Levant becoming
increasingly precarious. But, even at this unpropitious time,
the Venetians were able to extend their island empire
further east than ever before. They acquired first a protectorate over Cyprus, and then direct dominion over the
island, through the marriage of Caterina Cornaro, daughter
of a rich Venetian house, to the last Lusignan monarch. On
his death Caterina was persuaded in 1489 to resign her
crown into the hands of the Republic. Cyprus was an
invaluable outpost on the voyage to Syria, and the island
itself was an important source of sugar, salt, cotton and
grain. Possession of a Kingdom, moreover, raised the diplomatic status and prestige of the Republic, which could now
claim formal equality with crowned heads.

The Turkish advance, the conquests of Tamerlane and
the instability of the Mongolian Khanates all had the

general effect of displacing trade with the Far East from the Black Sea termini to the more southerly trade routes debouching at Beirut, Damascus and Alexandria. Here the Venetians were firmly established. To some extent they depended perilously on the goodwill of the Soldan of Egypt, but the Venetian government had sufficiently tight control over its own merchants to be able to launch effective retaliatory measures. Towards 1430, when nearly all the spices reaching Europe were passing through the Red Sea, the Soldan determined to increase his income by establishing a firm monopoly, not only over spices but also over cotton grown in Syria. But the Venetian Senate's reaction – which eventually brought the Soldan to terms – was to forbid the export to his territories of coin, bullion, or any of the more valuable sorts of merchandise save on fleets commanded by admirals forbidden to let merchandise ashore unless they had first received assurances of total freedom of trade.

Holding this strong position, the Venetians encountered no effective rivals among western merchants in the Levant. The Genoese were developing other interests, and the Florentines did not present a really serious challenge. After annexing Pisa in 1406 and acquiring its outports of Porto Pisano and Livorno (otherwise Leghorn) in 1421, they launched a state-controlled galley system in imitation of the Venetian. A newly founded magistracy, the Sea Consuls, built and equipped a fleet of galleys, auctioned them for specific voyages to private buyers, and sent them to sea under the command of a captain appointed by the state. By the 1460s the Florentines were annually dispatching about half as many galleys as the Venetians, and this was no mean feat. But they did not succeed in breaking into the Venetian spice markets, and were chiefly concerned with the transport of industrial primary materials. Neither their organization nor their capacity for protecting their fleets against pirates and other aggressors was sufficient to transform them into really formidable rivals. By 1473 and 1480, only four or five of the state's great galleys were still in service.

The merchant-capitalists of Genoa had ceased to compete directly with the Venetians. Even in the early fifteenth century the value of Genoese maritime trade in terms of gold weight was rather higher than it had been in 1274 and 1334: though the figures registered a very steep decline over the years from about 1410 to 1470, with a partial – but only partial – recovery from 1480 to 1510. The decline was too great to be countered by any likely variations in the purchasing power of gold. By the late 1450s Genoese colonies in the Aegean had all fallen to the Turks, with the solitary exception of the island of Chios, now burdened with heavy tribute; so, by 1462, had all the possessions of the Gattilusii, a powerful Genoese family which had willingly collaborated with the company or Maona exploiting Chios. Caffa, the last Genoese outpost in the Black Sea, survived the conquest of Constantinople by more than twenty years at the cost of some collaboration with the Turks to the detriment of Christendom: it supplied the Sultan, when engaged after 1463 in the struggle against Venice and her Hungarian and Albanian allies, with slaves, with Ukrainian corn, and with timber from the Caucasus to build his ships. But in 1475, Caffa too fell at last. In the 1470s a Florentine jubilantly recalled how the Genoese fleet had declined from the proud force of sixty-three great ships active in 1424. Indeed, there were only about thirty great ships left in 1458 and twenty-four in 1466 – though the tonnage of individual vessels had probably grown, and may have compensated in part for the decrease in their overall number.

Nevertheless, the ancient port of Genoa was not merely declining into inactivity: the Genoese were adapting to circumstance, and becoming specialists in the transport of cheap and bulky goods, both foodstuffs and dyestuffs. Showing far less conservatism than the Venetians, they were turning increasingly to the Spanish peninsula, the Atlantic and the North Sea. The Black Sea had once been the Mediterranean's 'window on the north'; the Genoese developed the Atlantic trade as compensation for its loss, especially after 1460. Virtually abandoning merchant galleys altogether, they launched huge roundships or cogs, frequently with a capacity of 700–800 tons, which were among the largest vessels known before the age of steam. Cogs were less manoeuvrable than galleys and therefore a little less safe, since they could less easily be negotiated into port in a storm. But they could manage with smaller crews, carry more fresh water and provisions, and hence make more direct voyages: overall, the services they provided were very cheap, and were excellently adapted to products whose value was small in relation to their volume. Cogs might commonly travel from Genoa to Southampton, with only one stop on the way, at Cadiz. Among the goods they carried were wine, grain, salt, woad from Lombardy, and above all alum. Alum was used in the textile industries for cleaning fibres and cloths, and as a mordant or fixative for dyes; it also had other industrial uses, in glassmaking and tanning. The Genoese had long controlled vital supplies of alum from Asia Minor from their island entrepôt of Chios, and for them the greatest casualties of Turkish conquest in the mid-fifteenth century were the alum mines of Phocaea. The Genoese failed to persuade the Sultan to contract with them for the exploitation of the mines, and by 1460 their accumulated stocks were exhausted. But meanwhile there had been a search for sources of alum in Italy itself, whose greatest success was the discovery of substantial deposits at Tolfa in the Papal States. Although the exploitation of these mines passed for a time to the Medici of Florence, they were still dependent on the Genoese for transport.

Indeed, the overall impression of the Genoese economy in the mid-fifteenth century created by Professor Heers's extensive survey of the surviving material is one of great ingenuity and sophisticated business organization, though the political instability of the town was liable to create short-term economic depressions in addition to the great hazards abroad to which the Genoese were exposed. Genoa's population may well have reached 120,000 in the mid-fifteenth century, and the city was able to cope successfully with the exceptionally difficult problem of providing itself with victuals and salt from fairly distant sources. Business was carried on by highly specialized long-term partnerships, which devoted themselves to the exploitation and marketing of particular products, such as alum, mercury, coral or salt, and behind these were ranged non-specialized capitalists prepared to invest their money in a variety of different commercial or industrial concerns. Genoese industries were capitalistically organized, though a system of putting out materials to artisans who worked upon them in their own homes was more in evidence than any tendency to concentrate industrial processes in factories. Insurance had also been developed to a high level – not only marine insurance, but also certain kinds of life assurance. It was possible, for example, to insure the lives of female slaves approaching childbirth, or those of such great personages as the Pope or the King of Aragon whose death might inflict financial loss on the person taking out the insurance (e.g. by the cessation of some cherished privilege). The Genoese disposed of extensive supplies of gold and silver for commercial purposes, and were able to supplement their cash through various forms of credit instrument. They did so by the use of cheques and letters of exchange; through a number of private banks which accepted deposits and so enabled payments to be made by simply recording transfers on the books; and through the use of credits registered with the Casa di San Giorgio, an association of lenders to the state which controlled the revenues assigned to servicing the various loan funds. Moreover, the interest of the Genoese in Atlantic navigation was to ensure that in future years the Italian peninsula would never be entirely cut off from the oceanic world of the great geographical discoveries. Already in the fifteenth century the Genoese were taking a hand in the discovery by the Portuguese of Madeira, the Canary Islands and the Azores – and the career of Columbus was to be by no means an untypical Genoese career.

No simple verdicts can ever be pronounced on the Italian economy of 1350–1450 and of the years which immediately followed. Decline in traditional sectors of economic activity was almost invariably balanced by some form of advance into new fields, and the absence of precise and comprehensive statistics makes it virtually impossible to assess the extent of the compensation. Nevertheless, the unfavourable impressions created by repeated epidemics, prolonged warfare and the high incidence of taxes on a reduced population do prove in the end to be extremely hard to eradicate. Even the story of Genoa is one of determined adaptation to unfavourable circumstances, rather than of renewed prosperity. The Visconti had a coherent economic policy, and Lombard agriculture may provide one of the strongest exceptions to the rule of general depression: but the Milanese state at times threw intolerable fiscal burdens upon its subjects. Even after the Peace of Venice (1454) had registered the existence of a more balanced and stable states-system, general prosperity did not return. Indeed, the period 1460–80 was marked by a depression probably general to much of western Europe. Its concomitants included the failure of the Medici bank, the collapse of many Florentine silk firms (five fell in November 1464 alone), profound depression in Genoa from 1461–3 especially, the collapse of the alum trade from Asia Minor, a reduction in Venetian and eventually also in Florentine galley sailings.

Nevertheless, it may be that the student of this period needs to cultivate a kind of bi-focal vision of it. For the historian it is comparatively easy to stride across a century or more, and to attempt comparisons between the early fourteenth and the mid-fifteenth centuries: but the society of fifteenth-century Italy was probably one with a fairly short memory which spanned few generations, and the short-term ups-and-downs may have mattered far more to contemporaries who were actually involved in these events. Perhaps few knew, for example, that even the proud Medici bank of fifteenth-century Florence was barely equal, in the extent of its working capital or the numbers of its staff, to the third of the great banks before the Black Death, the Acciaiuoli; and that it could not rank with the Bardi or the Peruzzi. Perhaps the historian must often be prepared to say: 'This seems like a depression to us, but probably did not do so to its contemporaries, because they are unlikely to have measured constantly by the standards of the early fourteenth century, but to have used their own personal experience and drawn on their own or their fathers' memories.'

*

The question of the influence of economic and social conditions upon art and architecture in this century is very complicated and uncertain, and only the vaguest speculations can be offered. But it does seem that the aftermath of the Black Death coincided with a striking change in the styles and preoccupations of Tuscan painters, especially in the pioneer cities of Florence and Siena. Between about 1350 and 1380, as Professor Meiss has argued, the younger masters were no longer using the techniqués of Giotto, and he was no longer regarded with the reverence and awe he had commanded in Dante's day. The tendency was no longer to stress the human qualities of Christ, the Madonna and the saints – Christ was no longer seen as a child or a wounded man, but portrayed in splendour and majesty, richly and opulently clad, and somewhat in the style of the great Byzantine mosaics of the thirteenth and earlier centuries. He was shown as a judge, as a fount of doctrine, as the source of ecclesiastical authority: and, as if to combat both mysticism and heresy, great stress was symbolically laid on the power of priests and the role of the institutional Church in procuring salvation. Sacred figures were depicted with much more stiffness and formality, seeming increasingly remote both from the viewer of the painting and from each other. In this retreat from realism the miraculous and the mysterious, the suspension or defiance of the laws of nature, began to play a much larger part. For example, in paintings of the Resurrection, Christ was no longer seen actually climbing out of his sarcophagus, but was portrayed in a state of levitation, suspended in air by miraculous forces. There had been hints even before the Black Death of attitudes hostile to the naturalistic presentation of sacred scenes – as the Augustinian preacher Simone Fidati, who was in Florence from 1333 to 1338, had declared that no midwives were present at the Nativity, because Christ was born without difficulty or pain. But only after 1350 did even the most accomplished artists seem to accept such an attitude – whether it reflected their own inclinations, or the altered tastes of their audience and patrons. Notoriously, contemporaneity and causality are not the same thing. But it may be that this change of style does reflect an increasing sense of the remoteness and inscrutability of the God who was believed to have inflicted the plagues on mankind as a divine punishment for sin and corruption. Not surprisingly, some of the benefactors who paid for these paintings had suffered personal loss on account of the epidemics – as Buonamico di Lapo Guidalotti, a Florentine merchant whose wife had died of the plague, gave a large part of his fortune to the Dominicans of Santa Maria Novella for the construction of a new chapter-house, the Spanish Chapel. Realism, naturalism, and a tendency to humanize Christ and the saints had not been permanently established by the genius and reputation of Giotto and his contemporaries: they had to be revived again, by the generation of Masaccio, in the early fifteenth century.

In at least one city, Siena, plague and economic depression cut short a major building project. In 1339–40, the Sienese had resolved to construct a new nave at right-angles to their existing cathedral, which would thus have been incorporated in a colossal new building and would have become its transept. But the ambitions of the architects greatly outstripped their technique, and financial difficulties and grave labour-shortages supervened. The government of the Nine, which had fostered the project, fell from power in 1355. Their successors ordered the abandonment of the nave two years later, letting all but the unsafe parts stand, as it does to this day. But some difficult work on the extension of the choir was in fact carried out and eventually completed in 1370.

In general the later fourteenth century was a time for the completion of projects already undertaken, rather than for the undertaking of new ones. There were, however, some very conspicuous exceptions to the rule – in the Palace of the Doges which housed the council chambers of Venice, in the cathedral begun at Milan in 1386, in the Certosa at Pavia designed as the splendid tomb of the Visconti family, in the church of San Petronio at Bologna. It is not easy to explain in economic terms the great flowering of literature, art, architecture and sculpture which occurred in Florence in the early decades of the fifteenth century, because – even if Florence enjoyed an important respite from war over the years 1414 to 1423 – there was no great economic recovery dramatic enough to account for it. However, certain very general reflections on this subject can be put forward. The relationship between the economic and the 'cultural boom' need not be a direct one. Art may be most generously supported in phases of relative economic uncertainty by the rich members of a society which has accumulated much capital – wealth no longer capable of finding outlets through further investment in commerce or industry.

It can be argued that in periods of economic expansion the businessman may be more strongly tempted to pursue wealth for its own sake without pausing to ask what he can do with it: to plough his profits back into the business, rather than to spend them on painting or building. It can also quite plausibly be suggested that for a society to patronize art it does not need to be generally prosperous, with a reasonably even distribution of wealth throughout the social hierarchy: what is most needed is a small number of rich men with a surplus of wealth, endowed either with feelings of guilt at possessing it, or with a lust to acquire lasting fame through raising monuments of their own magnificence, or with both. Perhaps (for these purposes) it does not matter if the total wealth of the community has shrunk, so long as it is still unevenly distributed, and so long as there are people concerned with spending and enjoying rather than merely with getting and working. It has already been suggested that the Florentine tax system, with its heavy reliance on forced loans serviced by gabelles weighing oppressively upon the poor, was hardly likely to create an even distribution of wealth. The expansion of the *Monte* may have slightly encouraged the formation of a more leisured society, since the state could now be used as a source of profit, and a part of one's income could now be drawn from its dividends. Palace-building may well be undertaken at a time when, owing to a reduced population, there is more space available in the central districts of the town. About 1427, Florence probably had less than half the number of inhabitants it had contained in 1338; in the course of the fifteenth century clusters of small houses and shops, and sometimes entire streets, were ripped down to make way for large family palaces – for the Medici, the Strozzi, the Pazzi, the Guidi, the Rucellai, the Pitti.

It may well be that fifteenth-century Florentines were not distinguished by an exceptionally ruthless economic individualism or a voracious appetite for gain, but rather by a greater willingness to spend, and to spend on objects of enduring quality, rather than on ephemeral ostentation. Lorenzo de' Medici wrote in a memorial to his sons:

I find we have spent a large sum of money from 1434 up to 1471, as appears from an account book covering that period. It shows an incredible sum, for it amounts to 663,755 florins spent on buildings, charities and taxes, not counting other expenses, nor would I complain about this, for though many a man would like to have even part of that sum in his purse I think it gave great lustre to the state and this money seems to be well spent and I am very satisfied.

It is now well known that humanists in the early fifteenth century, not only in Florence but also in Venice, Milan and Naples, began to state openly that wealth could possess some positive value, and need not be officially regarded solely as a trap or a hindrance to salvation. But it does not seem, to judge by Professor Baron's account, that they encouraged their readers to regard wealth as an end in itself, in the manner of Max Weber's ideal capitalist: rather, they praised it for what could be done with it, and were sometimes very vague about how it should be obtained. In 1415 the Venetian Francesco Barbaro wrote that gratitude, charitable sentiments and the joy of giving were without true value 'if we are unable to prove our feelings by deeds',

and it was for such practical generosity, especially in helping friends or children, that wealth was especially valuable.
A few years later Leonardo Bruni, the chancellor of Florence,
translating Aristotle's *Economics* for Cosimo de' Medici,
declared that the quintessence of Aristotelianism was the
doctrine that only the possession of external goods afforded
'an opportunity for the exercise of virtue'. Such sentiments
were shared by Pier Candido Decembrio in Milan and by
Giovanni Pontano in Naples – Pontano, indeed, did not
believe in the dignity of commerce, and thought much more
highly of those who became rich through the munificence
of their prince. Perhaps this accent on munificence and
spending even in the midst of economic contraction – of
which it may have been both a cause and a consequence –
was most responsible for the flourishing of art and architecture in these years, though it cannot of course explain the
particular forms that the fine arts took. As the Florentine
Giovanni Rucellai was later to write: 'I have now done
nothing for fifty years but earn and spend money, and it has
become clear to me that spending money gives more
pleasure than earning it.'

Expansion and Conflict

13

In retrospect, the outstanding political development in Italy between 1350 and 1450 seems to have been the establishment of five large territorial states, each with anything from 800,000 to about two million Italian subjects. These states came to balance one another in such a way that further significant expansion on the part of any one of them became impracticable. Often considered, it was invariably to be frustrated by highly flexible combinations or 'leagues' of watchful opponents, ready to re-group themselves when any of their number achieved too startling successes. The old patterns of alliance, very approximately based on Guelf and Ghibelline, lost their force and relevance. Efficient imperial or German intervention in Italy disappeared almost completely; the Pope himself became much less of a universal spiritual lord, and – having settled at last in Rome – took on increasingly the attributes of a native Italian prince, increasingly concerned with exploiting his temporal dominions in order to compensate for the loss of 'spiritual' revenues from the Church abroad.

Such patterns may seem clear enough to the twentieth-century observer of Renaissance power politics. But there was, of course, no smooth evolutionary process or 'trend' visible at the time and leading inevitably towards the 'balanced states-system' of the 1450s and later years. Detailed chronological accounts of the power-struggles in Italy abound with inconclusive episodes, with tales of frustrated intentions, false starts, brittle conquests, and shady diplomatic deals which never came off. Accidents of birth and death, pointless acts of treachery, the caprice of such inconstant and fickle rulers as the Joannas of Naples or Filippo Maria of Milan, the cynical opportunism of mercenary captains and the uneasy distrust of their dubious employers: such things loom large in any close examination of the innumerable and intricate struggles. In a history such as this, their ramifications are too complex to describe, and only the most conclusive episodes can be brought to the fore – though such a method inevitably entails some risk of representing Renaissance politics as more orderly and logical in their development than they could ever have been in the confused reality.

*

Emperors and imperial claimants had not severed all connections with Italy, but they no longer came as enemies of the Pope and Ghibelline leaders. No more did they constitute a serious threat to the *de facto* power and property of communes or small seigneurs. Their role was not to oust and depose, but to confirm and acquiesce – in return for substantial cash payments. The belief that the Emperor was the ultimate source of legal authority survived, and it became reasonably clear that his function would in future be that of distributor of privileges in exchange for money. When, in 1354–5, Charles IV of Bohemia journeyed southwards to Rome to claim his crown, the Visconti of Milan deemed it worth their while to offer him 50,000 florins towards his coronation expenses, and a further 150,000 for the confirmation of their vicariate. Another measure of the respect still accorded in some quarters to the Emperor lay in the readiness of other cities to bribe Charles handsomely for cancelling sentences passed some forty years earlier by Henry VII. But Petrarch, who had met Charles at Mantua, soon had occasion to reprove the Emperor for his swift retreat from Italy, saying, 'You take with you crowns of iron and gold and the sterile name of Empire. You may be called Emperor of the Romans, but in truth you are King of Bohemia and nothing more!'

At first the Emperors confined themselves to dealing in the title of Vicar, which soon became virtually hereditary – for imperial vicars were not deposed as were some of the small seigneurs in the Papal States. But in 1395 Wenceslaus, King of the Romans, went a stage further and supplied the ambitious Giangaleazzo Visconti with the title of Duke of Milan – thus promoting him from the status of a theoretically dismissable official to that of a hereditary prince of the Empire. The action of Wenceslaus proved highly unpopular with the German princes, who challenged its validity; but they were quite unable to muster the military force necessary to reducing the Milanese upstart. Rupert of Bavaria, Count Palatine of the Rhine, was sent to recover the rights which Giangaleazzo was supposed to have usurped. But his armies were hopelessly disorganized, and he was forced into ignominious retreat in 1402 after a farcical skirmish near Brescia. It was clear that the Germans could only confirm, and not revoke, authority: for some time to come, it would be their task to observe the course of Italian history and not to divert it.

Meanwhile, the pillars of the old Guelf alliance – the Pope, the King of Naples, the commune of Florence – began to weaken or to separate. Most dynastic states became subject, sooner or later, to the devastating effects of succession disputes, royal minorities, personal incompetence or mental instability on the part of the ruler. On the death of Robert of Anjou in 1343 the Neapolitan Kingdom passed to his granddaughter Joanna (1343–82), and under her nominal government royal authority dissolved in a series of disputes over the succession. The Kingdom was ripped apart by conflicts between the Hungarian branch of the

Angevin family and the cadet branches of the Neapolitan Angevins – the houses of Taranto and Durazzo. The consequence of this was that for fifty or sixty years the power of the ruler of Naples abroad in Italy became negligible – although it was to revive suddenly, dramatically but briefly in the early fifteenth century through the military adventures of a skyrocket conqueror, Ladislao of Durazzo (1390–1414). When one of his own subjects was elected Pope in Rome in 1404, he was to seize the opportunity of becoming not merely the protector but the master of the Papal States: not the vassal of the Pope, but his effective lord.

Meanwhile, between the early 1340s and the mid-1370s, relations between Florence and the Papacy deteriorated. Both Neapolitans and subjects of the Pope contributed something to the great failures of the early 1340s, which reduced the largest Florentine banking houses, the Bardi, Peruzzi and Acciaiuoli. In 1341 the Florentines found Robert of Anjou unwilling to support them in a local war within Tuscany, and they then provoked a grave crisis of confidence by launching an ill-advised appeal to Ludwig of Bavaria. Subjects of the Pope and Angevin reacted by demanding payment in full of their deposits in Florentine banks, and these concerns proved to have insufficient liquid reserves to withstand the strain. Litigation over the repayment of deposits accounted for some tension in subsequent years between the Florentines, the clergy and the Papacy; the financial stake of the Florentines in the affairs of the Popes had been diminished, for although Florentine bankers still conducted business at Avignon and Naples they seem to have done so on a reduced scale.

Unhappiness was also caused by the reconstruction of the temporal power of the Papacy, for not all Florentines were prepared to look enthusiastically upon the restoration of a strong state in their own immediate neighbourhood – even if it might herald the return of the Papacy from Avignon to Rome. The essential preliminary to this event would, of course, be the pacification of central Italy. Some years before, even John XXII's able and vigorous legate, Cardinal Bertrand du Poujet, had tried and failed to restore order in the centre. But now the temporal authority of the Pope found a successful champion in Cardinal Gil Albornoz, Archbishop of Toledo and a former servant of the kings of Castile. For most of the time between 1353 and 1367 Albornoz was engaged in a prolonged struggle to reconquer the Papal States from adventurous barons and usurpers of power. It was he who codified the legislation of his predecessors for the good government of the Papal States by a system of legates, rectors and treasurers in the various provinces. His work was promulgated as the 'Egidian Constitutions' at Fano in 1357, and it was to provide a model (or at least a goal) for the administration of the Papal States until the early nineteenth century. Albornoz fought strenuously to restore central control in the province of the Patrimony and in the Romagna, where he collided with the local dynasts, the Malatesta and the Ordelaffi.

But at this the Florentines looked askance, for they were friendly with the Malatesta and were in the habit of employing them as military captains. They also feared the mercenary companies – especially the German troops of Conrad, Count of Landau, and of Anechin von Bongartz – who came to take part in the campaigns of Albornoz, and were engaged by both sides. They felt that Albornoz was not guaranteeing Tuscany sufficient protection against the plundering expeditions of these unsavoury gangs of foreigners. For their part, they remained persistently neutral in the quarrel which was in progress in the mid-fourteenth century between the Popes and the Visconti. The territorial ambitions of both the contenders intersected at Bologna: a large city with a prestigious university, semi-independent and strategically vital, which in theory formed part of the Papal States. By the 1390s the Florentines were to recognize the lord of Milan as a deadly enemy; but that was in the future, and when war came in 1375 it was war between Florence and the Papacy – a war ironically known, from the board of eight Florentines who directed its conduct, as the War of the Eight Saints. A substantial anticlerical faction had been much in evidence in Florence in the years preceding the outbreak of this conflict, though it was countered both by the capacity of the Pope for buying off his opponents with the great reserves of patronage at his disposal and by the survival of the ultra-conservative Guelf Party – which had still at this time been rather imperfectly subordinated to the commune. Reasonable relations between Florence and the Papacy were eventually restored after the War of the Eight Saints, and the Medici eventually became bankers to the Papacy. But the new relationship was not of the same kind, for the Papacy was greatly weakened by the schism which began in 1378 and by the turbulent conditions which could still drive it, as late as the 1430s, into exile from the Papal States. The highly articulate civic patriotism of the early fifteenth century tended to portray Florence, not as a link or partner in the Guelf alliance, but as an independent republic and a self-contained entity.

The successes of Albornoz had beaten flat the path for the Papacy to return to Rome. In the past it could have been argued that Rome was geographically placed on the edge of western Christendom, farther from the centre than was Avignon. But there was now some prospect of reunion between the Catholic and the Greek Orthodox Churches, and hence of the renewal of a great Christian commonwealth which would have embraced the whole of the Mediterranean world and stretched into the Levant. Hard pressed by the advancing Turks, the Byzantine Emperors of the house of Palaeologos were anxious to open negotiations for reunion, in the belief that this might improve their prospects of obtaining military aid from the west. Italy would be the ideal site for discussions, and Rome might hope to become the capital of a new Church centred once more in the south. From 1367, Pope Urban V returned for three years to Rome – although, in view of the very grave administrative problems which would have been created by moving all the archives and the other apparatus of government, the curia was effectively cut in half and papal finance continued to be administered from Avignon. The move was neither complete nor permanent, but Urban's successor, Gregory XI, decided to move from Avignon during the War of the Eight Saints and made his solemn entry into Rome in January 1377.

But soon after this second return, the western Church was bisected by schism, and the Papacy was entering its gravest crisis since the terrible humiliation of Boniface VIII at the hands of the King of France. The Great Schism was to enfeeble the Pope's position both as a spiritual lord and as a ruler of central Italy, and he was to become an object rather than an instigator of international intrigues and diplomatic machinations. When Gregory XI died in Rome in 1378, the non-Italian cardinals (who formed the great majority among members of the college present in Rome) were so divided by mutual jealousies that they were prepared to compromise on an outsider. Their choice fell on Bartolomeo Prignano, Archbishop of Bari: he was an Italian by birth, but could be called French in the somewhat remote sense of being a subject of the Angevin Queen of Naples. The cardinals saw their nominee, now Pope Urban VI, as a nonentity whom they could easily bend to their will: but they had misjudged him. He proved to be a man of violent and despotic temperament, with little personal dignity and even a streak of sadism. He now took the line that the Papacy was to remain in Rome and emancipate itself from

French influence. Concentrating on the Cardinal of Amiens, he began criticizing the corrupt and vicious life of several members of the college of cardinals.

Certain cardinals then adopted a drastic remedy. Withdrawing to Anagni, some distance from Rome, they declared Urban's election null and void. For this their pretext was that they had been intimidated in conclave by the Roman crowd outside the walls, bellowing for a Roman or at least an Italian Pope. Allegedly they had elected the Archbishop of Bari solely in order to pacify the mob outside, 'but never with the intention that he should be true Pope'. There was no reason to doubt that the Romans had been anxious for the election of a Pope who would keep the curia in Rome – but some cause to wonder whether presumably responsible churchmen could really have behaved in such an erratic manner. The rebellious cardinals elected Cardinal Robert of Geneva, now called Clement VII, as rival Pope, and they soon succeeded in entrenching themselves once more at Avignon. In this confused situation, two parallel 'obediences' were created, 'Urbanist' and 'Clementine', Roman and Avignonese, and each obedience managed to win some support from among the rulers of Europe and of Italy. The Schism was perpetuated into a second generation of rival pontiffs when in 1389 the Roman obedience chose a successor to Urban, in Pope Boniface IX; and in 1394 Clement VII was succeeded by a Spanish antiPope, who called himself Benedict XIII.

Schisms in the papal office had occurred in earlier generations, for Emperors and imperial candidates (including Ludwig of Bavaria) had in the past tried to discomfit recalcitrant opponents by disputing their title to be the true Pope. But this division was to last the unprecedented term of thirty-nine years, and it was to create a much deeper cleft in the whole of Catholic Christendom than had any of its predecessors. Moreover, this dispute was to call in ques-

tion the whole nature of the papal office and even to challenge the Pope's ultimate sovereignty over Catholics. There
were major issues of principle beyond the incompatibility
of Urban and his cardinals, even beyond the question of
whether the Papacy should settle in Rome or in Avignon.
Should the Church be subjected to absolute government by
the Pope alone, or to a form of constitutional oligarchy in
which the college of cardinals would exercise considerable
control over him? The Schism created a pressing need to
discover in the Church a sovereign authority greater and
more stable than the Pope himself, and publicists and
canonists began to formulate – and even to act upon – the
theory that ultimate sovereignty ought to rest with a council
of the whole Church: for surely the whole Church was
mightier than any single part of it, greater even than the
city of Rome and the Apostolic See.

The Popes in Rome suffered grave loss of revenue as well
as of spiritual prestige, and their control over the Papal
States was badly shaken, so that they lacked the material
resources which could have made them a force in Italian
politics. At its disposal the Roman obedience had far more
territory than the Avignonese, but its fiscal administration
was a good deal less efficient and stable. Since the Apostolic
Treasury of Gregory XI had passed to the Avignonese
obedience, the Roman curia suffered from a painful lack
of tried administrators and of experienced collectors of
revenue from abroad. It was difficult to communicate with
the far-flung countries of the Roman obedience, with
Guyenne and England, or with Poland and Sweden:
especially as France and Spain were adhering to Clement
and his successor. In Italy, the tribute due from the vassal
King of Naples, originally fixed at 8,000 gold ounces a year,
had to be formally reduced and in fact remitted altogether
up to the year 1413. Among the Pope's 'apostolic vicars'
during the first years of the Schism only the Malatesta

proved to be loyal subjects and prompt prayers of tribute. In most of the other regions of central Italy – Umbria, the Campagna, the Maremma, the Patrimony – the Pope faced prolonged and obstinate resistance.

Admittedly, the situation did improve quite considerably during the pontificate of Boniface IX (1389–1404), the second Pope of the Roman obedience. But the heavy defence and running costs of the Papal States proved sufficient to swallow up the revenue yielded by tribute from the apostolic vicars, by duties levied on trade and consumption, and by direct taxation. Boniface died with his treasury empty; during and after the reign of his successor, Innocent VII, the Papal States were threatened with dismemberment at the hands of the Neapolitan King, Ladislao of Durazzo. Their slow reconstruction could only be undertaken when the Schism itself had ended.

In the early fifteenth century, despite the eagerness of some European kings to make capital out of the division of Christendom by playing off one rival pontiff against another and extracting concessions from both, there was a growing desire for the restoration of unity within the Catholic Church. For a time, the most practicable method of bringing this about appeared to be the so-called 'way of cession', which would have entailed the simultaneous abdication of both the claimants. Indeed, at the conclave held in Rome in 1406, each cardinal swore that if elected Pope he would be prepared to abdicate to end the Schism – so long as the antiPope and his cardinals were prepared to cooperate. On this understanding the Venetian Angelo Correr became Pope Gregory XII, but he soon betrayed his promise; he may have been pressed by his Correr nephews not to forgo this opportunity – so earnestly desired by ecclesiastical careerists and their relatives – for enriching his own family with the patronage of which he disposed. Both Angelo Correr and the antiPope began to hedge.

Plans were hatched for them to meet and lay down their tiaras, but they contrived with some skill to avoid doing so. It seemed increasingly plain that nothing could be expected from strictly constitutional action and that only irregular methods would succeed; traditional respect for papal supremacy was wearing thin.

When Gregory XII forgot his undertakings so far as to appoint some new cardinals, seven of his followers broke away and leagued themselves with other cardinals of the antiPope. Despite warnings that their action might lead, not to unity, but to a threefold division, they summoned a council to meet at Pisa in 1409. There they declared both the Popes deposed, on the grounds that they were promoters of schism and – since their conduct had subverted the article of faith concerning the One Holy Catholic and Apostolic Church – heretics. But the well-intentioned cardinals at Pisa did indeed fail to clarify the situation, and they could do no more than conjure up a third obedience, since the two senior claimants refused to consider themselves deprived. The first Pisan creation was Petros Filargis, the Cretan Archbishop of Milan, who became Pope Alexander V; and on his death in 1410 Cardinal Baldassare Cossa succeeded him as John XXIII. It seemed briefly as though John XXIII might be capable of offering the only effective resistance to King Ladislao, the invader of the Papal States; but he found his strength sapped by inevitable but dangerous reliance on hired mercenary captains, who proved all too capable of switching sides.

The body which did succeed in terminating the Schism was a general council of the Catholic Church which met in Constance, on the Swiss–German border, between 1414 and 1418. Some canonists, including the Paduan Zabarella (one of John XXIII's cardinals), had argued that the Emperor or King of the Romans, as protector and defender of the Holy See and head of the laity within the all-embracing Christian commonwealth, ought to be responsible for the summoning of such a council. Sigismund of Luxemburg, King of Hungary and King of the Romans, was prepared to take his duties seriously; only when the Schism had ended would he be able to obtain a satisfactory coronation as Emperor. The uncertainties of John XXIII's position prompted him to agree to a council, which he vainly hoped to be able to steer in a direction favourable to himself. In the course of the next three years the Council's deliberations did in fact bring the Schism to an end. John XXIII lost his nerve, took to flight, and was subsequently deposed by the Council. Gregory XII, Pope of the Roman obedience, abdicated in a relatively dignified manner. The Council now elected as Pope a member of the Roman aristocracy, Cardinal Oddone Colonna, who became Pope Martin V and proved to be a competent and formidable administrator. Both John and Gregory were reconciled with Martin and were compensated by honourable appointments; but the Pope of the former 'Clementine' obedience clung obstinately to his shadowy title although his following dwindled away, retreating to the Spanish fortress of Peñiscola and calling himself Benedict XIII until his death in 1424.

Although the Council of Constance had ended the Schism, it had still created new problems about the location of sovereignty within the Church. It had boldly asserted its own supreme authority, but there was little chance that the Popes would accept so revolutionary a claim. Furthermore, to ensure the survival of conciliar authority the Council had provided that in future general councils should be held at fairly frequent intervals to review the state of Christendom – that they should become a regular part of the Church's governmental machinery, and should not be treated as an extraordinary measure only to be invoked in emergencies. No serious difficulties arose with the first of these general councils, which assembled at Pavia and later

at Siena in 1423-4 and, on account of the troubled condition of Europe, was poorly attended. But Eugenius IV, who
reigned from 1431 to 1447, ran into serious trouble with
the Council meeting at Basel which set itself up as a parallel
authority within the Catholic Church. Apart from its
impact on the Church at large, the conflict with the fathers
of Basel had embarrassing consequences for the Pope's
temporal government; for the Duke of Milan, seeing the
loosely structured Papal States as a land of promise and
opportunity for himself, intervened in their affairs on the
dubious pretext that he and his hired captains were agents
of the Council of Basel.

Although Sigismund had offered the Pope the chance to
reside in Basel, Mainz or Strasbourg, and although the
French had proposed a return to Avignon, Martin V was
determined to go back to Rome. Conditions in central
Italy were still so uncertain that he could not enter his
capital until September 1420. But the fact that he came of a
local family and could employ powerful relatives as
governors and generals undoubtedly helped him to restore
order in central Italy; although family rule could never
offer a permanent solution to problems of government, and
the Colonna proved unwilling to accept the authority of
Martin's successor. In these years the Papacy was to become
more of an Italian prince, more firmly identified with
Rome – at least after Eugenius IV's return from exile in
1443 – than in any previous epoch of its history. Its concern
for the wider problems of Christianity did not diminish,
for it was Eugenius who at Florence in 1439 succeeded in
effecting a form of reconciliation between the Catholic and
Orthodox Churches, and he and later Popes faced up to
their daunting, self-imposed task of trying to induce the
powers of Italy and Catholic Europe to sink their enmities
and combine in a new international crusade against the
advancing Turks. The sacred college of cardinals remained

fairly cosmopolitan for the time being, and in 1447 there were still only eleven Italian cardinals in a total of twenty-four. There was certainly a strong German element in the various branches of the curial bureaucracy, and between 1417 and 1455 the office of Master of the Sacred Palace was held three times by a Spaniard, once by a German, and once by an Italian. But, on the other hand, the Pope's temporal dominions in Italy became much more important to him as a source of revenue, and the need for the efficient exploitation of the Papal States consequently increased.

In the course of the damaging Schism, revenues from the universal Church, outside the Papal States, had been greatly reduced: indeed, a commission of cardinals concluded in 1429 that they had dropped to only about one-third of the level attained before the Schism. Zealous in their efforts to prune the Pope's income from the Church at large, the Councils did nothing to provide alternative means of support for the curial bureaucracy. During the pontificate of Gregory XI (1370–78) the income of the Papacy had been 200–300,000 gold cameral florins per annum, and of this not more than a quarter had derived from the Papal States. But the revenue of Martin V in 1426–7 was about 170,000 gold cameral florins, of which some 80,000 or nearly a half came from the Papal States. Thus the yield from the Papal States had probably increased in absolute terms, and had certainly done so in its relationship to the total receipts of the Papacy. By the time of Pope Sixtus IV (1471–84) the return from the Papal States was to account for approximately 63 per cent of total papal income.

The Pope had become, not the pivot of the Guelf faction, so much as one among the five major powers within the peninsula. However, unlike the Venetians, the Visconti or the Florentine Republic, he was not concerned with the expansion of his frontiers and the absorption of new conquests so much as with the consolidation of authority within traditional boundaries, and with the seemingly endless struggle to assert direct rule and limit the uneconomical practice of relying on local vicars.

*

In this century, the overall pattern of Italian politics in the north had changed quite considerably. So had the terms in which the struggle between states was conventionally represented by the propagandists of those involved in it. With great over-simplification, it was portrayed by Florentines of the late fourteenth and early fifteenth centuries as a confrontation between the republican way of life and the despotic or 'tyrannical' state personified in the Visconti or in Ladislao of Naples. The watchword of the Milanese was 'peace', the condition of order and stability which could only be achieved under a just, authoritarian régime; and the Duke and the King were seen by their humanist partisans as new Caesars, whilst the Florentines rejoiced in their descent from the Roman Republic and claimed to be defenders of 'liberty'. This new situation arose out of the vigorous expansion of the Milanese state and out of its collisions first with Florence in Tuscany and then with Venice in Lombardy. It was true, especially between the early 1420s and the late 1440s, that the greatest seigneurial régime in Italy was being opposed by the two greatest powers that happened to be republics. On the other hand there was no solid alignment of the small tyrannies of Italy against the republics – the contrast between living in a republican and living in a tyrannical state was not, perhaps, as great as contemporaries liked to depict it; and in the end the Republics of Florence and Venice failed to show much solicitude for the short-lived 'Republic of St Ambrose' which was proclaimed when the last Visconti died in Milan in August 1447. It may be that an acute sense of self-interest and some appreciation of the need to preserve a balance of power had, even in these years, more influence upon diplomacy than had loyal adherence to principle.

In the middle and late fourteenth century the Visconti state became the prime mover in Italian politics. It passed through phases of expansion which were then cancelled out by almost equally dramatic phases of dismemberment and disintegration, in which the Visconti forfeited their most recent conquests to their uneasy and frightened neighbours. Visconti aggression prompted other states to expand, if only as a means to greater security, and helped to transform the landscape of communes, *contadi* and *Signorotti* into one of much larger territorial blocs. At intervals the Visconti dominions were partitioned among members of the family, and a second capital was established at Pavia; at intervals Visconti gains were obliterated by the consequences of succession crises and minorities to which the government of republican states was less liable. It may be that the strongest contrast between republic and 'tyranny' lay, less in any greater degree of 'liberty' which the republican oligarchies may have extended to their subjects, than in the greater stability and continuity of their régimes. Hence, when he described the collision between Giangaleazzo Visconti and the Florentines at the start of the fifteenth century, the Florentine Gregorio Dati could write:

Always they comforted themselves with the hope, which in their eyes was a certainty on which they could count, that a Commonwealth (*il Comune*) cannot die, while the Duke was one single mortal man, whose end would mean the end of his empire ... And consequently ... the Florentines never rested; when one remedy had worn thin or failed, they immediately resorted to some other.

After 1339 the Visconti clearly emerged as the most dangerous of the Lombard lords. A huge and wealthy dominion had been built up in the past few years by the

della Scala of Verona, and (since it came to include Lucca)
it had spread into Tuscany and impinged on the security of
the Florentines. But it had proved surprisingly brittle, and
was never renewed to the full. The Visconti were liable to
aim at four or five major objectives, and sometimes proved
capable of attaining them. Mastery of Genoa would be
highly desirable for the Milanese economy, and would help
to secure vital supplies of salt and grain. Opportunities to
realize this ambition were sometimes forthcoming, for the
Genoese state was highly unstable and the people were
occasionally willing to submit to some foreign lord who
might be expected to guarantee them peace and order. The
Milanese did become lords of Genoa for a brief spell in the
early 1350s and again betwen 1421 and 1436 – though on
the second occasion the Genoese came to feel that land-
locked Milan was insufficiently sensitive to their maritime
interests, and threw off Visconti rule. To the south-east lay
Bologna, and their designs on this city brought the Visconti
into direct collision with the still powerful Papacy in the
days of the legate Albornoz. The mouth of the Po and the
Alpine passes – St Gotthard, Lukmanier, Splügen, Septimer,
Simplon – were vital outlets for the state's economy, to
whose claims the Visconti were never indifferent. There was
also the possibility of thrusting still further to the south and
invading the Florentine sphere of influence.

In 1385 the Pavian and Milanese sectors of the Visconti
lands, which had for some time been ruled by different
members of the family, were united by the successful conspiracy hatched by Giangaleazzo, lord of Pavia, against his
uncle Bernabò in Milan. Bernabò was thrown into prison,
where he soon died, and his nephew systematically dis-
credited him by publishing a 'Processus', an indictment or
trial of Bernabò, which listed his subjects' grievances
against him and speciously claimed that he had been
dethroned for failure to obtain the cancellation of a sen-

tence of deposition uttered by the Emperor in 1372. Gian-galeazzo's ambitions were strongly focused on the east and south, and his immediate victims were two of the east Lombard seigneurs – the della Scala of Verona and the Carraresi of Padua. These small principalities were soon to be expunged from the map, when the Venetian Republic began to involve itself in the power-struggle on the main-land by way of reaction to the Visconti. But for the time being the Venetians did not intervene wholeheartedly, although they did begin to sense the desirability of preserv-ing small buffer states in Padua, Mantua and Ferrara to cushion them against Visconti's advance. They were certainly alarmed when Giangaleazzo began intriguing in Friuli, the gateway to Austria and Hungary so essential to Venice's role as entrepôt between central Europe and the Middle East.

Much more vociferous in opposing the Visconti, and far readier to anticipate dire consequences from Milanese aggression, were the rulers of Florence – or a section of them. From 1390 Florentine propagandists, headed by the humanist chancellor Coluccio Salutati, proclaimed the struggle between 'tyranny' and 'liberty', and began to put about manifestoes which rhetorically accused Giangaleazzo of aspiring to the monarchy of Italy – 'he has formed the notion of embellishing his tyranny with the splendours of the royal title.' In this context the term 'liberty' implied both freedom from foreign domination and the preservation of independent communes from being engulfed by a single vaster lordship. The Florentines' attachment to the prin-ciples of republicanism and 'liberty' may well appear exaggerated and even hypocritical, because they had not in the past objected either to tolerating the presence of seigneurs in neighbouring towns or to negotiating with them when it seemed appropriate. They had been happy to form relations with authoritarian governments in Bologna and glad to see Pietro Gambacorta – whose sympathies were pro-Florentine – reign as lord of Pisa from 1370 to 1392. Attachment to 'liberty' did not restrain the Florentines from expanding locally and annexing other cities, though they had been known (as at Volterra) to justify such actions on the score that they were rescuing the inhabitants from a tyranny. In their defence, however, it can be fairly argued that history has known few concepts of freedom divorced from the self-interest of those who formulate them. In any case the Florentines had been following a consistent policy of preserving Tuscany from interference from abroad, and it was in this spirit that they now acted.

But not all the peoples of Tuscany shared Florence's xenophobia, and in most of the rival cities there were anti-Florentine factions prepared to offer Visconti the leverage he required: for he did not achieve his successes by sheer armed might so much as by subsidizing partisans in the chief Tuscan cities – myrmidons who, once they had gained control, proved ready to hand them over and make Visconti their lord. Giangaleazzo was not always seen as a tyrant: he had a certain reputation for clemency, and newly acquired towns were allowed a measure of autonomy and some control over their own finances – they could not, perhaps, have hoped for more if the Florentines had become their masters. Furthermore, in the region of the Casentino and in the Apennines to the east of Florence, there were several feudal lords ready to shrug off their allegiance to the city. Although Giangaleazzo's advance had been delayed for about ten years, it was resumed in 1399–1402, when Visconti partisans engineered a series of take-overs in Pisa, Siena, Perugia, and (finally and most devastatingly) in Bologna – which the Florentines had long regarded as their indispensable ally.

As it happened, Visconti's advance ended in the anti-climax of Giangaleazzo's death of a fever in September 1402.

At this point his state began to crumble, as a mentally unstable minor, Giovanni Maria, inherited the ducal title, intrigue swirled around the Council of Regency, and the realm was shaken by the competing ambitions of the generals. For another ten years there could be little attempt at reconstructing the Milanese state, and it could offer no serious threat abroad. But despite this inconclusive ending to the drama the consequences of Giangaleazzo's aggressions and of his state's collapse were arguably very far-reaching – and not only for political history in the narrowest sense of the term. For it has been seriously maintained by a modern scholar, Dr Hans Baron, that the crisis of 1402 evoked in certain Florentines an acute sense of the value of the republican way of life, and served as a powerful stimulus to literary and artistic achievement: though not all scholars have proved ready to accept such contentions. Be this as it may, Giangaleazzo's successes had instilled in some Florentine and Venetian politicians a sense of insecurity which inspired them to adopt a more aggressive territorial policy, as if to protect their threatened commercial interests and their communications with the outside world. During the recent crisis Florence had found itself encircled and blockaded, and most of its links with Rome and the sea had been cut. Admittedly, one route had remained open, in the road across the Apennines to Rimini, where the Malatesta lords preserved their neutrality. But this was capable of handling only a small proportion of Florence's trade. In 1406 the Florentines took the precaution of annexing Pisa, though fifteen years had still to pass before they gained possession of the outports of Livorno and Porto Pisano and were able to launch their famous experiment with merchant galleys.

Still more momentous was the decision of the Venetian government to embark on territorial conquest on the Italian mainland. They began the construction of a state which, through its combination of great wealth, great area, dense population and prosperous towns, had probably become the greatest individual power in Italy by the middle of the fifteenth century. This resolution to become a continental power was not quite without precedent, for sixty years earlier Venice had joined a league which dismembered the extensive dominions of Mastino II della Scala, seigneur of Verona; and the Venetians had then annexed the province of Treviso. But the imperialism of the early fifteenth century was both more sweeping and more enduring. The Venetians had a strong interest in keeping their hinterland divided among evenly balanced potentates who could if necessary be played off against one another by clever diplomacy: a single super-power, astride the whole Veneto, could much more easily have held the Venetians to ransom by controlling their transit-trade up the Po, Brenta and Adige, or by cutting them off from Lombardy and the Julian Alps. There was good reason to fear that the power-vacuum created by the temporary collapse of the Visconti might be filled by the revival of the Carraresi. Furthermore, the uncertain situation in eastern Lombardy began to impede Venice's lucrative salt trade with the Milanese Duchy, the Council of Regency choosing to renew its supplies chiefly by way of Genoa.

It seems rather less likely that the Venetians were strongly moved by the need to find an outlet, in dominions of their own on the Italian mainland, for accumulated capital they could no longer invest in maritime commerce; or that they were seriously perturbed by the food situation and chose this method of securing supplies for the metropolis. Arguably, there was no really massive transfer of capital to the mainland until the mid-sixteenth century, when Venice had to face again the social and economic problems connected with a growing population. Rather, it seems as though the Venetians had begun to realize that if they were to survive as an entrepôt they could not go on ignoring the question of overland communications or continue to divorce the sea from the land. These could no longer be treated as two entirely separate spheres of action, competing for investment and attention. They must be regarded as complementary to each other, although perhaps there would always be a segment of opinion (compounded of puritanism and traditionalism) which distrusted the Venetian entanglement in the territorial politics of Italy: one which held that Venice should have been content with an island empire, for the sea was the source of her ancient greatness.

Unlike their Genoese rivals, the Venetians now annexed a large territorial dominion capable of securing their communications into Italy and into Europe. In 1405 the Republic seized the lands of the Carraresi and pushed its own frontiers westwards to include the province of Verona. Determined to erase all memory of the Carraresi, the Venetian government had the last lord of Padua strangled in prison and the tombs of his dynasty defaced.

Some years later, in 1419–20, the Venetians conducted further successful campaigns in Friuli, where they were anxious to protect transit – especially the routes through the Valle del Ferro to Pontebbio, Tarvisio and Villach. As a result of these operations the Patriarchs of Aquileia, once perhaps the richest landed prelates in Italy, were left in possession of small tracts of territory with limited jurisdiction over them, and granted an annual stipend of 3,000 ducats – now to be paid by the Republic. In the north-east of Italy the political map was being drastically simplified. By 1423, according to Doge Tommaso Mocenigo, the mainland provinces already accounted for 25–30 per cent of the revenue of the Venetian state. 464,000 ducats accrued to the treasury from the Terra Ferma, as compared with 774,000 from Venice itself and environs, and 376,000 from the maritime empire to the east of the city. Venice came to dominate the Veneto as Florence could not dominate Tuscany – for, despite the absorption of Pisa and Arezzo, Lucca continued to elude the grasp of the Florentines, and Siena was to remain an independent state until the mid-sixteenth century.

It was in the 1420s that a combination of the two major republics against a north Italian 'tyranny' did take place at last. The Milanese state had revived, its old frontiers with Switzerland had been restored, and its lord was again the lord of Genoa. In the aftermath of Giangaleazzo's death, Visconti rule had been threatened by the expanding dominions of a landed adventurer, Facino Cane, Count of Biandrate, who had forced the incompetent Duke Giovanni Maria to accept him as governor of Milan and as virtual co-regent. But both Facino Cane and Giovanni Maria had died in 1412, and the realm had passed into the hands of Giangaleazzo's younger son – the suspicious, inconstant but very able Duke Filippo Maria Visconti. He had solved some of his problems by the simple expedient of marrying Facino Cane's widow. Once his state had been reconstructed he showed a malignant interest in the affairs of others – in Tuscany, in the Papal States, and even in the apparently endless succession crises of the Neapolitan Kingdom.

By the early 1420s the threat of renewed Milanese aggression had become ominous enough to bring about the triumph of war parties over the advocates of appeasement, both in Florence and in Venice. For the first time the Florentines obtained the thoroughgoing collaboration they had vainly urged in the days of Giangaleazzo. As they tersely put it: 'The Genoese, unaided by us, made Filippo Maria lord; we, unless we are assisted by you, will be forced to make him King; and you, when you can no longer be succoured by anyone, will find yourselves making him Emperor.' There was no longer much room for debate as to whether

Venice ought to acquire a territorial state or not – the central issue was whether or not the interests of Venice could best be promoted by pressing further to the west, rather than by preserving the friendship of Milan and Genoa. How far was the fate of Venice bound to that of Florence? In Venice, Francesco Foscari said of the Florentines that 'their weal is our weal, and, by the same token, harm to them is harm to us'; it was he who triumphed over the warnings and mis-givings put about by the dying Doge Tommaso Mocenigo and rose to take his place. Venetian expansion into Lom-bardy continued: the growing state absorbed the pros-perous metal-working regions of Brescia and the poor mountain valleys of the textile-town of Bergamo. Eventually, in the mid-fifteenth century, the Venetian frontier was stabilized on the banks of the Adda, after the failure of further attempts at land-grabbing amid the uncertainties which followed the death of Filippo Maria Visconti.

A modern historian, Dr Baron, has seen the formation of this alliance as 'the crowning success of the policy Florence had pursued from the 1390s onwards'; a combination of the free peoples of the peninsula against tyranny had taken place at last. However, there must be some doubt as to whether the alliance was really inspired by much more than the exigencies of power politics. In the mid-fifteenth century the Florentines were to turn against the Venetians when they recognized them, and not the Milanese, as the most dangerous aggressors in northern Italy: perhaps this action did not mark a real change of principle on the part of the Florentines, though it did involve a change of ally. It is true that in 1436 other republics, those of Genoa and Siena, joined the alliance; but princes from Mantua and Ferrara fought on the side of Florence and Venice, and so at one time or another did the Duke of Savoy and the Marquess of Monferrato, whose adhesion might help to outflank the Visconti. But even though there was in reality no simple alignment of 'free' republics against 'tyrannies' or 'despotisms', it was natural that some publicists – including the Venetian Francesco Barbaro – should dignify the struggle by depicting it in these terms.

The relatively balanced 'states-system' which characterized Italy in the middle and later fifteenth century could not have come into being without the settlement of the quarrels which had so long torn the ruling house of Naples, and without the return of a king in the south who was feared in other parts of the peninsula. After the death of Ladislao in 1414, the most significant development south of Rome was the extension of Aragonese dominion from the island of Sicily to the mainland, so that the Kingdom of Naples became a part, and the city the administrative capital, of the west Mediterranean empire of Alfonso, King of Aragon, Valencia, Sicily, Majorca, Sardinia and Corsica, and lord of Catalonia, Rosellón and Cerdaña. Ladislao was succeeded by Queen Joanna II; she proved to be childless, and veered erratically between nominating an Aragonese and an Angevin heir. In the end she favoured the Angevin, but still kept him at a distance and made no practical arrangements for him to participate in government so as to ensure a smooth take-over on her death. For a time Joanna had leaned towards Alfonso of Aragon, who was already (by 1420) betraying his interest in consolidating his rule over Sardinia and Corsica. Within a few years of Joanna's death in 1435 Alfonso had triumphed over the current Angevin claimant, and by 1442 he had completed the conquest of the south and was installed in Naples itself.

Since the Pope was still theoretically overlord of the Kingdom of Sicily – now reunited under Alfonso for the first time in a century and a half – the régime of the conqueror could not become legitimate without his recognition. This demanded a change of front on the part of the Papacy, which had hitherto been more inclined to favour the less formidable Angevins, or to keep the Kingdom divided. But Pope Eugenius's own insecurity, together with any inclination he may have felt to acknowledge a *fait accompli*, made him ready to negotiate. By the Terracina treaty of 1443 Alfonso obtained recognition on the understanding that he would himself withdraw support from the Council of Basel, which was contesting the Pope's sovereignty over the Catholic world. The King also undertook to furnish aid against an ambitious and talented adventurer, the mercenary captain Francesco Sforza, who had vivisected the Papal States by occupying the March of Ancona and compelling the Pope to recognize his usurpation.

Alfonso's conquest of Naples implied that the formidable navies of the Aragonese were now equipped with further bases in the south. Since Aragonese power was now identified to some extent with the commercial progress of Catalan traders, the Italian states most likely to collide with Alfonso were the ancient sea-going republics of Venice and Genoa and the emergent maritime power of Florence. The Aragonese conquests of Sardinia and Corsica had in the past been achieved at the expense of the Tyrrhenean ports of Genoa and Pisa. But the lord of the inland state of Milan, Filippo Maria Visconti, found Alfonso less of a menace and came to see him as a potential ally, a protector for the Milanese state both against Venetian aggression and against the possibility of French invasion. Indeed, Filippo Maria went so far, just before his death, as to attempt to consign the Milanese state to Alfonso's representative in the north and to make a will leaving his dominions to the King. But Alfonso found the bequest embarrassing and was in no position to claim it. At the time his real interests lay in combined military and naval operations designed to win harbours on the Tuscan coast. These might serve as bases for his galleys and enable him to harass the shipping lines of Florence and Genoa. By 1450 Alfonso had managed laboriously to earn recognition of his conquest – achieved mostly by bribery – of the small but potentially valuable port of Castiglione della Pescaia. But neither his financial resources nor his skill as a strategist had enabled him to go any further, and his prestige suffered from his failure to take the harbour of Piombino, on which he had also entertained designs. Not even the King of Aragon was in a position to jolt the growing political equilibrium in Italy, which was now further guaranteed by the general recognition of Francesco Sforza as Duke of a reduced Milanese state.

Francesco Sforza was the hero of the most spectacular political and military success story of the fifteenth century: a soldier of undistinguished birth who, by sheer native skill and opportunism, raised himself and his heirs to become Dukes of Milan. Chronic feebleness, financial inadequacy or periodic collapse on the part of the Milanese, Neapolitan or papal governments offered exciting chances at intervals throughout the fifteenth century for the mercenary captains who commanded their armies; generals and freelance colonels who could employ their troops during interregna to carve out little states for themselves, slicing substantial chunks of territory off the larger dominions. An able *condottiere*, without permanent allegiance to any one master, could extract special favours and concessions as well as subsidies from employers anxious to retain his services. The opportunism of mercenary captains was only matched by their employers' suspicion of the most successful among them – as witness the Venetians' execution of their captain Carmagnola in 1432, and the unhappy relations between Francesco Sforza and the Ambrosian Republic. In the reign of Eugenius IV the Pope's lack of ready cash was still compelling him to compensate mercenary captains by authorizing them – rather than state officials – to exact taxation in particular areas. Of these, by virtue of assuming the state's functions in this way, they became virtual lords.

Even Martin V had been forced for a time to tolerate the rule of a terrible Perugian captain, Braccio da Montone, over the greater part of Umbria, and even to concede him vicariates and engage him as a soldier of the Church.

Francesco Sforza, born in 1401, was the eldest son of a mercenary captain, Muzio Attendolo, who hailed from the small town of Cotignola in the Romagna. The greatest successes of Muzio Attendolo had been achieved in the unstable Papal States and the Neapolitan Kingdom, where he was the great rival and counter to Braccio da Montone; and he acquired the additional surname of 'Sforza' as a tribute to his toughness and resolution. His son maintained the family's reputation after the death of Muzio at Aquila in 1424, and a year later he began his checkered career in the service of Filippo Maria Visconti. To keep Sforza on his side, the Duke was compelled to bribe him with the hand of his illegitimate daughter, Bianca Maria Visconti, although he took care to postpone the wedding as long as possible in order to keep a carrot dangling before Sforza's eyes, and thereby increase his tractability. Since Filippo Maria had no male heirs, this would certainly give Sforza a claim on the Duchy which he might well be able to back by military force.

But for the moment the ambitions of Sforza lay further to the south. In 1433, with some encouragement from the subtle Filippo Maria, he crossed the Papal States on the pretext that he was going to attend to his fiefs in the Kingdom of Naples, where the Sforza had been rewarded with estates. But he halted in the March of Ancona and from Jesi proclaimed that he was the representative of the Council of Basel, sent to free the province from the rule of Eugenius IV. For over thirteen years he was able to maintain a multiple seigneurie over the March, and to defy all attempts to dislodge him on the part of the Papacy and other Italian powers. For a time, indeed, the Pope was forced to concede him the official position of Marquess of the March of Ancona and to give him command of the papal armies, with the title of *Gonfalonier* or Standard-Bearer of the Church. But Eugenius could not be permanently reconciled to the presence of a Sforza lordship like a malignant growth in the Papal States. In Sforza's person rule over Milan might soon be combined with rule over the March. Sforza had also to reckon with Filippo Maria's alternate bouts of uneasy sympathy and active enmity, which made him now friend, now foe. At length, in 1441, the marriage with Bianca Maria Visconti did take place, and she brought as her dowry two border towns, Cremona and Pontremoli, which the Duke had found it difficult to hold against the Florentines and Venetians.

The rule of Francesco Sforza in the March did not endure, and he had to abandon it at last in 1447, only to secure the richer prize of Milan despite the decision of his father-in-law to disinherit him. Shortly after the death of Filippo Maria, four members of the Milanese College of Jurisprudence proclaimed the Republic of St Ambrose, so christened in honour of the city's patron saint. But most of the subject towns were reluctant to accept this Milanese régime, and the new Republic soon found itself compelled to engage Francesco Sforza, a highly interested party, as its defender against the Venetians. Understandably, there was little mutual trust between Sforza and his employers, especially as Lombard cities proved willing to yield to Sforza himself rather than to the Milanese, and he could hardly escape the charge of working for himself. For some time he was poised between the Venetians and the Milanese. Eventually, as the régime in Milan grew increasingly unstable, subject to witch-hunts, reigns of terror ·and at last to outbreaks of popular violence, he was able to plan and carry through a successful siege and to enter Milan in February 1450. To other Italian powers, and especially to Cosimo de' Medici in Florence, the triumph of Sforza seemed the best guarantee against further Venetian aggression.

The reasonable if somewhat precarious balance between the major territorial states was recognized by the terms of the Peace of Venice of August 1454. In the first instance this was signed by Florence, Venice and the Duke of Milan, the three chief belligerents of northern Italy. But in the next few months all other Italian powers also signed it. Its object was to stabilize existing frontiers, and to guarantee Italian states against aggression either from outside Italy or from within. The powers joined together in a defensive alliance which was to last for twenty-five years, with the possibility of further renewal. Any state in the alliance which attacked a fellow member was to be disciplined by common military action. Such measures by no means prevented wars from breaking out, for they did so five times in the next thirty years, and each lasted on average about two years. But mutual jealousies and the multilateral distribution of strength did ensure that no individual state could bid for unlimited gains, much less secure them.

*

Southern Italy had certainly not broken with its ancient tradition of foreign monarchy; it had merely become part of a different 'power-aggregate', and its King proved unable to dominate the politics of the whole peninsula to the same extent as Charles or even Robert of Anjou. But the north and centre had ceased for the time being to be the most invaded areas in Europe or the theatre of war between universalist authorities. Admittedly, the exclusion of foreigners was never absolute, and traditional attitudes to the Emperor as the ultimate source of respectability, the fount of legal authority, died very hard. Wenceslaus made the lord of Milan a Duke, Sigismund promoted the ruler of Mantua to the rank of Marquess. Even the Venetians (in

1437) took the precaution of swearing fealty to Sigismund for the imperial fiefs they had conquered: an uncharacteristic action, for Venice's independence both from the Byzantine and from the western Empire was to become an essential part of its 'myth' or legend, and homage was to be withheld from future Emperors. The Emperor Frederick III could still, with a modest retinue, make the traditional journey to the south to be crowned in Rome in 1452; being harmless enough, he made a pleasant impression, and some Florentines noted that he was much busier choosing presents for his bride than in attending to public business.

The terms Guelf and Ghibelline were still in use, and were current (for example) during the Milanese succession crises which began in 1402 and 1447. But their meaning derived only from local enmities and was not tied to papal-imperial conflict, for the fifteenth century knew no successor to Henry VII – let alone to Frederick II. In the words of Bernardino of Siena, the great Franciscan preacher and an enemy to all factions, 'Some silly people take the Church to be Guelf; but, as experience tells us, the Guelfs will fight against the Church and the Ghibellines against the Empire seven times a day to gain their own ends.'

It is true that the possibility of intervention from beyond the Alps could seldom be forgotten; true that the Angevins had not abandoned hope after Alfonso's victory; true that for some years about 1400 Genoa surrendered its independence to live under a French governor, Boucicault. The Visconti intermarried with the ruling houses of France and Austria: indeed, the marriage of Giangaleazzo's daughter Valentina with Louis of Valois formed the basis of French claims to the Duchy of Milan which were to be made good at the close of the fifteenth century. Between 1425 and 1432 Filippo Maria Visconti and Sigismund of Hungary, King of the Romans, maintained resident ambassadors at each other's courts, with the object of preparing for common action against Venice. But invasions from across the Alps were not distinguished by their resolution or their military effectiveness. The prime movers in Italian politics and diplomacy were now Italian states: even the Pope himself was forced to become more of an Italian prince, depending heavily on the yield of his temporal power.

Monarchs and
Oligarchs

14

Of the Italian powers in the fifteenth century, the great German historian Ranke wrote: 'They were neither nations nor races; neither cities nor kingdoms; they were the first States in the world.' Contemporaries involved in the struggles of the late fourteenth and early fifteenth centuries had seen them as a war between the principles of republicanism and 'tyranny' or 'despotism', between corporate rule and the government of one man, between arbitrary and responsible power. Two major questions are implied here. How far can the territorial states of the fifteenth century legitimately be related to the centralized modern state? What were the practical differences which distinguished republicanism from 'despotism'? To the majority of people, what difference did it make whether they lived under a republican or a monarchic form of government?

The contrast between the two was not as clear as propagandists represented it. The so-called despotisms were not despotic or tyrannical in any simple sense – the stabler dynastic states justified themselves by offering their subjects peace from factional strife and not by reckless disregard for law and order. Nor did they wantonly destroy or override hereditary privilege. If their power originally rested on naked force or the cunning intrigue with which they outwitted and banished enemies, they had a passion for legitimating it through the acquisition of papal or imperial vicariates or still more resonant titles. And for its part, republican government knew no manhood suffrage. Most

Italian communes restricted the franchise to burgess proprietors who had either been born in the town or resided there for long periods. With the passage of the fifteenth century ruling groups tended if anything to become more rigid and less willing to admit new recruits, even though the acquisition of new territory had greatly increased the number of subjects affected by political and administrative decisions. This exclusiveness naturally retarded the process of interpenetration between the conquering and the dependent cities, and prevented them from being drawn together into a homogeneous unit. On the other hand, opportunities for subjects from newly annexed areas may actually have been greater in the monarchic state of the Duchy of Milan, where there was no narrow sovereign people to monopolize the most important offices, and the rulers were accustomed to choose their servants and advisers from all over their dominions.

It may be that, as one English historian has argued, all Italian governments – whatever their external form – were in reality oligarchic. It is also true that in fifteenth-century Florence there emerged a régime which came, as it were, to straddle republicanism and despotism – through the dominance of the Medici faction or clientele, through the gradual strengthening of the unofficial semi-dictatorship of the heads of the Medici family. Let it be said that so-called despots were quite capable of retaining the administrative machinery and even the legislative councils of the communal era, so long as they could pack them to a suitable extent with reliable nominees, and circumscribe their functions. As suggested in the previous chapter, it may be that the real distinction between republics and despotisms lay in the firmer foundations of republics, and their comparative immunity from succession crises. But by no means all republics enjoyed the rock-like stability for which Venice became legendary, or the continuity of Florence under the

Albizzi and the Medici. The instability of Genoa was such that it havered constantly on the borderline between republic and seigneurie, and was hardly a state at all, but an agglomeration of families and business enterprises with little sense of being subordinate to the whole community. But it was surely no coincidence that by the mid-fifteenth century the most formidable Italian state was the Venetian Republic. It had gained more slowly than the Visconti, but had lost far less.

*

To the Visconti régime the term 'absolute monarchy' is more appropriate than the pejorative 'despotism', with its connotations of arbitrary and irresponsible power. The Visconti were, and they declared themselves to be, above the law: they possessed the power to alter it, but not the moral right to ignore it capriciously. Early in the fifteenth century the government issued a declaration apropos of the statutes of Cremona that the will of the Duke and his heir was like a living and acting law, a *lex animata* with authority to make and interpret statutes, to declare the law, and to rescind statutes which it deemed useless. But it was the ruler's business to use this authority responsibly: as it was stated in 1480, 'to dispense from decrees and ordinances, for the well-being of our subjects, in cases where no wrong ensues to anybody from our doing so'.

Other Lombard cities had passed under the sovereignty of the Visconti for the formal reason that the Visconti proposed to guarantee them peace. Order had become more important to these communes – Como, Vercelli, Bergamo and others – than an abused and factious liberty. Without complete success, the Visconti tried to eradicate the party labels Guelf and Ghibelline, and to erect a state free of the disturbances of faction. Sometimes they had to compromise – as did Giangaleazzo in his Pavian lordship in 1378 – by merely ordaining that municipal office should be evenly shared between Guelfs and Ghibellines. Between 1428 and 1440 Filippo Maria Visconti made further attempts at this kind of pacification, and in 1440 he issued a general decree forbidding municipal authorities to distribute offices according to factions. Instead, where possible, they should create 'pools' of candidates, divided into three categories according to how much property they owned, and should select from these classes in determinate proportions. Wealth, not traditional allegiances, must become the new criterion. The Visconti also tried to insist that feudatories should collaborate with state officials in the pursuit of criminals, and in the course of the fourteenth century forced a number of them to destroy private fortresses inessential to the defence of the realm. Retinues must be reduced – in 1386, for example, Giangaleazzo issued a decree designed to forbid any one to present himself before a public official with a squad of more than four retainers at his back. Admittedly, it is easier to grasp what the Visconti aspired to do than to estimate the real extent of their success; and it does appear that by anything approximating to modern standards the Visconti police force was ineffectual. Between 1385 and 1429 the court of the *Podestà* in Milan had to condemn in their absence more than two-thirds of the accused persons cited before it.

Seeking to centralize the administration of their territory, the Visconti were forced to take much notice of local particularism and to acknowledge that they were often dealing with cities which possessed a long tradition of independence. Usually they would either send 'vicars' to govern the cities for them, or else choose the local *Podestà*. They reinforced this measure of control, in the fourteenth century at least, by employing officials known as 'referendaries' to keep watch on communal finance and administration, and to act in this as the 'eye of Milan'. Filippo Maria per-

petuated this system in 1423 through the despatch of state
commissars to hold a watching-brief on his behalf, attending
to the 'security and preservation of the cities' but not
otherwise interfering with their government. Their function
was evidently to report back to Milan if they saw grave
cause for concern. But Visconti control of finance in the
communes became especially tight from the days of Giangaleazzo onwards. He insisted on nominating the city
treasurers, and would allow the communes to retain only a
small proportion of their revenues to defray local expenditure. Moreover, the Visconti established their own central
councils to wield authority either over the entire Milanese
state or over a large section of it. Hence, a provincial organization began to rise above the narrower institutions of
the separate communes and their surrounding jurisdictional
areas. Giangaleazzo had his own privy council and council
of justice.

The Visconti did not rely upon the Milanese alone to
assist them in the work of government; they may, indeed,
have been anxious to prevent them from becoming a
privileged section of the community that might limit the
prince's freedom of action. Some recent biographical studies
have shown in detail that a large proportion of the fifty-three
chancellors and secretaries known to have served Giovanni
Maria and Filippo Maria between 1402 and 1447 came
from other regions of the Duchy. Perhaps the most conspicuous dynasty of servants was the Barbavara, of the family
of the Counts of Castello, from the city of Novara. Francesco Barbavara was in the service of Giangaleazzo from
about 1390 with his brother Manfredo, and rose to become
first chamberlain, to be richly rewarded with fiefs and
castles, and to be married to Antonia Visconti, a relative
of the ruler himself. In his will, Giangaleazzo designated
him tutor to his sons and adviser to the regent Duchess,
although this mark of esteem earned him spells of exile

before he was eventually reconciled with Filippo Maria.
Uberto Decembrio was born about 1370 in Vigevano, and
was originally in the service of Petros Filargis, Bishop of
Novara, later to become Archbishop of Milan and Pope
Alexander V of the Pisan obedience. For a time Decembrio
was imprisoned by Facino Cane for his loyalty to the Visconti brothers; under Filippo Maria he served for a time as
Podestà in Treviglio. His son, Pier Candido Decembrio
(1399–1477), was like himself a distinguished humanist,
and followed him in the Duke's service. Zanino Riccio, one
of Filippo Maria's closest servants, was a native of Castello
di Borgo San Martino in the district of Casale, and a former
servant of Facino Cane. Another humanist, Antonio Loschi,
came from newly conquered Vicenza to enter Giangaleazzo's
service, in which he compiled a famous Ciceronian *Invective
against the Florentines*. Other servants of the Dukes came not
only from Milan itself but also from Pavia, Tortona, Monza,
Alessandria, Varese, Brescia and Bergamo. These chancellors and secretaries provided the Duke with an important
reserve or pool from which he could draw administrators,
counsellors and diplomats. For diplomatic missions to kings,
princes or Emperor, the Dukes would normally retain
eminent prelates or decorous noblemen of respectable
lineage; but for negotiations with other Italian states they
were often prepared to employ 'new men', lay careerists of
no very distinguished antecedents. Hence, the service of the
Dukes began to provide a ladder of promotion and a means
to social mobility for subjects from all over the state, and
sometimes for persons born outside it – such as Giovanni
Corvini of Arezzo, occasional diplomat, member of the
secret council, and some time Master of the Revenues.

In this particular respect the Milanese state was certainly more broadly based, more fully centralized and more
homogeneous than the Venetian. Servants of the Dukes of
Milan were not in their own right part of a governing

corporation, a conquering people, as were the Venetians or Florentines: their authority derived from their master above them. But to the non-Venetian subjects of the Venetian Republic it probably made little difference that they had come to live under a republican rather than a princely régime. Venetian sovereignty over the mainland or Terra Ferma was based on conquest – in the phrase of Marc' Antonio Pellegrini, a Paduan lawyer, it had been acquired 'by right of a just war'. The cities of the Veneto were not admitted to equal partnership in the Republic. Relations between the Venetian Signory and the local administration were regulated by agreements known as *capitoli* which were only issued after the surrender of the town, so that they became not bargains struck between equals but 'privileges' issued by the conqueror. In the words of the Golden Bull issued in 1406 by Doge Michele Steno, the Paduans were to be treated as 'good and law-abiding subjects'.

In much the same way as the Visconti Dukes, the Venetians claimed the ultimate right to alter the statutes of subject cities, as at Padua in 1419–20. Their principal method of control was to take over the ancient offices of *Podestà* and *Capitano* in all large cities and towns, and assign them to Venetian patricians. These Venetian noblemen were to govern the city in consultation with prominent local men, referring when appropriate back to the government in Venice. The Venetians lacked the bureaucratic apparatus for more extensive centralization, and in local matters they relied heavily on local oligarchs and administrative organs. Significantly, they made use of a form of magistracy known as the *Deputati ad Utilia* which had originally been introduced into Verona by a seigneur, Cangrande II della Scala, in 1350. In deliberations on local affairs this organ came to replace the old communal council known as the *Anziani*. The duty of its members, who were chosen by the *Podestà* himself, was to inform him of the

interests of the commune; and he, in the words of the
regulations introduced at Padua in the early fifteenth
century, 'must examine all aspects of the matter, put them
down in writing, add his own opinion and inform our
government, so that it may take such action as it sees fit'.
It was the business of the city council to decide which
matters ought to be forwarded to Venice for adjudication,
to consider those which Venice had entrusted to them to
resolve, and to deal with purely domestic matters which
did not interfere with the administration of the state as a
whole.

Significantly, again, these city councils continued to be
dominated by the families which had already been prominent in the days of the Scaligeri and Carraresi lords – a
symptom of how little the social and political structure had
really been disturbed by the absorption of Verona and
Padua into a republican régime. The Bevilacqua and the
Nogarola, who had been great men in Verona in the days
of the della Scala, became the leaders of the two principal
local factions under the Republic. A list of 334 members of
the council of Vicenza, drawn up in 1321, contains the
names of almost all the chief families who were to participate in the government of the commune, up to the time
when the Venetian Republic fell at last in the late eighteenth century. In Padua the Zabarella, the Scrovegni, the
Dottori, the Conti, the Capodilista and the Capodivacca
lost little of their former eminence in local affairs. At least
forty-nine of the eighty-three families summoned to an
important council by Francesco I da Carrara in 1372 were
still present in the civic council between 1430 and 1446.

Furthermore there was a strong tendency for these local
oligarchies to become both self-contained and self-
perpetuating; they became 'closed' like the ruling aristocracy
in Venice itself, and the Venetian state thus tended to
remain a series of separate compartments or cells within

and between which social mobility was seriously hindered. From the crisis year 1381 to the crisis year 1646 the Venetian patriciate became a virtually closed caste, and if it admitted any new recruits it was tacitly understood that they were only to be honorary members of the patriciate. The new admissions of 1381 and 1646–69 were block admissions of families prepared to pay handsomely for the privilege and thus bolster up finances strained by war. There was certainly no regular recruitment, and patricians or noblemen from the mainland were admitted to the ranks of the Venetian aristocracy only in the later eighteenth century. Venetian 'citizenship' could be acquired by immigrants from the mainland or elsewhere in Italy after a very prolonged period of residence. But it conferred only economic privileges (especially the coveted right to trade from Venice directly with the Levant) and the right to be considered for posts of trust in the Ducal Chancery and the rest of the permanent civil service: it did not bestow the formal right to a part in decision-making. The Venetian patriciate was numerous, having more than 2,500 members at the start of the sixteenth century, and it may be that the ruling class refused to entertain the idea of further competition for a restricted number of lucrative jobs: magisterial posts were plentiful, but were counted in hundreds rather than thousands, and a great many of these – certainly in the sixteenth century – involved their occupants in heavy expenditure. Admittedly, in 1411 the Venetian Senate did consider a proposal from a member of the Cabinet that eighteen noblemen of Zara, an important Venetian possession on the coast of Dalmatia, should be employed in the government of eighteen cities of the Italian mainland, of Istria and of Albania. They would have been given positions of trust outside their own particular locality. But nothing came of this.

The local civic councils remained as narrowly based as

the Venetian, and showed signs of becoming equally resis-
tant to change. In Brescia in 1488, entry to the civic council
was effectively restricted to those whose ancestors had
resided in the city since 1438 – the year when a great siege
had been laid to Brescia by the Visconti armies. Between
1430 and 1446, when the population of Padua was 16–
18,000, 222 citizens from 149 families took part in the civic
council, and only forty-two families supplied just over half
the members of that assembly. These councillors were
mostly landed proprietors, having goods or capital valued
at 2,000 lire or more. Effective authority in Verona had
devolved on the *Podestà* and on the local Councils of Fifty
and Seventy-Two. By the end of the fifteenth century
thirty-four families controlled two-thirds of the seats in these
assemblies, and seventy-seven per cent of the councillors
belonged to the top nine per cent of the taxpayers listed in the
Estimo. Within these local oligarchies there was a strong
tendency in the course of the fifteenth century towards
social exclusiveness, so that the majority of the councillors
were either rentiers or professional men, rather than merchants or industrialists. In Venice itself, however, the connection between the nobility and international commerce
remained largely unimpaired: many noblemen took part
in commercial activity, directly or indirectly, at some stage
in their lives, and Andrea Barbarigo (1399–1449) redeemed
his family's sunken fortunes by means of it.

Republicanism and social fluidity did not necessarily go
together; a republican state could be just as authoritarian
as a so-called 'tyranny' or 'despotism' in its treatment of
its dominions, and the relationship between the dominant
city of Venice and its territories was not one of a capital and
provinces so much as that of a city state and a thinly
colonized empire. The local oligarchs, however, had not
been rudely dispossessed of all power: the Venetian governors held office for terms only of sixteen–eighteen months,

and in the sixteenth century they were regularly to complain in their reports that in so short a period they could not fathom all the intricacies of local politics, or see the implications of proposals sprung on them by local men. Local autonomy may well have been greater in practice than it appeared on paper.

The rigidity of ruling groups was less extreme in the Tuscan republics of Florence and Siena, though even in Florence after 1400 and Siena after about 1440 there was a marked tendency to admit fewer new families to the highest political honours. Despite (or perhaps because of) the broader basis of the patriciate, real power in Florence was usually acknowledged to lie in a comparatively small and well-defined group of leading families – revolving round the Albizzi, Capponi, Uzzano and others in the years between 1382 and 1434, and round the Medici and their associates thereafter. The rapid turnover in the principal Florentine magistracies created a doubly urgent need for an influential group of politicians behind the scenes to maintain continuity. Florence inclined to family rule where Venice, whose leaders were more anonymous, inclined to the corporate rule of a legally defined aristocracy. Both in Florence and in Siena the organization of the state was tightened so as to ensure the subordination of all corporate bodies to the republic, and the powers of the executive were strengthened at the expense of the open legislative councils.

After the failure of the revolt of the Ciompi – workers in the woollen industry – the Florentine government did become more narrow and more suspicious in certain respects. A new police magistracy, the Otto di Guardia or Eight of Ward, was set up in 1378. It maintained an efficient network of spies, and Florence was now equipped with a standing committee of public safety similar to the Venetian Council of Ten, and likewise dedicated to preserving the existing oligarchic régime. After 1382 the

Florentines proceeded to abolish the most recently formed guilds, those of dyers and doublet-makers, and to concentrate authority in the hands of the so-called Greater Guilds or *Arti Maggiori*. Their members were bankers, industrialists, merchants, or the leisured men of wealth known as *scioperati*. Office in the chief legislative councils and executive bodies was chiefly their preserve, and between 1382 and 1387 they were entitled to three-quarters of the seats in them. After 1387 their portion increased to four-fifths, and the Lesser Guilds (*Arti Minori*) were allowed only a small share in office as a palliative. At the same time, Florence's involvements in war and the danger from marauding mercenary companies demanded the freer use of *Balìe*, executive commissions equipped with special powers to ensure rapidity of decision. *Balìe* had been used to some extent since the late thirteenth century, but their terms of office had always been strictly limited. The first *Balìa* with no time-limit was the commission of the *Ottantuno*, the Eighty-One, which was created in 1393. It was entitled to impose taxes for the maintenance of the commune's armies, both in the form of forced loans which bore no interest and in that of outright direct taxes. To it, also, was assigned the task of determining when other *Balìe* were to be instituted, and it acquired control of another special commission, the *Dieci di Balìa*. This body of ten defence commissioners in fact remained in existence for over twenty years, from 1384 to 1406. Such *Balìe* were unpopular with the Florentines and highly suspect in their eyes, although they performed the valuable function of providing continuity, and they did compel the Florentine people to make financial sacrifices for the common weal. Indeed, after 1404 the powers of the *Ottantuno* were curtailed, and the structure of government returned to its pre-1393 form.

Generally, the Florentine state was becoming more monolithic in the late fourteenth and early fifteenth centuries. The Guelf party lost many of its powers and privileges, so that it ceased to form a state within the Florentine state. The government began to exercise tighter control over the guilds, and in the late fourteenth century it also extended its competence further into the realms of economic policy. For the first time it introduced measures to protect Florentine manufactures from foreign competition. During the wars against Milan in the 1420s, despite its general aversion to direct taxes, the ruling oligarchy introduced an exceptionally far-reaching system of taxation known as the *Catasto*. This was not based on landed wealth and house property alone, but was designed to take account of movable goods, business investments at home and abroad, holdings in the state debt, and other assets which had usually been regarded as too elusive, too fluid and perhaps too ephemeral to track down and to tax. Eight revisions, between 1430 and 1480–81, on the basis of returns submitted by heads of households, helped to ensure that the *Catasto* was kept reasonably up to date.

Furthermore the government proved ready to attack at least some of the special exemptions or immunities from normal legal processes which were enjoyed by ecclesiastics, so that the clergy could increasingly be treated as ordinary citizens and not as persons who stood partially outside the state. The powers of church courts were somewhat curtailed, so that there was less of an alternative jurisdiction to compete with the state's own. Religious confraternities were strictly forbidden to engage even in the most trivial political activities, and there were spells of persecution in 1419 and 1426 in which their books were confiscated and their property sold or distributed to the poor. On the other hand, it is doubtful whether the Florentine state permanently secured such gains as it made at the expense of clerical independence – for from the mid-fifteenth century papal authority was reviving and the activity of papal law courts growing more intense. In this there was nothing hollow, for the Pope could always enforce sanctions against Florentine merchants abroad, and so ensure that his courts' decisions commanded some respect.

Despite this tightening of the state and strengthening of the executive, access to the principal magistracies of the Republic remained quite open in the last two decades of the fifteenth century. According to statistics compiled by Dr Anthony Molho, 4,500 Florentines were matriculated in the Greater Guilds at the close of the fifteenth century: on the assumption that they were sensitive to the opinions of adult members of their immediate families, they could be said to have 'represented' some 13,500 persons or nearly 20 per cent of the total population of Florence. Over the years 1382–99 many new families obtained access to the supreme magistracy of the Priorate, and by such a criterion social mobility in Florence was greater over this period than at any time since the plague-ridden decade 1340–49, when there had naturally been a very great number of new recruits. Members of the Priorate and other leading magistracies were, after 1393, *ex officio* members of the *Ottantuno*. Under the régime of the Albizzi from 1382 to 1434 the Priorate was almost invariably chosen in the most democratic way possible – by lottery from those qualified – and only once was it chosen by a *Balìa*: in October 1393, after the discovery of a conspiracy by some members of the Alberti family. Dr Molho's studies further suggest that office in the Priorate was being circulated reasonably rapidly in the decades 1393–1402 and 1410–1419, which he has taken as specimens. Compared with earlier sample decades, it seems that relatively few families and individuals were repeatedly holding office. On the other hand, the number of new admissions to the Priorate did begin to fall abruptly from the beginning of the fifteenth century onwards, and this may indicate a stronger tendency towards oligarchy and towards closure of the ruling group. Whereas 249 new families had been admitted over the eighteen years from 1382 to 1399, only 101 others gained admission over the first three decades of the fifteenth century.

It was characteristic of Florence that its real lords were 'unofficial' rulers, who did not openly monopolize office or claim the title of *Signore* or seek vicariates from Pope or Emperor. In the early 1430s a change of régime occurred as a result of the close identification of the Albizzi with the unsuccessful campaign to subdue Lucca in 1429–33. Spokesmen for the war party, Rinaldo degli Albizzi and Neri Capponi, promised a brief and decisive war; they claimed that Paolo Guinigi, lord of Lucca, had secretly supported the Visconti of Milan during the recent conflict. Foreign policy was the acid test of a régime's stability – and when the unsuccessful war had dragged on for several years, it brought down the Albizzi leaders. In 1434 members of the rich Medici clan, who had fallen out with Rinaldo degli Albizzi and were less directly implicated in the Lucchese war, returned in triumph from the exile imposed on them the previous year. It was they who now displaced the Albizzi, as the leaders of a restricted group of families at the heart of the state.

Tax returns had recently shown that the Medici were the third richest family in Florence, falling some way behind certain of the Panciatichi and behind Palla di Nofri Strozzi, an immensely wealthy associate of Rinaldo degli Albizzi, who was now exiled in his turn. By 1457 the Medici were outdistancing all rivals. In the days when Cosimo was first citizen of Florence, to 1464, the private wealth of the unofficial rulers derived chiefly from the bank founded in 1397 by Giovanni di Bicci de' Medici, which in 1451 had seven branches outside Florence. To a lesser extent the riches of the Medici came from textile manufacturing (two woolshops and a silkshop), and from international trade in a wide variety of merchandise. The superior financial resources the Medici gained from their banking activities enabled them to build up extensive clienteles of persons with good reason to be grateful to them – and their patronage of artists, architects and sculptors was only one facet of this. In building and dress, however, they were careful in the early days not to be too immodest or ostentatious. Certainly Cosimo tried to present himself as a first among equals rather than as the master of the state. For thirty years, indeed, writers praised Cosimo as if he were a citizen of Greece or Rome, a prominent republican statesman; and the title of *Pater Patriae*, or 'father of his country', was inscribed on his tombstone in the church of San Lorenzo. In these years Cosimo held the most prominent office in the state on only three occasions, and for a total of only about six months. His authority was not clearly defined or circumscribed by constitutional forms.

Institutionally, Medicean control of Florence was based on manipulating elections to the Priorate (which, among other things, initiated legislation) and to the committee of public security, the Eight of Ward. Such elections were now controlled by a small group of officials known as *Accoppiatori*, who edited the lists of those eligible. By careful screening, they ensured that leading officers of state should be selected from a greatly reduced number of candidates. The Medici also made further use of *Balìe*, which with their extraordinary powers temporarily superseded the existing councils, and (notably) took control of taxation. Both the *Accoppiatori* and the members of the *Balìe* sometimes held office for a few years at a stretch, instead of a few months only, as had most of the officials of the ancient communal organs. Many individuals or families, collaborators of the Medici, served in one *Balìa* after another. Naturally, this system was one most easily justified in times of tension or war, and on the occasions when no such stresses existed and none could be invented public opinion had frequently to be pacified by reverting to the older system whereby leading magistrates were chosen by an open lottery, rather than through selection by the *Accoppiatori*. There were occasional reactions in favour of a more liberal régime, the most serious in 1465–6, and these invariably entailed demands for a return to the lottery and for some reduction in the extra-ordinary authority conceded to prominent magistracies. Then, from 1458 onwards, the Medici began to introduce special permanent councils of their own into the framework of the constitution. First, the régime came to rely on a per-manent Council of One Hundred, to pass legislation and elect to vital offices. It assumed some of the functions of the temporary *Balìe*, and eventually acquired control over the public loan-funds, the *Monte*, the financial core of the state. By the mid-fifteenth century the public debt stood at about eight million florins, and most of the more well-to-do Florentines had a stake in this and were personally affected by the government's capacity to meet its financial commit-ments. By 1480 another council, the Council of Seventy, had made its appearance, and the Priorate could now initiate no legislation without this Council's approval. Two new magistracies dealing with foreign and domestic policy branched out from it, and it elected to the Priorate and the Eight of Ward.

It has also been suggested that the power of the Medicean oligarchy was partly founded on its control over the pro-cesses of justice, which enabled it to intimidate opponents – for the older courts of justice, including that of the *Podestà*, were losing their status, and government standing com-missions showed signs of encroaching on their competence. Many magistracies were acquiring judicial powers, and in the days of the Medici the more prominent lawyers were willing to uphold the increasing power of the executive, so that an independent judiciary (which is a standard guarantee against authoritarian government) became a thing of the past. Lawyers took a prominent role in the Medicean régime: they were not notaries, who very seldom appeared among the highest magistrates after 1433, but representatives of the higher branch of the legal profession, 'judges' or jurisconsults who had undergone a prolonged and expensive university education and had now become the complaisant technicians of the régime.

Throughout sixty years of authority the Medici worked circumspectly and delicately preserved their balance: as Lorenzo de' Medici, chieftain from 1469 to 1492, once told a Milanese ambassador, they operated 'by an indirect way'. Florence, indeed, presents a curious and paradoxical instance of a self-proclaimed republic which succumbed to the dominance of an unofficial, though not an unrecognized, seigneurie. The Florentine patriciate was less exclusive than the Venetian, and during the fifteenth century an average of some thirty-five new families per decade found its way into the Priorate for the first time. But this compared poorly with the high average of nearly 130 new families per decade over the much more fluid period 1340–1400, and the dominance of one particular family was far more marked in Florence than in Venice. When after Lorenzo's death in 1492 the Medici were no longer able to provide competent leadership the Florentines were driven to experiment with institutions developed in Venice, and to look to the Venetian constitution to save them.

In the dominant city of Florence the tendency was, then, towards exclusive and oligarchic rule. There seems little reason to think that Florence any more than Venice treated her subject cities as equal partners in the régime, even though she had sometimes claimed to be saving them from tyranny. Annexation by Florence in the late fourteenth or early fifteenth century meant subjection to very heavy fiscal demands, and the rural district subject to Florence was forced at that time to begin paying disproportionately heavy taxation. Some of the cities temporarily or permanently lost control over their own finances. For example, between 1351 and 1398 the Florentines had not directly imposed taxes on Pistoia, but had merely required subventions which were raised by the local authorities as they chose. But in 1401–3, when Pistoia was unable to meet the demands upon it, the Florentine government temporarily removed the fiscal administration from local control. Subsequently they restored to the Pistoiese the authority to administer indirect taxation, but they forbade them to levy new direct taxes on the countryside. In 1427 the Pistoiese found themselves compelled to adopt the same methods of tax-assessment as the Florentines, and this too restricted their freedom of action.

But it would be misleading to represent the economic and financial effects of Florentine dominion in Tuscany as essentially deleterious. Conquering republican cities have sometimes been accused of ruthlessly promoting their own interests at the expense of competing industrial and other activities in subject cities, and have been charged with inability to see their dominions as part of a single all-embracing state. But it does seem to be true that the annexation of Pistoia by Florence meant its being absorbed into a bigger economic unit, within which men, beasts and agricultural produce were allowed to move more freely. The old system of restricting the export of food and raw material from the district of Pistoia had to be modified, and tariff barriers were overthrown: as in 1386 the trade in cereals, wine and oils between Florence and Pistoia was freed of tolls.

Still more conspicuously, the Florentines did enhance the prosperity of Pisa and Livorno, and when these towns became the site for the Florentine experiment in the launching of state galleys the Pisans themselves seem to have been able to benefit. Many of the local families which had been wealthiest in 1402 were still the wealthiest in 1412 and 1428, so the Florentines can scarcely be accused – any more than the Venetians in Verona or Padua – of organizing whole-sale proscriptions or of drastically altering the social and economic structure. Most of the leading taxpayers were merchants, who must have had some part in the commerce promoted by Florence. The Florentines were anxious to bring new wealth and manpower into Pisa and Livorno, and they encouraged immigrants by the offer of tax-exemptions and rent-free housing.

On the other hand the Florentines did exercise rigorous control over industries and crafts throughout their terri-torial state, chiefly through their tight rein on the guilds. Alterations of Pisan guild statutes had to be approved in Florence, and only in the later fifteenth century did the Pisan guilds show signs of recovering their autonomy and of being relieved of the obligation to pay dues to their Florentine counterparts. Florence was not prepared to tolerate competition in the woollen industry from her own subject cities, and tried to limit local industries to producing cloth for home consumption only. But the Florentines were prepared to encourage the industries of tanning, soap-making and hat-making in Pisa. Indeed, Dr Michael Mallett has credited them with 'a move towards a planned economy with certain industries allotted to the subject cities even at the expense of parallel industries in Florence'. Nor was the Pisan *contado* neglected, for in 1455 the Sea Consuls were instructed to supervise the work of repairing roads and dikes and clearing irrigation ditches, and soon afterwards a board of officials was appointed to implement plans for a canal running from Pisa to Florence.

During the fifteenth century, developments in the smaller Tuscan republic of Siena were broadly similar to those within the Florentine state. The Sienese régime in the fifteenth century was probably the most broadly based in all Italy, but there were fewer admissions to the franchise in the second half of the fifteenth century; likewise, there was a determined move towards the tightening of the state's organization and towards the more extensive use of *Balìe* to circumvent the long-winded procedures of the traditional magistracies and councils. Entry to political life in Siena depended on membership of certain of the associations of families confusingly known as *Monti* – for here the term *Monte* could be applied to an agglomeration of families as much as to an accumulation of wealth or debt. Each *Monte* was desscended from one of the régimes which had for a time governed Siena in the thirteenth and fourteenth centuries, and was initially identified with a particular socio-economic group – though in the course of the fifteenth century social distinctions tended to become blurred and shaded over by the fact that most members of the *Monti* were landowners and a fair proportion of them leisured rentiers who no longer took an active part in business enterprise. From 1403 onwards the *Monti* or parties known as the *Nove*, *Riformatori* and *Popolari* bore the main burden of government, and between 1385 and 1425 there were seventy-six new admissions to their ranks, each new recruit bringing his descendants with him, down to the farthest generation. But from 1440 to 1480 no more than twenty-one new admissions took place. Siena was experiencing the same tendency as the Venetian subject cities of Padua and Verona towards the formation of a restricted ruling group consisting to a large extent of landowners and rentiers.

Like the Florentines the Sienese were also trying to establish a more decisive form of administration, with a strong executive. Finally, from 1455 onwards, they erected a *Balìa* of fifteen citizens .(five from each of the three dominant *Monti*) to conclude the current war, and this *Balìa* became permanent: in 1456, its members were elected 'for

the safety of the city and *contado* and of the men and jurisdiction of Siena, and for the conservation of peace and
liberty'. In the territory, many of the small communes were
equipped in the early fifteenth century with new statutes,
and these were drafted with Sienese help and on the
Sienese pattern. Far-reaching authority was delegated to the
Sienese official in residence. In the early fifteenth century the
Aldobrandeschi, the surviving family of great feudatories in
the region, submitted to the commune at last.

However, the political history of all Italy cannot be seen
in terms of city-states consolidating authority over newly
annexed territories, or of a prevailing 'trend' towards more
tightly organized, monolithic, centralized states with strong
executive bodies. There were some moves towards greater
centralization in the Papal States, especially under Martin
V, but seldom were permanent gains made by the central
government – and some of Martin's progress was undone
during the pontificate of Eugenius IV. For much of his
reign, Eugenius was an exile from Rome and from his own
state, expelled from the capital by a rising against papal
taxation in 1434; though after his return nine years later no
other Pope was to suffer such a humiliation until the days
of Napoleon.

To over-simplify a little, the Popes could be said to be
faced with two methods of mastering their temporal
dominions in Italy. The 'direct method' consisted of trying
to implement the administrative system envisaged in the
famous 'Egidian Constitutions' codified by Cardinal
Albornoz and promulgated in 1357. Hence, the territory
would be subjected to legates, rectors, treasurers and
governors (preferably cardinals or other ecclesiastics)
appointed directly from Rome. Moreover, the Papacy would
also assert its claim to appoint the chief officials, the
Treasurer and *Podestà*, in the cities. The 'indirect method',
which always had to be employed to a certain extent, was

to make a virtue out of necessity and simply to recognize the *de facto* position established by a local secular potentate. The Papacy could adopt the well-known device of recognizing such a man by appointing him vicar of the Church in the region for a limited period (preferably not more than a three-year stretch), and charging him a substantial sum in annual tribute or *census*. It might also be advisable to concede a great deal of administrative autonomy to such prominent towns as Bologna.

But the 'indirect method', which was not adopted as a free choice, had clear disadvantages. Many of the vicars were mercenary captains, and it was difficult to prevent them from contracting and taking service with other Italian powers. Even under the able Martin V, in 1428–9, the Papacy was able to secure only about half the tribute it should officially have received from the remaining 'apostolic vicars'. The incentives to extend direct government were therefore very great.

After the death in 1424 of Braccio da Montone, the redoubtable warlord of Perugia, Martin V did achieve some very fair successes. The Abbot of Rosazzo, an ecclesiastic appointed from Rome, successfully took over the government of the March of Ancona. In this province, it did prove practicable to abstain from confirming certain vicariates after their term had expired, and the lords of Ascoli were actually deprived for taking service without permission under the Milanese. However, independent *Signori* were still left in the March – the Varano of Camerino, the Montefeltro, the Malatesta. Under Eugenius IV (as an earlier chapter has described) the whole March of Ancona succumbed in 1433 to Francesco Sforza's successful acts of effrontery and brigandage, and he was not evicted for more than thirteen years – for some of which the Papacy was obliged to grant him official titles in recognition of his presence in the province. Local seigneurs still reigned supreme in a large part of the Romagna, and even though Forlì and Imola were brought under direct dominion in the days of Martin they did not remain so permanently. No really determined and systematic attempt to displace the vicars of the Romagna, the weakest point in the Papal States, was to be made until the pontificate of Alexander VI, at the start of the sixteenth century.

Some of the larger cities – Bologna, Perugia, Orvieto, Ancona – were left to enjoy a fair degree of independence, officials of the commune dividing authority with the Pope's representative. There was a further risk that direct control from the centre might break down through the practice of allowing mercenary soldiers, as distinct from state officials, to collect the military subsidies allocated to their own support. However, the finances of Martin V did prove sound enough for him to drop the dangerous habit of making grants of territory to mercenary captains in lieu of cash payments from the Apostolic Treasury. His successor was less well situated.

Under Martin, the government of the Papal States was therefore distinguished by significant extension of the Pope's direct dominion. Moreover, he was equipped with a small but very useful pool of dependent trained administrators, in the clerks and notaries of the Apostolic Treasury. Their function was to receive and disburse revenues, and to write certain important categories of papal letters. Determined to preserve his freedom of action, Martin asserted his own authority at the expense of the cardinals. He refused to appoint them to the chief posts within the Apostolic Treasury (as Popes of the Roman obedience had done in the days of the Schism); and he stubbornly resisted their claims to enjoy, automatically, an independent share in the revenues of the Papal States. But the achievements of Martin V did not rest entirely or even chiefly on his ability to run a bureaucratic system, staffed by persons of modest standing, which would survive his own death. They depended too much on the entrenched position of his own aristocratic family, the Colonna, in the Papal States, and on the services they were prepared to render as soldiers of the Church. Their influence was further extended into the mainland south, the vassal-kingdom where Martin claimed to determine the succession to Queen Joanna II. Here they served as commissioners and tax-collectors and obtained great lands and sonorous titles, including the Principate of Salerno and the County of Celano. Implicit in such family rule was the danger that the Colonna would refuse to submit to Martin's successor. This was demonstrated to the full when Gabriele Condulmer, a Venetian nobleman with no family roots in the Papal States, became Pope Eugenius IV in 1431. The Colonna clan rose in rebellion, and their great power in the provinces of Campania and Marittima threatened to cut communications between Rome and Naples. Several years were partially occupied in containing the Colonna with the aid of the rival clans of Conti and Orsini – although it did eventually prove possible to bring them to heel and, in 1436, to destroy their stronghold of Palestrina.

Only limited, and by no means continuous, progress was therefore made towards the centralization of the Papal States. At the north-western gateway to Italy the region of Liguria was highly fragmented, and the Republic of Genoa was far less stable than its counterparts in Venice and Florence. Indeed, the contrast between Venice and Genoa had never been starker. By the early sixteenth century, territories outside the city but under the direct dominion of the Genoese commune supported no more than 95,000 inhabitants. In 1548 (the nearest year for which a statistic is available) the Venetian Terra Ferma contained $1\frac{1}{2}$ million subjects, and even if one makes allowance for a fairly steep population increase in the early sixteenth century the difference between the two territorial states is still very striking. Genoa and the other communes of the Riviera controlled only a narrow coastal strip and a few isolated mountain villages. The rest of Liguria consisted chiefly of large estates centring on seigneurial castles. Ligurian feudatories retained some link with Genoa and might take command of its armies and fleets, but they were often very far from being urbanized, and few of them now engaged in intensive commercial activity. Some fiefs were bound to Genoa by ties of vassalage, and the Doge invested their holders; but others were completely independent, especially those of the Malaspina and the Fieschi, who dominated the interior of the Lunigiana and were in a position to threaten Genoese communications across the Apennines. The Fieschi were said to be able to raise a military force of 4,000 men from their own lands, and they exerted strong influence over the Fregosi, one of the families from which the Doges of Genoa were habitually recruited. To the west, Genoese sovereignty in Liguria was greatly restricted by the presence of the Counts of Venti-miglia.

In Genoa itself, authority was still divided between the commune and other parallel bodies whose competition had never been eliminated. In the mid-fifteenth century the revenues of the commune were very scanty. Its main source of income was the *avaria mobili*, a direct tax assessed on the basis of the capital and the income from sources other than land or real property which people were believed to enjoy. Most indirect and other taxes were controlled by the so-called Casa di San Giorgio, a powerful association of state creditors. The state had long been in the habit of raising money by loans known as *compere*, and the proceeds of certain taxes were assigned to repaying them and to paying interest on them. The Casa di San Giorgio was formed by the amalgamation of several of the principal loan funds in 1407, when interest rates were standardized at 7 per cent.

There were precedents for this, for a similar merger had taken place in 1340: but the Casa di San Giorgio developed into a much more extensive organization than any of its forebears. By the mid-fifteenth century it had incorporated most other *compere* in Genoa, though this process of absorption was not to be finally completed until 1539. Though a considerable proportion of the capital belonged to foreign investors from Chieri, Asti or Milan, the government of the Casa di San Giorgio was in the hands of the Genoese themselves. The constitution of the Casa favoured a much higher degree of stability and continuity than could be found in the feeble and incoherent commune, in that its chief officers served for longer terms and were formally advised by committees of persons who had previously held the same office.

It was, perhaps, this greater stability that equipped the Casa di San Giorgio, rather than the commune, to take over control of Cyprus for a time in the mid-fifteenth century. It was also charged with the government of Genoa's Black Sea possessions after the fall of the colony of Pera in 1453, and with the government of Corsica. These were not the only Genoese possessions which escaped communal control – for Chios, the vital entrepôt in the Aegean, was subject to a private association known as the Maona, which originally consisted of the ship-owners and capitalists who had borne the expense of the expedition to conquer the island in the mid-fourteenth century.

Some modern historians have suggested that in fifteenth-century Florence allegiances to the extended family or clan became rather less binding, and that in Siena loyalty to the *Monti* was properly subordinate to loyalty to the state. But in Genoa clan organizations were still very powerful in the mid-fifteenth century, and were embodied in institutions. Clans in Genoa were known as *alberghi* or 'great houses', and were associations of families which settled in the same districts, both within Genoa itself and in the adjacent countryside. They banded together for the purposes of self-defence or to promote common interests, and adopted the same surname – as, to take a conspicuous example, families involved in the Maona of Chios almost all adopted the name of Giustiniani when they decided to form an *albergo* of their own. Before the mid-fifteenth century there were as many as sixty *alberghi* among those families which were technically deemed to be noble, but these tended to coalesce into larger and fewer units, and by about 1467 there were only thirty-five of them. The strength of the *albergo* and of such powerful clans as the Spinola implied the existence in Genoa of one more allegiance competing with loyalty to the commune, and further hindered the formation of a stable political organization; though the Casa di San Giorgio came much closer to this than did the commune itself.

Fragmentation, instability, a very feeble sense of devotion to the common weal or allegiance to the state: these things were also found to an equal or greater degree in the very different environment of the Kingdoms of Naples and Sicily. In 1372, ninety years after the xenophobic Sicilian Vespers had first separated the government of Sicily from that of the mainland, the Angevins of Naples had at last been forced to accept Sicilian independence; though they had done so only on the understanding that Frederick IV should call himself King of Trinacria (the old Roman name for Sicily), pay tribute to Naples, and recognize the Pope as his feudal overlord. For diplomatic purposes the name of Kingdom of Sicily was still reserved to the Neapolitan mainland, though in the later fifteenth century the alternative name of Kingdom of Naples became increasingly popular in ordinary usage, expressing as it did the increasing bond of affection between the people of Naples and their sovereign. Temporarily, the island and the mainland were united in the person of the great conqueror, Alfonso of

Aragon, a restless, ambitious military adventurer who used the island as his base for the conquest of the south Italian mainland. On the death of Alfonso in 1458 the mainland passed to his bastard son Ferrante, and Sicily with Alfonso's other Kingdoms to Alfonso's brother John, who proclaimed that the island should never again be severed politically from Aragon.

The endless succession disputes on the mainland between 1345 and 1442 had helped to deprive the provincial baronage of any sense of cohesion or class interest: in the absence of any unchallenged claimant with a clear legal right to the throne, the barons could only be guided by self-interest and personal ambition, rather than by any higher loyalty. Their diverse national origins – Norman, French, Provençal, Catalan, Aragonese, heirs to a long history of invasion – also helped to divide them. Moreover, since the late thirteenth century the demands made by the King upon the feudatories had been diminishing and their rights to exercise jurisdiction (even criminal jurisdiction) on their estates had been increasing. In effect the functions of the state had been taken over to a large extent by private men in their own localities, jurisdiction was fragmented among a number of individuals, and the shadow of the feudatory was falling between the King and his subjects. In the late fourteenth century on the island of Sicily the Aragonese commander Bernardo Cabrera received full rights of criminal jurisdiction in the County of Modica, which had been confiscated from the pro-Angevin family of Chiara-monte; in the reign of Alfonso a grant of full criminal juris-diction was made to the family of Ventimiglia in the County of Geraci. Alfonso was compelled to make very generous concessions in order to win the support of a section of the barons. In Sicily, purchasing support for his expedition, he granted that estates and privileges held by a baron for a period of thirty years should become legally his by prescriptive right even if they had been illegally acquired in the first place. Barons would be permitted to exact oaths of allegiance, to impose private taxation, and to hear an increasingly wide variety of cases in their own courts.

On the mainland also, Alfonso, needing to purchase support, had to connive at and even legitimize the usurpations of the barons and nobles. The parliament, which was essentially the preserve of the barons, was preoccupied with maintaining and even extending their jurisdictional authority, especially over criminals. Most of the communes in the realm were no longer directly subject to royal authority, but had fallen into the power of the provincial nobility, so that the King had no immediate relationship with a large number of his subjects. Indeed in the mid-fifteenth century only 102 of the 1,550 communes remained part of the royal demesne, whilst one of the great lords of the Kingdom, the Prince of Taranto, held more than 300. His lands comprised six archbishoprics and thirty other dioceses, and he received from Alfonso the port of Bari with a licence to export freely from it. The Prince's vast properties in the regions of Bari and Otranto may have accounted for the suppression of the office of royal justiciar in the Terra d'Otranto, and for the Terra di Bari having to be entrusted to a magistrate with more limited powers. In 1456 the King recognized the barons' privilege of nominating magistrates in infeudated towns, and he also went so far as to waive the requirement that they must be dependent on royal confirmation: henceforth it would be sufficient for the nominee to swear fealty to the provincial justiciar and to pay a tax to the royal chancery. Some communes, moreover, were exempted even from this comparatively light obligation. Admittedly there was still a *Capitano* representing the King both in domainal and in infeudated towns – but he had often to contend uneasily with the authority of the local lord. The King also confirmed the barons in their right to nominate the fiscal officers in infeudated communes.

The King's liberality earned him the name of Alfonso the Magnanimous, but his was a generosity which most greatly benefited the barons. He was prepared to abolish the *adoa*, a subsidy paid in lieu of military service, without reimposing military obligations on the barons; and instead he introduced other burdens which weighed more heavily on ordinary people – in the shape of a capitation tax and of an obligation that each household must purchase a determinate quantity of salt, which was a state monopoly. Alfonso was also prepared to grant to barons, churches and monasteries rights of free grazing for specified numbers of beasts on the state-controlled pasture grounds in Apulia, and thereby to reduce the income of the fisc from this very valuable source.

On the other hand, the monarchy did make some attempts to recover direct control over products whose extraction, manufacture or distribution were supposed to be royal monopolies. Hence the *Sacro Consiglio* issued in 1446 a decree requiring feudatories to show their titles to the possession of salteries or iron works, and to prove that they had not usurped them.

No very high degree of loyal service or public spirit could be expected of the baronage in general. As one group of noblemen frankly expressed it, 'So long as the King has war and trouble, we shall be safe, sound and prosperous.' Hence the King could only hope to divide and conquer, and to put down by force and cunning those whose loyalty he failed to win by concessions. But the corollary of this was that the barons were too divided to offer any really constraining opposition to Alfonso, and the General Parliament in Naples did not share his authority. The General Parliament was essentially a consultative organ summoned at times of financial stress, when the King wanted it to share the responsibility for fiscal innovations. It could suggest new measures, ask for privileges and favours, and air grievances about such matters as the administration of justice; but it did not actually share in the legislative process.

In 1443, when the King negotiated with an assembly of 'all the princes, dukes, marquesses, counts and barons of the Kingdom', he agreed to parliamentary proposals by his 'gracious will' and did not treat them as contracts with the parliament which could only be revoked with the consent of both parties. The position in Sicily, however, seems to have been rather different, and the King did show more inclination to regard as binding contracts the concessions he made to his parliament of barons, town-representatives and ecclesiastics in return for their subsidies. On the mainland, too, there was hope in the communes, and the rulers seem to have encouraged those prepared to defend their rights against the feudatories. Hence, in 1419 Joanna II granted a pardon to the people of Capri who had demolished the baronial castle, for she recognized that 'nothing is more burdensome to peoples, especially to those subject to royalty, than to be subjected to some lordship other than the Queen's majesty.'

The centralized, bureaucratized dominion so neatly sketched in Frederick II's Constitutions of Melfi two hundred years earlier had certainly disappeared – if, indeed, it was ever a reality. But although concessions to the barons had circumscribed the power of the state, it would be wrong to suppose that this was non-existent, that there was no move towards centralization, or that the state had no bureaucracy or civil service. Although the Neapolitans could feel for Alfonso little of the affection they had for Joanna II or for his son Ferrante, and although they regarded him as a foreign conqueror, nevertheless he did make Naples for a time the capital of a vast west Mediterranean empire and the seat of judicial and financial organs which served all his dominions. A consequence of this was that offices and officials of Spanish origin were imported into southern Italy. Alfonso's other dominions were governed either through lieutenants-general recruited from the royal family or through viceroys, and he also appointed viceroys as each new Neapolitan province fell into his hands. They were given control over the royal forces, over the local militia, and over the regular provincial administration. By the time of Alfonso's death the provincial viceroys were being replaced by officials of a more traditional type – the justiciars.

Alfonso was in fact able to find some counterweight to the barons by making extensive use of lawyers and salaried bureaucrats in the central councils of Naples which derived their authority from his own person. Such professional administrators depended heavily on the King's pleasure rather than on their own prestigious social position or private wealth. The far-reaching bureaucratic machinery of the Regia Camera della Sommaria exerted financial control over the administrative organs of the Kingdom. Great Neapolitan barons ceased to enjoy automatically a right of entry to the most powerful royal councils. Traditionally, the seven branches of the royal administration were presided over by seven dignitaries selected from the baronage and known as the Collateral Officials, but their posts began to turn into decorative sinecures whose effective functions became the responsibility of other officers. As Grand Constable, the mighty Prince of Taranto should in theory have been commander of the army, but in practice Alfonso preferred to lead his troops himself, or to entrust them to his son or to military contractors in his confidence. The Grand Admiral, Giovanni Antonio Marzano, Duke of Sessa, had been a loyal supporter in Alfonso's struggle against the Angevin candidate – but Alfonso was careful not to entrust command at sea to him. This task he transferred to an experienced sailor, Bernardo Villamarino, leaving the Grand Admiral with jurisdiction only over such matters as piracy, and over naval personnel, arsenal workers and watchmen. The Great Chamberlain had in practice little influence over the Camera della Sommaria, of which he was nominally the head, and the Great Seneschal lost control of crown lands to the Conservator of the Royal Patrimony, a Spanish official whose jurisdiction extended over all Aragonese lands and lordships, and not merely over the Kingdom of Sicily.

Moreover, after 1449, the great nobles and the Collateral Officers were unable to claim the right to sit, *ex officio*, in the *Sacro Consiglio*. This was the supreme civil tribunal of the Aragonese empire, and among much else had the duty of resolving disputes between feudatories over the possession of land. Alfonso was, however, prepared to appoint some eminent nobles to serve on this body at his pleasure and in return for salaries which he himself determined. But towards the middle of the century the court was also staffed with lawyer-bureaucrats, including three Neapolitans, two Catalans and a Sicilian, who had distinguished themselves in diplomacy and administration as well as in legal practice.

Furthermore, by 1455 the monarchy was beginning to tighten its grasp on the financial administration of the Kingdom. The offices of Conservator and Advocate of the Royal Patrimony were imported into the Kingdom from Spain, and the King also introduced a *Consilium Pecuniae* or supreme financial council which launched a series of inquests into the titles by which various tolls and offices were held in the Kingdom. Here there was no uncomplicated drift towards further baronial anarchy and the further abdication of the state's powers. The way was open for a long period of reconstruction under Alfonso's son Ferrante.

Formally, the Kingdom of Sicily was a vassal-kingdom of the Papacy, and Alfonso still found it necessary to shore up his conquests by securing official recognition from Pope Eugenius IV. But he pressed hard to get the Terracina treaty interpreted in such a way as to take the sting out of his vassal status. For example, the King would no longer be bound to pay the permanently fixed sum of 8,000 gold ounces per annum in tribute, but this sum would be subject to adjustment; and he would no longer be subject even in theory to the drastic punishment of deposition for defaulting on these obligations, but only to financial penalties and milder ecclesiastical sanctions. Alfonso also bombarded Eugenius with requests for the promotion or transfer of favoured clerics within the realm, and he tried to insist that the Pope should not promote to dignities of any importance there without consulting him. His correspondence with Eugenius often included intimations that certain proposed appointments would not be acceptable to the King. So long as the Pope depended on Alfonso's military efforts in the Papal States, he was obliged to accommodate him to some extent, and to concede him representation in the college of cardinals. Hence the austere Alonso Borja, Bishop of Valencia, negotiator of the Terracina treaty and some time President of Alfonso's *Sacro Consiglio*, received a cardinal's hat; he was later to become Pope Calixtus III, and to establish the Spanish–Italian dynasty of Borgia. In these respects the King was, if not claiming virtual royal supremacy, at least asserting his independence in an aggressive manner – though after the accession of Nicholas V in 1447 relations with the Papacy became more amiable and relaxed.

*

In certain respects the greater Italian powers of the mid-fifteenth century justified the claim, made so categorically on their behalf by Ranke, that they were 'the first States in the world'. In others, they were clearly still far from anything approaching the concept of 'the modern state'. The greater powers, unlike the petty lordships within the Papal States, were finite and self-contained territorial areas whose rulers were in practice independent of the great supra-national authorities of Empire and Papacy – though they might, like the Visconti, derive their legal authority from the Emperor, or (like the Kings of Naples and Sicily) theoretically be vassals of the Pope. Some progress was made towards the establishment of a single sovereign authority within these territorial states, one supreme over competitors, and somewhat less limited than before by traditional privileges or immunities from its power, on the part of guilds, corporations or clergy. Professional bureau-crats were beginning to appear, loyal servants of the monarch in Milan and Naples, and the great hereditary offices were declining in importance. On the other hand there were obvious limitations on the process of 'bureau-cratizing' in certain parts of Italy: in the Venetian Republic there was no question of the whole administration being penetrated by a body of civil servants recruited from all over the state. Instead it was entrusted to a combination of the elected representatives of the sovereign and exclusive Venetian patriciate, chosen in Venice itself, and of local oligarchs, who were consulted on essentially local matters. It was true that in Naples government was often a matter of negotiating and conceding rather than commanding, that much of the power of judging and maintaining order was in private rather than public hands, and that the barons had little sense of belonging to any sort of community – let alone of allegiance to a state. But even where fragmentation and instability were greatest, as in southern Italy or Liguria or Genoa, there were some compensations for it – in the growth of the royal bureaucracy in Naples, or in the efficiency and continuity of the Genoese Casa di San Giorgio.

Among the Italian powers, the contrast between republicanism and despotism was, understandably, less stark and dramatic than contemporary publicists liked to suggest. For all their cant of liberty, the Republics of Florence and Venice needed their committees of public safety, their spies and secret denunciations, their Council of Ten and Eight of Ward, to maintain their oligarchic régimes. They displayed a marked tendency towards restricting membership of the ruling groups, even towards the formation of virtually closed castes – especially in Venice and the Veneto, but to a smaller extent in Florence and Siena. The struggle abroad demanded the strengthening of the executive, and the *Balìa* or its equivalent flourished in the republics. A republican take-over could make remarkably little difference to a city formerly under the rule of a so-called 'tyrant' or 'despot': for its people there was, perhaps, little to choose between the corporate authoritarianism of a dominant city and the personal absolutism of a monarchic ruler – save that the first was more enduring.

PART FIVE

The Early Renaissance

Classical Renaissance and Religious Revival

15

In the first half of the fifteenth century there were exciting changes in intellectual life and in the fine arts. Like their predecessors, they still came in the guise of revivals, of a return to nature or of a return to the idealized world of classical antiquity. But they were not mere slavish imitations or laborious efforts to resurrect wholesale a vanished culture. They were, rather, the fruits of an attempt to apply principles discovered by the ancients to the needs of the contemporary world.

Knowledge of antiquity was greatly extended, not only by the discovery of more and better texts in the libraries of Europe, not only by the appearance of something approaching a science of archaeology, but also by much fuller acquaintance with classical Greek and by its insertion into the curricula of universities and secondary schools. Greek was both studied in the original and made available by humanists in Latin translation. The early fifteenth century saw the development – at least on a small scale – of a liberal education based on direct acquaintance with the writings of ancient authors and designed not to offer professional training so much as to prepare pupils to be citizens and to hold posts of public responsibility. The preoccupations of a sizeable group of humanists turned on relatively down-to-

earth practical problems, many of them connected with
civic life. In general, the *avant-garde* philosophy of this half-
century pleaded for a measured, rationalistic approach to
life, showing a determination to introduce balance, harmony and reason into all branches of human activity, the
fine arts included.

Certainly there was a marked increase in non-religious
interests on the part of intellectuals, in that they spent more
of their time in considering problems which could be
detached from religious preconceptions. But this did not
mean that the outlook of all men became indifferent or
hostile to conventional Christianity, or that intellectuals
had taken any irrevocable steps down the road towards a
general secularization of values. Indeed, after the middle of
the century, growing interest in Platonism was to bring
them back to a renewed concern with things beyond the
physical world. Even in the early fifteenth century the
worldly philosophies of the humanists coexisted with another
culture, and with the spread of the movement of the
Observant Franciscans and their great impact on popular
life. These years saw not only the revival of classical culture
but also a determined attempt to return to the original
Rule of St Francis – this time a respectable effort, which
earned the seal of the Pope's approval and was not sent to
join the Fraticelli in the outer wilderness. Much classical
scholarship was devoted to the recovery of the works of the
early Christian Fathers, and a modern Catholic historian,
Ludwig von Pastor, was impelled in his vast *History of the
Popes* to make a somewhat prim distinction between this
'true Christian Renaissance' and the 'false Renaissance'
shot through with paganism and anti-clerical ribaldry.
Historians have, perhaps, an understandable tendency to
concentrate on the elements of change and innovation in a
society, and to understress those of stability and continuity. In the fifteenth century, literary classicism still

coexisted with considerable respect for the vernacular, and Gothic styles in painting and architecture did not suddenly disappear. Within the universities, the educational programme of humanism was certainly competing for recognition with the rather older intellectual system known as scholasticism and based on the writings of Aristotle. But it did not displace it, or succeed in launching any real attack upon its foundations.

*

By the early fifteenth century, the most conspicuous development in humanism surely lay in the greater concern of certain of its practitioners with specific and practical problems of politics, society and human conduct – they thought and wrote of such matters as the family, civic life, the possibility of organizing a citizen army, or the means of planning an orderly and beautiful town. Drawing inspiration from classical antiquity, they began to formulate clearly arguments which exalted marriage, family life and the active exchange of ideas; which expressed the belief that the greatest happiness could only be attained in community life, and not in solitude or withdrawal, asceticism or contemplation. Symptomatic of this development was a marked change of attitude to certain revered figures from the past. Fifty years earlier Petrarch had been greatly disconcerted by discovering (in Cicero's *Letters to Atticus*) the feverish interest with which Cicero had followed the course of political events during his enforced retirement after Caesar came to power. But by the close of the fourteenth century the humanist chancellor of Florence, Salutati, began to admire precisely those characteristics of Cicero which Petrarch had thought unworthy of a philosopher; and Cicero was enthusiastically praised in the years which followed for combining the skills and attributes of a philosopher with those of an active man of affairs who was never afraid to assume public responsibility. It might, admittedly, be rash to suppose that the humanists who wrote of those things were themselves personally committed to a belief in, for example, the absolute superiority of the active to the contemplative life. As Professor Kristeller and Professor Seigel have maintained, the humanists were by training rhetoricians, and as such probably prided themselves on their ability to argue for and against a particular point of view – with this they were no more personally identified than a barrister is personally identified with the case he puts for his client. But it was in itself remarkable that such contentions could be put forward at all – whether or not they embodied the final opinions of their authors.

In Florence the connection between humanism and active political life was especially close – since many Florentine humanists or supporters of the movement were members of the most prosperous Florentine clans, forming a part of the governing patriciate, and appearing in the tax registers among the richest 10–12 per cent of all the city's families. Others, of comparatively humble birth, made their own way by holding important public office – as Coluccio Salutati, Leonardo Bruni of Arezzo and Poggio Bracciolini all rose to become chancellor, and to serve in effect as permanent foreign secretary to the Republic. The high-ranking humanists of Florence, in that they were active citizens and men of independent means rather than paid secretaries or salaried bureaucrats, had few counterparts elsewhere. In Venice Francesco Barbaro (who had several Florentine friends) undertook to translate Plutarch's *Lives* in the belief that they would provide models for Venetian politicians, and showed some sense of the relevance of Ciceronian writings to contemporary life: indeed, he sent to a friend appointed governor of Zara a copy of a letter of Cicero's on Roman provincial administration. But even in Venice his was a comparatively isolated figure.

In their political and historical writings Florentine intellectuals began to focus their attention increasingly on the ancient republics, and to see their city as the heiress not of the Roman Empire but of the Roman Republic. A new version of history was put forward, which extolled the republican virtues, and portrayed the republic as the political form most favourable to the flowering of talent and genius. Leonardo Bruni, from about 1415 onwards, devoted himself to a *History of the Florentine People*, in which he strove to do for Florence what Livy had done for Rome. In 1428, as chancellor, he composed a modern imitation of the funeral oration of Pericles on victims of the Peloponnesian war, in which Florence was triumphantly presented as a modern Athens, which had led the way in the revival of the humane studies in Italy and especially in the knowledge of Greek. Not surprisingly, great significance became attached to a new historical theory about the origins of the city. It was now believed to have been founded in the days of the Republic – by veterans of the victorious Roman army under Sulla, soon after the beginning of the first century B.C. Florentine chauvinism had always concentrated on the Roman origins of the city, but legend had previously stressed its imperial past by asserting that it was a colony founded in the time of Julius Caesar, and that after being destroyed by the Gothic general Totila it had later been restored by Charlemagne. Elsewhere in Italy, at the courts of princes, there was a parallel literature which praised the authoritarian and monarchic forms of government descended from the Caesars, and greeted their reincarnations in the Visconti or the kings of Naples. To the Paduan humanist Giovanni Conversino, writing in the late fourteenth century, government by the people could imply only civil strife and instability. In his professed opinion, princes and monarchs in modern Italy were the greatest patrons of learning – Robert of Naples, Nicolò d'Este of Ferrara,

Giangaleazzo Visconti, or Francesco II da Carrara of Padua.

None the less, it should perhaps be said that by no means all the humanists connected with Florence were strongly committed to republicanism, civic patriotism or the assumption of public burdens. Some of them, including the learned bibliophile Niccolò Niccoli, were primarily anti-quarians, and saw their passionate study of the ancient world as a means of escape from the vanities of the present life. Indeed one critic, Cino Rinuccini, attacked them for this very reason (among others) in 1417. The most versatile of intellectuals, the humanist and architect Leon Battista Alberti, has often been claimed by modern scholars as a Florentine civic humanist. But in fact he was born of a family whose sentence of exile from Florence was lifted only in 1432, when he was twenty-eight years of age, and he spent most of his life in the papal secretariate. The achievement of Florentine artists, sculptors and architects inspired him to write his treatise on the theory of painting and design during the 1430s; but his greatest work as a theorist and practitioner of architecture was done in the service of Pope Nicholas V and in the princely cities of Rimini and Mantua, as well as in Florence.

Educational pioneering, the new practice of educating young men essentially to be citizens, was not confined to republics. Professors of rhetoric employed by universities or cities sometimes began to take pupils into their own homes and to offer them a coherent system of elementary and secondary education based on first-hand knowledge of the Latin and Greek classics. Training in grammar and rhetoric was followed by instruction in the mathematical disciplines and subsequently in philosophy. These establishments – or the best of them – were boarding-schools or *contubernia* throwing a heavy emphasis on an active community life. The curriculum, in which the study of literature was the study of life through history and poetry, was varied by physical exercise, and heavy stress was thrown on finding out and developing the natural aptitudes of individual pupils. Since some professors introduced their charges to the philosophy of Plato and Aristotle and kept them till the age of twenty-one, some of these schools came to rival the universities themselves, and to acquire higher prestige in the teaching of classics.

A theoretical foundation for these experiments was provided by Pier Paolo Vergerio of Capodistria in a treatise dedicated in the early years of the century to Martino da Carrara, a member of the doomed ruling house of Padua. Here Vergerio asserted that the education of children was a matter of supreme importance to the state, and that children must be saved by constant activity from mental or physical idleness. Among the practical pioneers was Gasparino Barzizza of Bergamo, a professor of rhetoric who ran a school for Venetian noblemen at Padua from 1408 to 1421 and subsequently removed to Milan. More famous educators followed him, in the shape of the distinguished Greek scholar Guarino of Verona (1374–1460) and of Vittorino of Feltre (1378–1446). Princely courts attracted them: in 1423, Vittorino accepted an invitation from the Marquess of Mantua, Gianfrancesco Gonzaga, and set up his school in a pleasure-house in the palace gardens. Formerly called the Gioiosa, it was now renamed the Giocosa, and came to accommodate about seventy pupils, who were educated together with the children of the ruling house; poorer pupils were subsidized partly by higher fees demanded of the rich. Guarino contracted for some years with the commune of Verona, but moved in 1429 to Ferrara to serve as tutor to Leonello, son of the Marquess Niccolò d'Este.

Nevertheless, in Florence in the early fifteenth century there was much to justify the proud claim that republicanism was peculiarly favourable to the arts and literature. The beginnings of civic humanism coincided with some splendid artistic achievement, much of which was financed by public institutions and directed towards beautifying the city as a whole. There was of course nothing new about such patriotism, but it was being clad in highly original forms. Soon after 1400 the *Signoria* held a famous public competition to design new bronze doors to be hung at the baptistery near the cathedral of Santa Maria del Fiore. It was judged by a panel of thirty-four experts from within and outside Florence, and the commission eventually went to Lorenzo Ghiberti, who spent the greater part of his working life executing the many scenes from the Old and New Testament which now adorn the building. The guilds commissioned statues of their patron saints to stand in the niches surrounding the church of Or San Michele, and Ghiberti and Donatello carved some of these figures. The Silk Guild financed the large foundlings' hospital, the Spedale degli Innocenti, whose loggia was designed between 1419 and 1424 by the architect Filippo Brunelleschi. Brunelleschi, too, performed the seemingly impossible feat of constructing the vast dome of the cathedral, which was completed in essentials between 1420 and 1436.

Even the personal patronage of the Medici family was at this time largely directed towards public and religious institutions – churches, monasteries, libraries, charities – and not towards the formation of private collections of art treasures. In the days of Cosimo it remained discreet and unostentatious, as if the Medici were anxious not to provoke jealousy by setting themselves too far above the general run of Florentine patricians. In 1418 and 1419 Cosimo and his father, Giovanni de' Medici (founder of the Medici bank), each contributed as one of several subscribers to the enlargement of the church of San Lorenzo and to commissioning a statue of St Matthew the Publican to represent the Bankers' Guild on the walls of Or San Michele. When Cosimo built his own family palace in the 1440s his chosen architect was not Brunelleschi (who had prepared him a model), but the more austere and submissive Michelozzo. Himself an avid book-collector, Cosimo prevented the dispersal of the extensive library of the antiquarian Niccoli on his death in 1436, and caused Michelozzo to build premises at the monastery of San Marco for what subsequently became the first public library in Italy, the Marciana. Cosimo's own library eventually passed to the monastery of San Lorenzo, and became the Laurenziana. He may also have put the facilities of the Medici bank at the disposal of some classical scholars: there were agents throughout Europe, as far afield as Lübeck, who could help to recover manuscripts newly unearthed. This, too, was a valuable but by no means a showy service to learning.

In Florence, a highly concentrated movement was beginning to develop, transcending the boundaries of the fine arts and literature and setting up a lasting model to be admired and imitated by future generations. As Giorgio Vasari, the sixteenth-century art historian, wrote in his Life of the painter Masaccio:

The appearance of a man of outstanding creative talent is very often accompanied by that of another great artist at the same time and in the same part of the world so that the two can inspire and emulate each other. Besides bringing considerable advantages to the two rivals themselves, this phenomenon of nature provides tremendous inspiration for later artists who strive as hard as they can to win the fine reputation and renown which they hear every day attributed to their predecessors. How true this is we can see from the fact that in the same period Florence produced Filippo Brunelleschi, Donatello, Lorenzo Ghiberti, Paolo Uccello, and Masaccio, each of whom was an outstanding artist and through whose efforts the crude and clumsy style which had persevered up to that time was finally discarded.

The movement was both a return to nature and a return to the principles of art and architecture which had been observed by the ancients – though the conquest of nature was greatly furthered by a contemporary invention, the art or science of drawing or painting in perspective so that scenes could with a new accuracy be represented exactly as they appeared to the eye of a human observer. The mathematical principles behind such representation, applied by Brunelleschi and by Masaccio, were formulated during the 1430s by Leon Battista Alberti in his theoretical treatise on painting. Perspective, the art of proportional depiction, was later to achieve a position of its own as one of the liberal arts and so to further the process by which painting came to be regarded as a scientific and imaginative pursuit fit for intellectuals rather than for artisans. At least one Florentine painter, Paolo Uccello, developed an obsessive interest in perspective and in the technical problems it posed. Vasari wrote of Donatello's power not only to represent the physical being of his creatures in stone or bronze but also to convey their emotional and moral qualities.

For the Armourers' Guild he made a very spirited figure of St George in armour, expressing in the head of this saint the beauty of youth, courage and valour in arms, and a terrible ardour. Life itself seems to be stirring vigorously within the stone.

It was said that when Donatello was working on a statue for the main front of the cathedral's belltower, he kept muttering to it 'Speak, damn you, speak!'

The impact of classicism was slighter in painting than in either sculpture or architecture – in some of the work of Masaccio and other artists there was still a contrast between the classical style of the setting and the non-classical or less classical appearance of the figures. But architecture gained most, both from the adoption of Roman techniques of construction, and from fresh adaptations of classical architectural theory. Brunelleschi's studies of the constructional principles of the great buildings whose shells survived in

Rome helped him to solve the technical problems of building the vast dome for Santa Maria del Fiore. Alberti, in the treatise on architecture which he dedicated to Pope Nicholas V soon after the middle of the century, sought to resurrect for his own age the architectural principles declared for the ancients by Vitruvius. Massive barrel-vaulting, triumphal arches and temple-like façades began to reappear, adapted to the needs of Christian churches, the antique sometimes blending with the Gothic. Beyond this lay a general preoccupation with symmetry and order and with geometrical principles of design – specifically, with the ancient 'modular' system of proportion, whereby the design of a whole building was related to the width of its columns at their base.

*

It may be that the flowering of genius is a phenomenon that can only be explained to a very limited extent in terms of its environment – that the historian can only draw attention to certain more or less favourable preconditions for the Renaissance, and that beyond that point he can only describe and analyse its progress rather than explain its origins. An economic historian can explain how the Medici amassed wealth through banking, but cannot account for their judgement in employing Donatello or Brunelleschi. Dr Hans Baron, the historian *par excellence* of civic humanism, has made one of the most precise attempts to relate this phase in the literary Renaissance to specific political events. He has attached crucial importance to the crisis of 1402; to the confrontation – especially at that point – between the forces of republicanism and tyranny; to the heightened patriotism of the Florentines and their fresh awareness of the way of life they were defending. He holds that before that time even Salutati was not completely committed to the ideals of civic humanism. However, Dr Baron's thesis hangs perilously on somewhat intricate and challengeable arguments about the dating of certain works of Leonardo Bruni, and it is uncertain whether Bruni, or indeed any humanist, can be totally identified with a particular philosophy or system of values. Among other historians, Professor Brucker attaches more significance to the crisis which occurred between 1409 and 1414, in the face of the threat from Ladislao of Naples. This, in particular, coincided with the development of a new intellectual habit on the part of politicians – in the practice of appealing for guidance to historical example, and particularly to the experience of the last Florentine century. At about this time, as Professor Rubinstein remarks, some flickerings of 'republicanism' appeared in Siena, which was then allied with Florence against the King of Naples. When the Sienese government commissioned Taddeo di Bartolo to paint 'beautiful and honourable figures' on the walls of the ante-chapel of the Palazzo Pubblico, he concentrated on depicting Roman republican statesmen, such as Cicero or Cato the Younger, who had resisted tyranny.

Explanations of this relatively precise kind can only claim to illuminate one particular sector of the Florentine Renaissance, and their particular value lies in the fields of political thought and historical writing. Some suggestions with broader implications and less reference to specific events have also been put forward by modern historians. As Professor Brucker again remarks, Florence may actually have profited from the absence of a powerful university and from the consequent lack of any dominant cultural or intellectual interest: intellectual life was less formalized and therefore perhaps less hide-bound by tradition than in Padua or Bologna. It may be important that Brunelleschi and Ghiberti, who served their apprenticeship as gold-smiths, had no formal training in the fields in which they most distinguished themselves. Indeed, Florentines were characterized by a kind of passionate and limitless curiosity, which led them on from one discipline to another as if to embrace the whole cultural field or to harness all knowledge to the service of their art. For example, Giannozzo Manetti, born in 1393, was originally trained to be an ordinary businessman and for some years contented himself with keeping the books of the family firm. But at the age of twenty-five he abruptly conceived an ambition to win fame and glory for himself and his family through the pursuit of letters, and with spectacular rapidity in the seclusion of his own home he mastered the liberal arts and went on from Latin to the study of Greek and Hebrew. It was said of Brunelleschi that he soon began to 'speculate about problems of motion and time, and of weights and wheels'. He himself made some very beautiful clocks, aspired to beat Donatello in his own art of sculpture, and took a great interest not only in geometry but also in the Scriptures and in the writings of Dante. His qualities as an organizer served him well as an architect – in the construction of the cathedral dome he had to prove his own ability to handle strikes among recalcitrant masons and to set up canteens in the dome itself so that the workers would not lose time by descending to eat and drink below.

Another tentative clue to the origins and character of the Florentine Renaissance may, as Dr George Holmes suggests, lie in the relationship between Florence and Rome in the early fifteenth century. After the War of the Eight Saints relations between the Florentine state and the Roman Papacy were usually reasonably good, and the weakening of the Papacy by the Schism or by revolt in Rome did mean that the Florentines no longer stood in awe of the Popes. Instead they were able to regard them with detachment, even at times with superiority, and there was little risk of Rome taking any form of repressive action against humanists suspected of departing from the norms of conventional Christianity. The disintegration of the old Guelf

alliance – a slow process already in motion in the 1340s –
may have prepared the way for the Florentines to think of
themselves as an independent republic, without severing all
useful ties and traditional bonds with Rome. Business connections were maintained, and the Medici first became
bankers to the Papacy during the troubled pontificate of
Baldassare Cossa, Pope John XXIII of the Pisan obedience.
On more than one occasion an exiled Papacy chose Florence
as its refuge. Martin V lived in the Dominican convent of
Santa Maria Novella in 1419–20. When Eugenius IV came
to occupy the same premises in 1434 he brought Alberti in
his retinue, and it was then that Alberti first became aware
of the achievements of his compatriots, which now seemed
to equal those of the ancient world. Tommaso Parentucelli
of Sarzana, who rose to become Nicholas V, the first
humanist on St Peter's throne, had as a young man been
tutor to the Florentine families of Rinaldo degli Albizzi and
Palla Strozzi for a spell of about two years. He was friendly
with Cosimo de' Medici, at whose request he drew up plans
for the library of the convent of San Marco in Florence
itself and for that of the abbey at Fiesole.

There was a good deal of interchange between Florence
and the papal curia. Of the Florentine chancellors, both
Bruni and Poggio served for years in Rome, and Poggio's
privileged status as a papal secretary enabled him (when
the Council of Constance was in session) to obtain access to
jealously guarded collections of classical manuscripts. With
the help of friends and colleagues he searched the libraries
of Reichenau, Weingarten, St Gallen and other monasteries, and made some remarkable discoveries. Ease of access
to Rome itself had great potential importance for artists,
especially at a time when employees of the curia were taking
a more intense interest in the ruins, and attempting to
reconstruct them mentally and understand the principles on
which they were built – though not, as yet, to restore them

physically or to excavate them systematically. The visits of Brunelleschi and Donatello to Rome are well known, and Brunelleschi's observations in Rome in the 1430s seem to have strongly influenced his later work in Florence. Furthermore, the Popes – whether in Florence itself or in their crumbling, rickety capital – gave generous employment to Florentine artists and craftsmen, since they could find few or none in Rome itself. A lover of ceremonial, Martin V relied on Florentines from Ghiberti downwards to provide him with its trappings. Both he and his successor, Eugenius, were of necessity concerned with repairing the damage to the city and undoing the ravages of years of neglect rather than with any new and far-reaching plans to dignify Rome. Taking responsibility himself for parish churches and the greater basilicas, he urged his cardinals to restore the churches from which they took their titles. Masaccio was on his payroll for a time, and he retained Gentile da Fabriano to paint the walls of the nave of St John Lateran. It was left to Nicholas V, with Alberti as his architectural adviser, to plan massive and large-scale reconstructions, especially of the Leonine City: although his dreams of rebuilding St Peter's came to nothing, it was he who began to demolish the dangerous, tottering fabric of the old church.

The outlook of Renaissance scholars was strongly influenced by growing first-hand knowledge of Greek literature and philosophy such as even Petrarch and Boccaccio had never possessed. This, in its turn, was an indirect result of a political and military situation in the Mediterranean at large which tended to encourage closer contacts and greater sympathy between Greeks and Italians. The Venetians, of course, had long maintained commercial relations with the eastern Mediterranean and had long possessed colonies in the Levant. This had tended to instil in them some knowledge of Greek, though it was usually colloquial and not literary. Mere proximity to Greeks did not produce a classical Renaissance any more than did the constant sight of Roman ruins – a change of attitude to them was necessary. In the late fourteenth and early fifteenth centuries, when Constantinople was hemmed in by the Turks, Emperors of the house of Palaeologos came to believe that their prospects of military aid from the west would improve if they did at least open negotiations with a view to reunion between the Catholic and Orthodox Churches. This could also be expected to discomfit the Turks by suggesting the possibility that the number of their foes might suddenly double. Some patriarchs and bishops desired union for its own sake – although, on the other hand, monks in the east tended to oppose it with fanatical obstinacy.

On the one hand, increasing knowledge of Greek culture in the west strengthened affection for those who preserved it and were its heirs. The Byzantine Empire had already had its own Renaissance, the 'Palaeologan revival', in the shape of a return to original classical Greek texts. Conversely, desire for union, negotiations to bring it about, and appeals from the east for military aid undoubtedly helped to encourage the interchange of ideas between Italians and Greeks. A most influential teacher of Greek was Manuel Chrysoloras, who was sent to the west by the Emperor Manuel II Palaeologos to beg for aid against the Turks. Partly through the influence of Salutati and his disciples, Chrysoloras was attracted to Florence, where he held the chair of Greek in the University from 1397 to 1400 and acquired an unusually talented circle of pupils, which included Niccoli, Poggio, Bruni and Vergerio. Other members of the Italian intelligentsia began to visit the Byzantine East for themselves – as Guarino of Verona went to Constantinople in the service of a Venetian merchant, Paolo Zane, and had the opportunity to study there in the household of Chrysoloras. Most distinguished of his followers when he returned to Venice was Francesco Barbaro, who had originally learnt Greek from Zaccaria Trevisan, a patrician back from a tour of duty as governor of Crete. An eager student of Greek antiquities was Ciriaco of Ancona. Unlike many advocates of union he felt no sympathy for his contemporaries in Greece, which to him was 'no more than a museum inhabited by people beyond contempt'. But he was inspired by determination to record the relics of antiquity before it was too late, saw Athens for the first time in 1436, and made drawings of the Parthenon.

Dialogue between the Greek and Latin Churches intensified when in 1437 Pope Eugenius IV brought off his most prestigious *coup* by attracting on to Italian soil a Greek delegation prepared to discuss union. The Greeks proved willing to take part in a Council under papal direction, rather than in the independent, rival assembly meeting at Basel. Ferrara was the original site of the Council, but the Florentine commune then offered to support the Greek delegation, thus relieving them of dependence on papal subsidies. The Council was transferred to Florence, and it was in Florence's cathedral that the Bull of Union signed by both sides was solemnly proclaimed in July 1439. It was in Florence that the Greek Patriarch Joseph II died and was buried, as a member of the Catholic Church, in Santa Maria Novella; and in Florence that the Pope bestowed cardinals' hats upon Isidore, Metropolitan of Kiev and of All Russia, and upon John Bessarion, Patriarch of Nicea.

It was, perhaps, significant that one of the most exciting achievements of the early fifteenth century should lie in effecting a brief reconciliation between estranged churches, and that the religious motives which led to union should also have furthered the development of the Renaissance. There was, admittedly, great difficulty in getting the actions of the Greek delegates endorsed in Constantinople, and in any case union failed to survive the Turkish conquest of

Constantinople in 1453. But the Council of Florence had succeeded in establishing the fundamental principle of 'unity of faith and diversity of rite', on which several subsequent unions were to be based.

Religion and the pursuit of beauty had been closely linked, and there was no need for the artist's quest for personal fame and recognition to be sharply detached from his zeal for the glory of God. Majestic and monumental architecture could immeasurably strengthen the Catholic faith – and the vision of Pope Nicholas V was eloquently set forth in a touched-up deathbed speech written by his biographer, Manetti:

A popular faith, sustained only on doctrines, will never be anything but feeble and vacillating. But if the authority of the Holy See were visibly displayed in majestic buildings, imperishable memorials and witnesses seemingly planted by the hand of God himself, belief would grow and strengthen like a tradition from one generation to another, and all the world would accept and revere it . . .

The gaze of the humanists was not trained only on the pre-Christian ancient world, and the architects of the fifteenth century probably did not distinguish clearly between early Christian basilicas and the monuments of the pagan Empire. New expertise in Latin or Greek could well be applied to discovering, interpreting and translating the works of the Fathers of the Church. Lorenzo Valla, a versatile travelling philologist, applied some of his skills to criticizing passages of the Latin Vulgate, St Jerome's translation, in the light of the original Greek New Testament. Some humanists were prepared to justify their interest in ancient philosophy or poetry on the grounds of its essential compatibility with the doctrines of Christianity. Among them Ambrogio Traversari, General of the Order of Camaldoli, was prepared to translate the *Lives of the Philosophers* of Diogenes Laertius on the grounds that the work contained inspiring examples of almost Christian behaviour, and that greater knowledge of the pagan philosophers would reveal their lack of agreement and drive the reader back to the clear truths of Christianity.

Not all humanists, however, displayed such exemplary piety. Some of the Florentines were accused of holding that virtuous and moral behaviour was an end in itself rather than a means of acquiring merit in the sight of God. In Alberti there seems to have been a certain rationalistic streak. He believed, for example, that God was constantly responsible for rational order in the universe, and could not be expected miraculously to vary the rules for the benefit of individuals in response to the promptings of prayer. He also revealed a certain tendency to underplay the mystical and sacramental aspects of religion, thus diminishing the role of the priesthood. A most aggressive defence of the classics and a challenge to certain commonplace Christian assumptions came from Francesco da Fiano, who for a time acted as mentor to some of the younger scholars and secretaries in Rome. Himself a cleric, he admitted having joined the profession merely in order to get a living, and allowed himself to argue, contrary to received opinion, that human nature had been very much the same in the Christian and the pagan eras. The Fathers of the Church had been as much inspired by lust for fame as were the great figures of antiquity, and there was plenty of superstitious saint-worship today – corresponding to the paganism attacked by the invectives of Augustine. What could be more unjust than to consign the ancient poets to hell, merely because they had no knowledge of Christ?

Some knowledge of the classics had survived throughout the Middle Ages, but it had normally been subordinated to Christian ends, and the eagerness of many of the humanists to study the ancient world in loving detail, as if it were an end in itself, was a thing bound to excite suspicion and

misgiving. Nevertheless, humanists were attacked by pole-
micists and pamphleteers, rather than suppressed by Inquisitors. Salutati, for example, had to defend Virgil from the
strictures of Zonarini, chancellor of Bologna, and classical
studies in general against the attacks of Giovanni Dominici,
lecturer on the Bible in the university of Florence. But even
Bernardino of Siena, the great Observant preacher, preserved a neutral attitude towards humanism in general
whilst objecting puritanically to the reading of erotica,
especially in the works of Ovid. In this period, official
ecclesiastical censorship was not much in evidence.

It would be very difficult to prove that the ecclesiastical
hierarchy or the doctrines of the Church were seriously
losing their authority over the minds and hearts of Italians
in the early fifteenth century, hard to maintain that an
unprecedented degree of contempt for the clergy was
opening the way to a more rationalistic or more pagan
outlook. Anticlericalism – contempt for the lax morals,
hypocrisy, ignorance or idleness of the clergy – was almost
a perpetual concomitant of Catholicism. It was not peculiar
to the fifteenth century, and was not synonymous with
irreligion. Satire on clerical morality or incompetence did
at least imply the existence of a society in which these things
were taken seriously; lewd or credulous friars were funny
because they fell short of an ideal standard which was still
important.

Information about the fluctuating wealth of the Church
does offer a rough guide, not only to the likely extent of its
worldly influence as a rich corporation, but also to its power
to attract gifts and bequests from those who still respected
it. On the one hand, Professor Carlo Cipolla has advanced
a famous thesis based on evidence drawn from the Milanese
state, and particularly from the region of Pavia. This main-
tains that the Church's losses in the Visconti and Sforza state
during the fourteenth and fifteenth centuries became so

serious that by about 1550 its share in the territory had fallen to no more than 10–15 per cent. The Church was heavily taxed by the Milanese lords, who did not shrink from laying heavy burdens even on the benefices of cardinals, and although its landed wealth was vast it kept at its disposal comparatively scanty supplies of ready cash. Hence its growing habit of granting out lands on long or even perpetual leases at derisory rents in order to obtain ready money. Although in 1401 the Duke tried to check the process by forbidding perpetual leases, it became easy enough to circumvent the law by introducing into contracts clauses which demanded that a tenant be reimbursed for any improvements he had made on his tenure. The monasteries or churches concerned, being frequently unable to reimburse, were then compelled to renew his lease at the same rate, and by the end of the century perpetual leases – if not a complete relaxation of control over lands – had again become quite normal.

However, the general applicability of this thesis is very much open to doubt. In the Venetian Republic, the house of Santa Giustina of Padua and other Benedictine abbeys showed great determination to reconstitute their landed property during the fifteenth century, and were eager to contract loans with Venetian patricians in order to recover lands previously leased or pledged. Subsequently, these loans were repaid out of the pious gifts or legacies which began to accumulate when the reputation of the abbeys as places of great holiness increased. In the Archbishopric of Genoa, the authorities tended as the fifteenth century advanced to show less enthusiasm for perpetual leases. These were certainly numerous in 1410, but by 1492 leases for periods of twenty-seven years had become more common. Moreover, many ecclesiastical foundations had substantial holdings of shares in the public debt controlled by the Casa di San Giorgio. Further south, in Tuscany, analysis of the tax registers of San Gimignano and its *contado* suggests that the landed wealth of religious institutions increased from 12 per cent of taxable property in 1315 to 25·7 per cent in 1419 and 28·8 per cent in 1475; though hospitals were gaining far more rapidly than were monasteries and convents. Ecclesiastical foundations made similar progress in various zones of the Florentine *contado* during the fifteenth century, where their share of the land rose from 13·5 per cent in 1427 to 23·2 per cent in 1498. Clearly, neither impiety nor mismanagement nor taxation was sufficient in these places to diminish the wealth of the Church, which was an indirect reflection of the esteem in which it was held by the public.

Clearly, too, the Church still wielded great influence in certain spheres of economic life, especially in banking and the money market – in which it was still necessary to take account of its official teachings with respect to usurious lending. The draconian usury laws of the twelfth and thirteenth centuries had been partly designed to prevent the diversion of funds from agricultural or other beneficial investment into sterile financial transactions. They were partly based on the assumption that borrowers were usually in some form of distress, of which no lender ought to take advantage by charging interest on his loan: they did not perhaps visualize the situation in which an investor might be lending to a rich man to help him become richer still. The usury laws were embarrassing to bankers, but on the other hand they had probably done little to hinder commercial partnerships in which the lenders who put up capital bore a substantial risk of loss. For this they might be allowed some compensation in the form of interest payments. Most severely condemned was lending which was in theory riskless. As late as the early sixteenth century, it was still deemed necessary to make restitution for usurious loans advanced in 1448–54 by Giuliano di Giovenco de'Medici, who had exacted from his debtors enormous securities far in excess of the sums he had lent.

The existence of the usury laws could still mean in the fifteenth century that loans at a profit made by bankers had to be decently disguised in a very complicated manner as exchange transactions. Interest paid on money deposited with a banker was not recoverable at law: hence it was called *discrezione*, and the fiction was maintained that it was a free gift. In practice a banker who got into difficulties was quite capable of withholding *discrezione*, so as not to depress his situation further by having to pay interest to his depositors. The banker who served as Depositary-General to the Apostolic Treasury was prevented from charging interest on its overdraft, and records of interest payments seem to have been kept strictly out of account books in Genoa. Lenders had to resort to various elaborate subterfuges. They might camouflage loans as leases; or they might lend in Currency A and recover an equal number of lire some time later in Currency B, another currency used in business transactions – one in which the lira was valued somewhat more highly.

The Church's economic doctrines, upheld by ecclesiastical or state courts or by the promptings of conscience or confessor, had plainly never procured a total suppression of capitalistic enterprise. But they did create inhibitions, and the sense of guilt oppressing Cosimo de' Medici may have been responsible for some of his most generous patronage. In the words of Vespasiano de' Bisticci, a Florentine bookseller:

He had prickings of conscience that certain portions of his wealth – where it came from I cannot say – had not been righteously gained, and to remove this weight from his shoulders he held conference with Pope Eugenius, who was then in Florence, as to the load which lay on his conscience. Pope Eugenius had settled the Observantist Order [of Dominicans] in San Marco;

but, as their lodging there was inadequate, he remarked to Cosimo that, if he was bent on unburdening his soul, he might build a monastery . . .

The doctrines of the Church did in their way contribute to the flowering of the Renaissance.

Moreover, the saints and evangelists of the late four-teenth and early fifteenth centuries helped to create a second culture which did not so much rival or challenge the assump-tions of the *avant-garde* intellectuals as coexist with them on equal terms. The half-century of the early Renaissance was also one of vigorous religious revival. The world and the flesh could still be denied as distractions from God, and wealth could still be renounced in the manner of St Francis, even as the humanists declared its positive value. Within the life-span of Coluccio Salutati, chancellor of Florence, there lived Catterina Benincasa, the dyer's daughter and Domini-can tertiary who as St Catherine of Siena was to be promoted five and a half centuries after her death in 1380 to the position of patron saint of all Italy. Her philosophy or 'wisdom' aimed at total immersion in God, at transforma-tion into him through the vision of divine love, whose corollary was 'holy hatred' of the flesh and of all sensuality:

The soul that sees its own nothingness and knows that its whole good is to be found in the Creator forsakes itself and all its powers and all other creatures and immerses itself wholly in him, directing all its operations towards him and never alienating itself from him, for it realizes that in him it can find all goodness and perfect happiness. Through this vision of love, increasing from day to day, the soul is so transformed into God that it cannot think or under-stand or remember anything but God and the things of God . . .

This total denial of the world and the flesh found expression in fantastic personal austerities and self-mortifica-tions recalling those of the early desert fathers of Egypt: Catherine was said for a time to have lived off no food other than the Eucharist, for which she experienced an appetite viewed with certain misgivings by more orthodox churchmen, embarrassed at the holy excesses of a potential saint. She was said to have undergone not only stigmatization but also the terrible experience of the re-enactment of the Passion in her own body. For her the laws of nature seemed frequently to have been suspended, for she was subject to ecstasies involving the most extreme physical rigidity, sometimes accompanied by levitation. Some of her experiences have been explained as a consequence of her responsiveness to images, for she tended to see visions of saints 'just as she had seen them painted in churches'. Her reputation in her own lifetime caused her to attract so great a concourse of pilgrims and sight-seers that Pope Gregory XI had to grant her confessor and two colleagues, by apostolic brief, 'faculties equivalent to a bishop's, to absolve all who came to see the virgin and wanted to confess their sins'.

Catherine of Siena and her cult were not merely the transitory products of the thirty years after the Black Death, when the world might well have felt itself to be at the mercy of divine or supernatural powers entirely beyond human understanding or control. During the fifteenth century, there was no generalized reform of the Catholic Church, stemming from Pope or Council and comparable with the Counter-Reformations of the thirteenth or of the sixteenth century. But there was some spontaneous localized reform, renewal of the tissues in certain parts of the body of the Church. A community of devout young men formed round two Venetian patricians, Gabriele Condulmer and his cousin Antonio Correr, on the lagoon island of San Giorgio in Alga, and both its leaders used their influence in Rome as nephews of Pope Gregory XII to get new benefices and monasteries attached to their congregation. Within the established religious orders, zealots began to return to the scrupulous and literal observance of the original Rules drawn up by the founders – to save the ideals of St Benedict, St Francis or St Dominic from being obscured by laxity, by the passage of time, by transmutation of the aim and character of the order. Failing to convert the whole order to their ways, the 'observant' movements were sometimes allowed, perhaps with misgivings on the part of the Papacy, to establish their own communities and to form separate organizations within or beside the parent body.

The Dominican Observants, strongly influenced by Catherine of Siena and her confessor Raymond of Capua, were prominent in Renaissance Florence and benefited by the generosity of its first citizen. An Observant friary had been founded at Fiesole in the early years of the century, but its occupants made earnest and even greedy attempts to secure premises in the city itself. At last, in 1436, they ousted the Silvestrine monks from the insalubrious buildings of the convent of San Marco. Cosimo de' Medici financed the new buildings there and chose them as the site of Niccoli's library. One of the friars was the artist Angelico of Fiesole, so much in demand as a painter of churches, who painted not only the public rooms of the convent but also the cells of the friars. There was a pleasant story that Fra Angelico, working on a chapel in Rome, put it into the head of Pope Eugenius to solve the current disputes over the Archbishopric of Florence by appointing to it Antonino Pierozzi, some time prior of San Marco and Vicar-General of the Italian Observants of the Dominican Order. In this high office Antonino followed two soldier Archbishops and an absentee diplomat. Retaining his personal simplicity and humility, he proved to be a tough and formidable prelate, and established himself as a guardian of public morals, a protector of the poor, a learned commentator on economic affairs and on the implications of the Church's teachings on usury. His visitations of his province pitilessly laid bare the dilapidation of churches and the shortcomings of the clergy in, for example, the diocese of Pistoia.

Monastic discipline in most of the Benedictine houses of Italy had decayed during the fourteenth century through the absence of effective supervision either from the diocesan bishop or from disciplinary mechanisms within the order itself. Especially pernicious was the practice of using abbacies or priories to provide financial support for secular prelates who were not monks, and frequently cared very little either about the community or about its buildings and estates. But in the early fifteenth century a Venetian, Ludovico Barbo, came forward with a practical solution to the problem which could be applied at least on a limited scale. It was he who had made the island of San Giorgio in Alga over to its devout canons, and in 1409 he was sent by the Venetian Pope Gregory XII to become Abbot of the decayed monastery of Santa Giustina of Padua. This had been in the hands of the now dispossessed Carraresi family, and was left with only three monks. Here Ludovico Barbo set in motion his own disciplinary reform. To some extent this was another 'observant' movement based on return to the literal interpretation of the Rule of St Benedict; but it also involved establishing a new organization which would bind monastic houses together and keep their monks and their property under strict supervision. By 1418 Barbo, able to recruit young men of high calibre from the university of Padua, had a following of about 200 disciples. Rather than extend their own premises or establish new foundations, the reformed Benedictines chose to occupy other empty or reduced monasteries, where they could obtain invitations to do so. From 1419 onwards these monasteries were united as equal members of a single congregation whose sovereign body was a chapter-general. This elected visitors to watch over the discipline of individual houses. Some abbots were shocked by the democratic leanings of the organization, and particularly by the fact that mere monks were entitled to take part in the chapter-general and even become visitors; indeed, by the middle 1430s abbots and priors were being elected or re-elected annually by the chapter-general. But the congregation survived its serious early difficulties, and by 1437 it was said to include eighteen monasteries and about 300 monks. Its influence was certainly not confined to Lombardy, for by the time of Barbo's death in 1443 the congregation had not only crossed the Apennines but even penetrated as far south as Naples and Gaeta.

But the most influential religious movements of these years were marked by a determination not only to improve the moral standards of the clergy but also to exert a civilizing and philanthropic influence on the world at large – and, in the Franciscan tradition, philanthropy involved not only tending the poor and sick but actually identifying with them. It was at this time that a movement for the strict observation of St Francis's Rule at last achieved respectability. Although in the fifteenth century the leaders of the Observance were to display uncompromising hostility towards the surviving irregulars or Fraticelli, their own movement was remotely descended from a branch of the heretic Spirituals. It began (officially, in 1368) at the hermitage of Brugliano, on the borders of Umbria and the Marches. This had been founded by a disciple of Angelo da Clareno, some time leader of the Spirituals of Ancona in the early fourteenth century. By 1389 there were twenty-one convents in Umbria, Roma and the Marches, and the first house in Tuscany was founded in the following year. By 1442 the Observants had more than 200 convents, which seem to have sheltered over 4,000 friars. Their progress was speeded by the personal prestige of certain very able preachers and evangelists recruited during the first two decades of the century – among them Bernardino of Siena, Giovanni da Capistrano, Alberto da Sarteano and Giacomo dalle Marche. As Giovanni da Capistrano proposed at a conference in Assisi in 1430, it was the desire of the Observants that all Franciscans should wear uniform habits, rid themselves of all landed property and cease to handle money themselves. Instead, they should put their financial affairs into the hands of agents or proctors. But Martin V was still prepared to allow the friars to continue to enjoy property so long as the legal fiction could be maintained that it really belonged to the Holy See. In effect, the Observants began to develop into a separate order or organization, permitted to choose its own provincial vicars and vicar-general apart from the other Franciscans, who became known as Conventuals.

For Bernardino of Siena (1380–1444) the preaching of the word was the supreme task of the Church on earth, and could even be regarded more highly than attendance at Mass.

There is less peril for your soul in not hearing Mass, than in not hearing the sermon. Tell me, How could you believe in the Holy Sacrament of the Altar but for the holy preaching you have heard? ... Nay more, how would you know what this was, but through preaching?

He may have borrowed his highly effective techniques from Vicente Ferrer, the Spanish Dominican whom he heard at Alessandria in 1401. Ferrer spoke from pulpits erected in open squares or fields and dealt with down-to-earth, practical subjects of instant relevance to his hearers' everyday lives. Bernardino broke with the practice of restricting the matter of sermons to the passage of Scripture appointed to be read as Epistle or Gospel for the day, and this enabled him to deal with the Bible as a whole. His influence extended far beyond the audiences who actually sat at his feet in the squares of Tuscan, Umbrian or Lombard towns, for it was his habit to write his sermons down and to make them available to other, less inspired performers. His campaigns to civilize social behaviour and to raise moral standards among laity as well as clergy formed an important parallel to the concern of many of the humanists with civic life and with education for it. Although the idiom was very different and the element of mystery far greater here, the aims of the two cultures were not wholly dissimilar.

In particular, Bernardino was determined to persuade citizens to live together in peace, and to eliminate factionalism and wanton violence, against which he spoke at times with almost fanatical vehemence. In a sense, he was returning to the traditional aims of the old Scuole dei Disciplinati, and of the flagellant movements of the late thirteenth century – having himself served an apprenticeship in a flagellant confraternity which met secretly in the basement of the Hospital of Santa Maria della Scala in Siena. At Treviglio in Lombardy, for example, he founded a Scuola dei Disciplinati pledged to maintain peace. Gambling, blasphemy, the desecration of religious festivals, heathen or pagan superstitions all earned his consistent denunciation. Agitating against sorcery, he once succeeded in procuring the destruction of a fountain near Arezzo, which had stood in a grove once sacred to Apollo and enjoyed a reputation for miraculous healing. He tried to counter the practice of buying charms and amulets by changing its direction and fostering the cult of the Holy Name of Jesus, encouraging his hearers to purchase tablets bearing the sacred monogram YHS and to use it as a substitute for the almost ubiquitous party emblems. To this day the sacred monogram blazes on the façade of the Palazzo Pubblico in Siena, where it replaced the emblem of the Visconti in 1425. Admittedly, the lengths to which this popular cult was carried by some of its enthusiasts caused Bernardino to be summoned to Rome in 1427 to face charges of idolatry before Pope Martin V. It was alleged that, as far afield as Messina, people would refuse to give alms when asked for God's sake or Christ's sake, but would do so immediately on hearing the name of Jesus; and that elsewhere in Sicily a preacher had been interrupted by the cry, 'Unless God is Jesus, say no more about God!' But Bernardino emerged unscathed from his ordeal, was revered as a saint at the time of his death in Aquila in 1444, and (despite the obstructive tactics of his personal enemies) was officially canonized by Pope Nicholas V within six years.

It may be that between the mid-fourteenth and the mid-fifteenth centuries religious fervour and piety began to adopt a more strongly philanthropic bent, and to focus attention more firmly on the needs of the poor and sick: they began to consider social problems, though these were certainly not clearly divorced from the religious preoccupation with the saving of souls. Hospitals were officially institutions with the cure of souls attached, places of shelter where the poor could be given every opportunity of dying with the sacraments of Holy Church. Catholic doctrine has often been accused of worsening the problem of poverty by encouraging indiscriminate almsgiving – the charitable Catholic is allegedly more preoccupied with the acquisition of merit for himself than concerned with the effect of his charity on its recipient, so that he is supposed to run the risk of corrupting the poor, depriving them of incentives to work, and of creating a 'class of professional paupers. But at least some of the admonitions of influential churchmen at this time were strongly in favour of carefully regulated almsgiving – as witness certain remarks in a sermon of Bernardino of Siena:

You should not give alms to every beggar and drunken vagabond; whence it is written (Ecclesiastes, xii, 5, 6) 'Give to a righteous man and give not to a sinner', that is, to the encouragement of sin; for many beggars haunt taverns and other disreputable places, setting examples of depravity.

More important, there was much highly organized philanthropy which depended upon institutions, and not upon casual almsgiving. For example, the old flagellant fraternities of Venice, the Scuole Grandi, developed from communities of equals into brotherhoods which embraced quite clearly defined orders of rich and poor – the rich administering the property of the Scuole for the benefit of the poorer members. Since almsgiving took place within the framework of a body whose members were known to each other, its casual and haphazard nature was reduced. In any case, the Scuole concerned themselves with forms of relief more sophisticated than simple almsgiving – and especially with the administration of funds intended to provide small dowries and make marriage economically feasible for girls of good character who could not otherwise have afforded it.

Furthermore, there was an increase both in the number and in the wealth of hospitals, at least in Tuscany. The town hospitals of Pistoia were prospering, and the Hospital of the Ceppo, founded about 1277, had by 1428 become the richest religious corporation in the city. Over the same period, the number of hospitals increased from four to eleven. Elsewhere, particularly in Milan and central Lombardy, campaigns were run by Observant Franciscans (including Alberto da Sarteano and Michele Carcano of Milan) to centralize the administration of hospitals by amalgamating the smaller institutions into a single larger one, to be controlled by civic and clerical authorities: the object being to increase efficiency through coordination, and to reduce the risk of funds being consumed by corrupt administrators. As many as eleven small hospitals were fused together to form the Great Hospital of San Marco in Bergamo in 1457, and such all-embracing institutions addressed themselves to the problem of caring for orphans and foundlings and sheltering the sick and aged. It seems likely that these general hospitals were sometimes modelled, architecturally and otherwise, on those of Florence and Siena.

The Franciscans, who publicized these institutions, were not only concerned with the outright relief of the poor, but also with the severe problem of controlling usurious lending and checking indebtedness: for there were innumerable occasions on which the poor people of Italy, possessing no reserves or savings, were compelled to contract petty loans to tide them over crises caused by sickness or accident, seasonal stoppages of work, inflated food prices or tax-demands which ignored the economic situation. Despite the canon laws which condemned public authorities contracting with usurers, some governments had retained the services of nominally Christian pawnbrokers to conduct the small-loan business and kept the letter of the law by ritually fining them each year for committing the sin of usury. In the late fourteenth and early fifteenth centuries it had become increasingly common to license Jews rather than Christians, on the uncertain grounds that they were outside the pale of the canon law – though even this practice caused much doubt and self-questioning, as at Brescia, where the propriety of contracting with Jewish lenders was long and earnestly debated. The Franciscans professed, not only compassion for the poor, but acute distrust of the Jews, and especially of their acquiring economic power over Christians by putting them in their debt.

The institutions which they eventually founded to meet the situation have survived in Italy to the present day. These were public pawnshops known as *Monti di Pietà* or 'Funds of charity', and accumulated a large part of their capital from charitable gifts and bequests; they were supposed to lend only to the genuinely poor, and never to do so to subsidize such immoral activities as drinking or gambling. They would also charge significantly lower rates of interest even than the Jews, who had been imported to many communities in the hope that they would undercut the more rapacious Christians. Such interest payments were justified as being designed to cover administrative costs, on the theory that the borrower was bound to make a payment to the officials of the *Monte* as compensation for their trouble in storing the pledge, making entries on the books, issuing a pawnticket, and so on. Since the borrower had no loan contract with the officials, but only with the commune which ran the bank, it could hardly be said that they were usuriously charging him for the use of their money. The first of the *Monti di Pietà* was erected at Perugia in 1462, and soon followed by other institutions at Orvieto and Gubbio. Standardized, exportable books of regulations were soon drawn up, and this greatly assisted the rapid spread of the new form of poor man's bank. Ugly methods, however, were sometimes used to discredit the Jews and clear a path for the Monti – especially the spreading of accusations of ritual murder supposed to have been committed during the Jewish Passover rites, which began to invade the Veneto from Trent in and after 1475. Much theological wrangling was still necessary before the *Monti di Pietà* obtained general recognition from a Lateran Council in 1515, and for a long time they merely coexisted with Jewish loan-banks without replacing them entirely. None the less, the *Monti di Pietà* survived to become perhaps the most lasting memorials to the social and religious concerns of the fifteenth-century revival.

*

The early fifteenth century had witnessed a revival, not only of classicism, but also of traditional Christian and especially Franciscan values; the beginnings, too, of a return to the pure original sources of Christian doctrine, in the Greek New Testament and the writings of the Fathers. Even for classical scholars Christianity often remained a central

point of reference. They tended, at least in public, to stress
the extent to which such doctrines as Platonism could be
reconciled with Christian teachings, rather than to extol
the ethics and beliefs of the ancients as an independent code
which could emancipate its followers from the constrictions
of Christian thought. With the culture of the scholarly élite,
in court and palace, republic and 'tyranny', chancery and
curia, there still coexisted the culture of the piazza and the
cult of the sermon. Artist, sculptor and architect were
pressed into the service of a Church alive to the splendour
of holiness; guilt at the evasion or defiance of canon law
could still prick the conscience of a generous patron;
fumbling towards Church union could help the west to
penetrate the secrets of ancient Greece. Growing ability to
focus on earthly problems did not obliterate all vision of a
world beyond, and the arguments of the civic humanists
had their counterpart in the less rationalistic moralizing,
peacemaking and philanthropy of the Franciscan Observants.

Maps

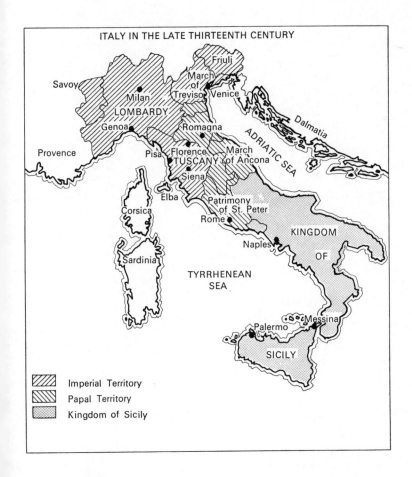

ITALY IN THE LATE THIRTEENTH CENTURY

Savoy
Friuli
March
of
Treviso
Venice
Milan
LOMBARDY
Dalmatia
Genoa
Romagna
ADRIATIC SEA
Provence
Pisa
Florence
TUSCANY
March
of Ancona
Siena
Elba
Corsica
Patrimony
of St. Peter
Rome
KINGDOM
Naples
OF
Sardinia
TYRRHENEAN
SEA
Messina
Palermo
SICILY

Imperial Territory
Papal Territory
Kingdom of Sicily

ITALY IN THE MID-FIFTEENTH CENTURY

DUCHY OF MILAN
Milan
REPUBLIC OF VENICE
REPUBLIC OF GENOA
REPUBLIC OF FLORENCE
REPUBLIC OF SIENA
STATES OF THE CHURCH
KINGDOM OF NAPLES
Corsica
Elba
Sardinia
KINGDOM OF SICILY

1. Marquisate of Monferrato
2. County of Asti
3. Territory of the Malaspina
4. Marquisate of Mantua
5. Dominions of the Estensi
6. Republic of Lucca
7. Duchy of Piombino

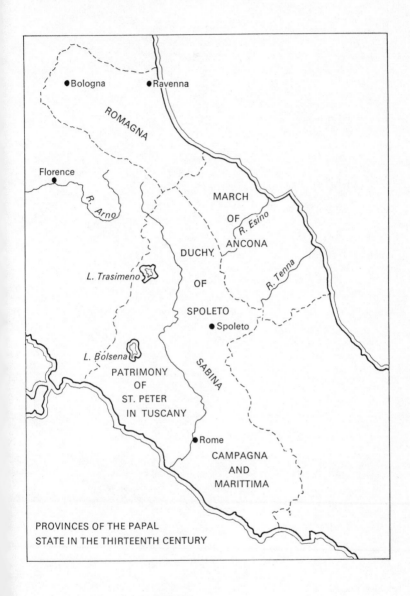

PROVINCES OF THE PAPAL
STATE IN THE THIRTEENTH CENTURY

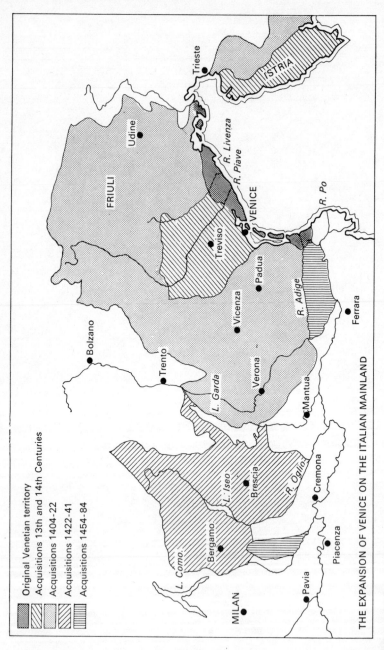

THE EXPANSION OF VENICE ON THE ITALIAN MAINLAND

Original Venetian territory
Acquisitions 13th and 14th Centuries
Acquisitions 1404-22
Acquisitions 1422-41
Acquisitions 1454-84

MILAN

Pavia

Piacenza

Cremona

R. Oglio

Bergamo

L. Como.

L. Iseo

Brescia

Mantua

L. Garda

Verona

Vicenza

R. Adige

Padua

Treviso

VENICE

R. Piave

R. Livenza

R. Po

Ferrara

Trento

Bolzano

Udine

FRIULI

Trieste

ISTRIA

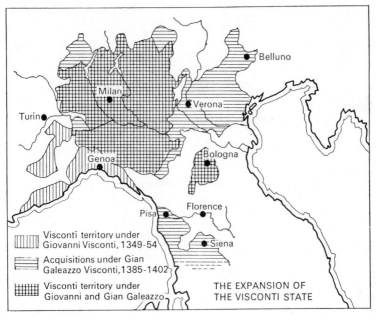

Visconti territory under
Giovanni Visconti, 1349-54

Acquisitions under Gian
Galeazzo Visconti, 1385-1402

Visconti territory under
Giovanni and Gian Galeazzo

THE EXPANSION OF
THE VISCONTI STATE

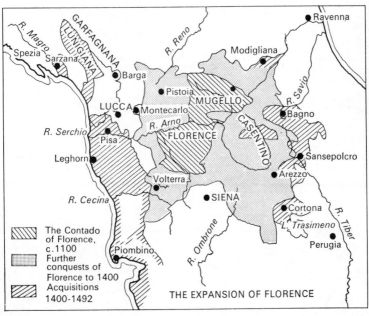

The Contado
of Florence,
c.1100

Further
conquests of
Florence to 1400

Acquisitions
1400-1492

THE EXPANSION OF FLORENCE

347

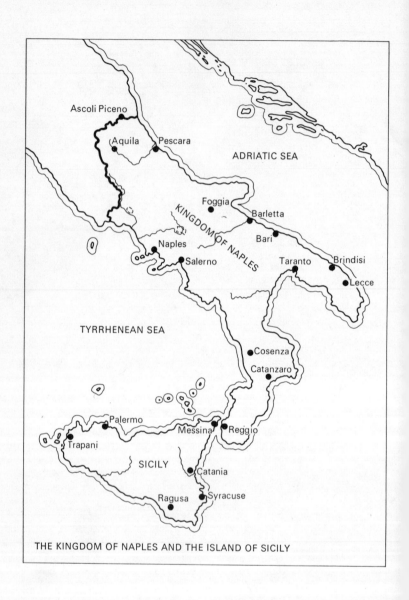

THE KINGDOM OF NAPLES AND THE ISLAND OF SICILY

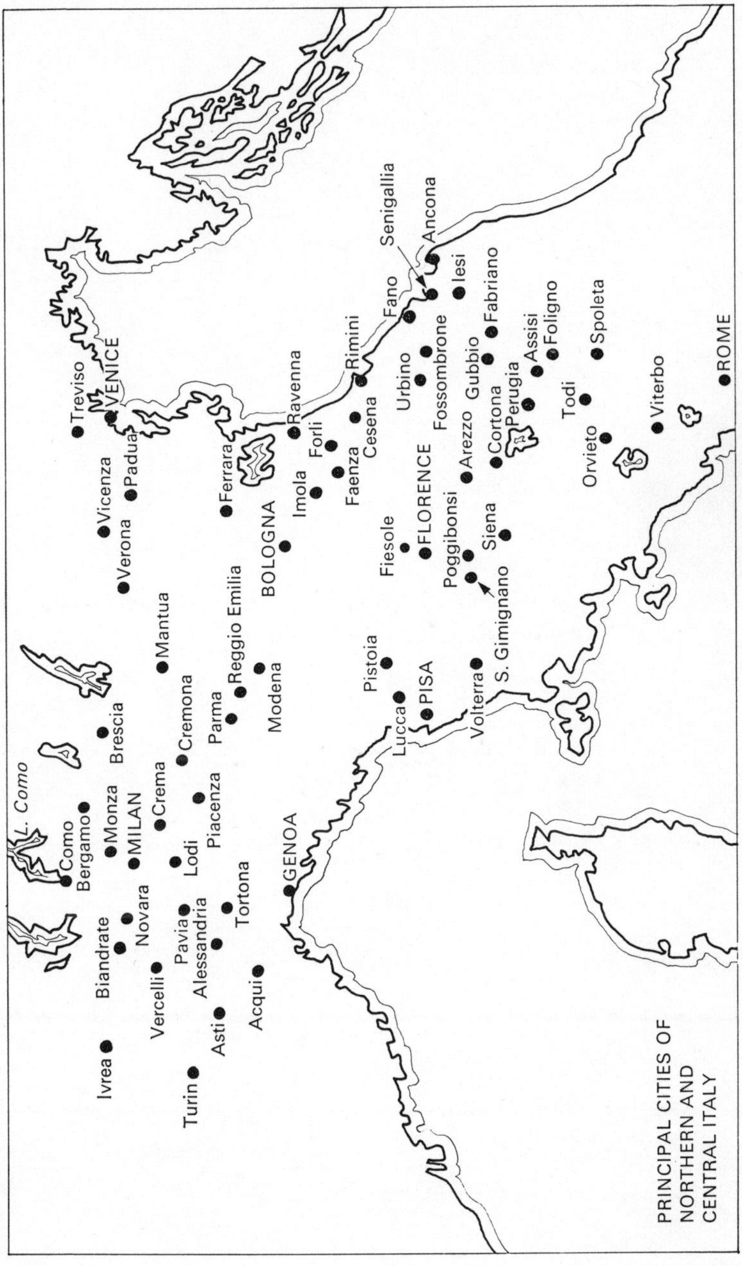
L. Como
Como
Bergamo
Monza
MILAN
Ivrea
Biandrate
Novara
Vercelli
Turin
Pavia
Alessandria
Asti
Lodi
Crema
Piacenza
Tortona
Acqui
Brescia
Cremona
Mantua
Parma
Reggio Emilia
Modena
GENOA
Verona
Vicenza
Padua
Treviso
VENICE
Ferrara
BOLOGNA
Imola
Faenza
Forlì
Ravenna
Cesena
Rimini
Lucca
PISA
Pistoia
Volterra
S. Gimignano
Poggibonsi
Fiesole
FLORENCE
Siena
Arezzo
Cortona
Urbino
Fossombrone
Fano
Senigallia
Ancona
Iesi
Fabriano
Gubbio
Perugia
Assisi
Foligno
Spoleta
Todi
Orvieto
Viterbo
ROME
PRINCIPAL CITIES OF NORTHERN AND CENTRAL ITALY

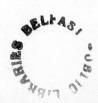

Select Bibliography

This bibliography is placed here partly by way of suggestions for further reading and partly by way of acknowledgement, for my debt to some of the works mentioned here is very great indeed. The emphasis lies on recent books and articles of manageable size and wide implications; and, wherever possible, on works available in the English language.

The following abbreviations have been used:

Ady Studies: JACOB, E. F., ed., *Italian Renaissance studies: a tribute to the late Cecilia M. Ady* (London, 1960)

Hale, *Europe*: HALE, J. R., HIGHFIELD, J. R. L., and SMALLEY, B., eds., *Europe in the late Middle Ages* (London, 1965)

General and General Political Histories

PROCACCI, G., *History of the Italian people* (London, 1970)

VALERI, N., ed., *Storia d'Italia* (2nd edition, 5 vols., Turin, 1965–7).

SIMEONI, L., ed., *Storia politica d'Italia: le Signorie* (2 vols., Milan, 1950)

Some Comparative Studies in Political and Social History

WALEY, D., *The Italian City-Republics* (London, 1969)

PREVITÉ-ORTON, C. W., 'The Italian cities till *c.* 1200', *Cambridge Mediaeval History*, vol. 5 (Cambridge, 1929)

SESTAN, E., 'La città comunale italiana dei secoli XI–XIII nelle sue note caratteristiche rispetto al movimento comunale europeo', *XIe Congrès International des Sciences Historiques, Rapports*, vol. 3 (Stockholm, 1961)

FASOLI, G., 'Le autonomie cittadine nel Medioevo', in *Nuove questioni di storia medioevale* (Milan, 1964)

FUIANO, M., 'Signorie e principati', ibid.

DIAZ, F., 'Di alcuni aspetti istituzionali dell' affermarsi delle Signorie', *Nuova Rivista Storica*, vol. 50 (1966)

JONES, P. J., 'Communes and despots: the city-state in late medieval Italy', *Transactions of the Royal Historical Society*, series 5, vol.15 (1965)

BUENO DE MESQUITA, D. M., 'The place of despotism in Italian politics', in Hale, *Europe*

MARONGIU, A., *Medieval Parliaments: a comparative study*, ed. Woolf, S. J. (London, 1968)

General Economic and Social History

LUZZATTO, G., *An economic history of Italy from the fall of the Roman Empire to the beginning of the sixteenth century* (London, 1961)

RENOUARD, Y., *Les hommes d'affaires italiens du Moyen Âge* (Paris, 1949)

JONES, P. J., 'Medieval agrarian society in its prime: Italy', *Cambridge Economic History of Europe*, new edition of vol. 1 (Cambridge, 1966)

LOPEZ, R. S., 'The trade of medieval Europe: the south', ibid., vol. 2 (Cambridge, 1952)

DE ROOVER, R., 'The organization of trade', ibid., vol. 3 (Cambridge, 1963)

CIPOLLA, C. M., 'The economic policies of governments: the Italian and Iberian peninsulas', ibid., vol. 3 (Cambridge, 1963)

CARUS-WILSON, E., 'The woollen industry', ibid., vol. 2 (Cambridge, 1952)

CIPOLLA, C. M., 'The trends in Italian economic history in the later Middle Ages', *Economic History Review*, 2nd series, vol. 2 (1949)

LOPEZ, R. S., and MISKIMIN, H. A., 'The economic depression of the Renaissance', *Economic History Review*, 2nd series, vol. 14 (1961–2)

CIPOLLA, C. M., LOPEZ, R. S., and MISKIMIN, H. A., 'Economic depression of the Renaissance?', *Economic History Review*, 2nd series, vol. 16 (1964)

KLAPISCH-ZUBER, C., and DAY, J., 'Villages désertés en Italie: esquisse', in *Villages désertés et histoire économique, XIe–XVIIIe siècle* (Paris, 1965)

ROMANO, R., 'L'Italia nella crisi del XIV secolo', *Nuova Rivista Storica*, vol. 50 (1966)

Some Collections of Essays on Italian Economic History

CIPOLLA, C. M., ed., *Storia dell' economia italiana: saggi di storia economica*, vol. 1 (Turin, 1959)

SAPORI, A., *Studi di storia economica – secoli XIII, XIV, XV* (3 vols., Florence, 1955–67)
Studi in onore di Armando Sapori (2 vols., Milan, 1957)

HERLIHY, D., LOPEZ, R. S., and SLESSAREV, V., eds., *Economy and society in medieval Italy: essays in memory of Robert L. Reynolds* (Kent, Ohio, 1969 – vol. 7 of *Explorations in Economic History*)

Emperors and Empire

BOWSKY, W. M., *Henry VII in Italy: the conflict of Empire and city-state, 1310–1313* (Lincoln, Nebraska, 1960)

OFFLER, H. S., 'Empire and Papacy: the last struggle', *Transactions of the Royal Historical Society*, series 5, vol. 6 (1956)

MOMMSEN, T. E., 'Castruccio Castracani and the Empire', in his *Medieval and Renaissance Studies* (Ithaca, N.Y., 1959)

DAVIS, C. T., *Dante and the idea of Rome* (Oxford, 1957)

GEWIRTH, A., *Marsilius of Padua and medieval political philosophy* (New York, 1951)

RUBINSTEIN, N., 'Marsilius of Padua and Italian political thought of his time', in Hale, *Europe*

The Papacy and the Papal States

WALEY, D., *The Papal State in the thirteenth century* (London, 1961)

DUPRÉ-THESEIDER, E., *Roma dal comune del popolo alla signoria pontificia (1252–1377)* (Bologna, 1952)

BOASE, T. S. R., *Boniface VIII* (London, 1933)

MOLLAT, G., *The Popes at Avignon, 1305–1378* (Edinburgh–London, 1963)

RENOUARD, Y., *The Avignon Papacy, 1305–1403* (London, 1970)

ULLMANN, W., *The origins of the Great Schism: a study in fourteenth-century ecclesiastical history* (London, 1948)

FAVIER, J., *Les finances pontificales à l'époque du Grand Schisme d'Occident, 1378–1409* (Paris, 1966)

PARTNER, P., *The Papal State under Martin V: the administration and government of the temporal power in the early fifteenth century* (London, 1958)

PARTNER, P., 'The "Budget" of the Roman Church in the Renaissance period', *Ady Studies*

GILL, J., *Eugenius IV, Pope of Christian union* (London, 1961)

GILL, J., *The Council of Florence* (Cambridge, 1959)

VON PASTOR, L., *The history of the Popes from the close of the Middle Ages*, ed. Antrobus, F. I., vols. 1–2 (London, 1891)

WALEY, D., *Mediaeval Orvieto: the political history of an Italian city-state, 1157–1334* (Cambridge, 1952)

CARPENTIER, E., *Une ville devant la peste: Orvieto et la peste noire de 1348* (Paris, 1962)

LARNER, J., *The lords of Romagna: Romagnol society and the origins of the Signorie* (London–New York, 1965)

JONES, P. J., 'The vicariate of the Malatesta of Rimini', *English Historical Review*, vol. 67 (1952)

JONES, P. J., 'The end of Malatesta rule in Rimini', *Ady Studies*

CHIAPPINI, L., *Gli Estensi* (Varese, 1967)

Naples and Sicily

CROCE, B., *History of the Kingdom of Naples*, ed. Hughes, H. S. (Chicago, 1970)

MACK SMITH, D., *A history of Sicily: medieval Sicily, 800–1713* (London, 1968)

MARONGIU, A., 'A model state in the Middle Ages: the Norman and Swabian Kingdom of Sicily', *Comparative Studies in Society and History*, vol. 6 (1963–4)

JORDAN, E., *Les origines de la domination angevine en Italie* (Paris, 1909)

RUNCIMAN, S., *The Sicilian Vespers: a history of the Mediterranean world in the late thirteenth century* (Cambridge, 1958; Penguin edition, 1960)

LÉONARD, E. G., *Les Angevins de Naples* (Paris, 1954)

GENTILE, P., 'Lo stato napoletano sotto Alfonso I d'Aragona', *Archivio Storico per le Provincie Napoletane, nuova serie, anni 23–4* (1937–8)

RYDER, A. J., 'The evolution of imperial government in Naples under Alfonso V of Aragon', in Hale, *Europe*

RYDER, G. F., and A. F. C., 'La politica italiana di Alfonso d'Aragona', *Archivio Storico per le Provincie Napoletane, nuova serie, anni 38–9* (1959–60)

RYDER, A. F. C., 'Alfonso d'Aragona e l'avvento di Francesco Sforza al Ducato di Milano', ibid., *nuova serie, anno 41* (1961)

Venice and the Venetian Republic

BATTISTELLA, A., *Storia della Repubblica di Venezia* (Venice, 1921)

CESSI, R., *Storia della Repubblica di Venezia* (2 vols., Milan-Messina, 1944–6)

LUZZATTO, G., *Storia economica di Venezia dall' XI al XVI secolo* (Venice, 1961)

LUZZATTO, G., *Studi di storia economica veneziana* (Padua, 1954)

CRACCO, G., *Società e stato nel medioevo veneziano* (Florence, 1967). This should be used with some caution – cf. the reviews by Lane, F. C., *Speculum*, vol. 43 (1968), and Pullan, B., *Rivista Storica Italiana, anno 81* (1969)

LANE, F. C., *Venice and history: the collected papers of Frederic C. Lane* (Baltimore, Md, 1966)

LANE, F. C., *Venetian ships and shipbuilders of the Renaissance* (Baltimore, Md, 1934; a new edition has been published as *Navires et constructeurs à Venise pendant la Renaissance*, Paris, 1965)

LANE, F. C., *Andrea Barbarigo, merchant of Venice (1418–1449)* (Baltimore, Md, 1944)

CHAMBERS, D. S., *The imperial age of Venice, 1380–1580* (London, 1970)

VENTURA, A., *Nobiltà e popolo nella società veneta del '400 e '500* (Bari, 1964)

PINO-BRANCA, A., 'Il comune di Padova sotto la Dominante nel secolo XV (rapporti amministrativi e finanziari)', *Atti del Reale Istituto Veneto di Scienze, Lettere ed Arti*, vols. 92 (1933–4), 96 (1936–7), 97 (1937–8)

Eastern Lombardy

HYDE, J. K., *Padua in the age of Dante* (Manchester, 1966)
CIPOLLA, C., *La storia politica di Verona* (revised edition, ed. Simeoni, L., and Pellegrini, O., Verona, 1954)
QUAZZA, R., *Mantova attraverso i secoli* (reprint, Mantua, 1966)

Milan and the Duchy

FRANCESCHINI, G., 'La vita sociale e politica nel Duecento', in Fondazione G. Treccani degli Alfieri, *Storia di Milano*, vol. 4 (Milan, 1954)
COGNASSO, F., 'Istituzioni comunali e signorili di Milano sotto i Visconti', ibid., vol. 4 (Milan, 1955)
BUENO DE MESQUITA, D. M., *Giangaleazzo Visconti, Duke of Milan (1351–1402): a study in the political career of an Italian despot* (Cambridge, 1941)
BARONI, M. F., 'I cancellieri di Giovanni Maria e di Filippo Maria Visconti', *Nuova Rivista Storica*, vol. 50 (1966)
RONDININI, G. S., 'Ambasciatori e ambascerie al tempo di Filippo Maria Visconti (1412–1426)', *Nuova Rivista Storica*, vol. 49 (1965)
ADY, C. M., *A history of Milan under the Sforza* (London, 1907)
CIPOLLA, C. M., 'I precedenti economici', in Fondazione G. Treccani degli Alfieri, *Storia di Milano*, vol. 8 (Milan, 1957)
DOWD, D. F., 'The economic expansion of Lombardy, 1300–1500: a study in political stimuli to economic change', *Journal of Economic History*, vol. 21 (1961)
MIANI, G., 'L'économie lombarde aux XIVe et XVe siècles: une exception à la règle?', *Annales: Économies, Sociétés, Civilisations*, vol. 19 (1964)
CIPOLLA, C. M., 'Une crise ignorée: comment s'est perdue la propriété ecclésiastique dans l'Italie du Nord entre le XIe et le XVIe siècle', *Annales: Économies, Sociétés, Civilisations*, vol. 2 (1947)

BORLANDI, F., 'Il commercio del guado nel Medioevo', in *Studi in onore di Gino Luzzatto*, vol. 1 (Milan, 1950); reprinted in Cipolla, *Storia economica*, cited above, p. 353

CIPOLLA, C. M., 'Per la storia delle epidemie in Italia: il caso di una borgata lombarda ai primi del Quattrocento', *Rivista Storica Italiana*, anno 75 (1963)

Genoa and Liguria

LOPEZ, R. S., 'Aux origines du capitalisme génois', *Annales d'Histoire Économique et Sociale*, vol. 9 (1937); also available in Italian translation in Cipolla, *Storia economica*, cited above, p. 353

LOPEZ, R. S., 'Market expansion: the case of Genoa', *Journal of Economic History*, vol. 24 (1964), with a critical note by Lane, F. C.

HEERS, J., 'Gênes', in Fanfani, A., ed., *Città, mercanti, dottrine nell' economia europea dal IV al XVIII secolo: saggi in memoria di Gino Luzzatto* (Milan, 1964)

HEERS, J., *Gênes au XVe siècle: activité économique et problèmes sociaux* (Paris, 1961)

Pisa

HERLIHY, D., *Pisa in the early Renaissance: a study of urban growth* (New Haven, Conn., 1958)

CRISTIANI, E., *Nobiltà e popolo nel comune di Pisa dalle origini del podestariato alla Signoria dei Donoratico* (Naples, 1962)

SILVA, P., 'Intorno all' industria e al commercio della lana in Pisa', reprinted in Cipolla, *Storia economica*, cited above, p. 353

RENOUARD, Y., 'Destin d'une grande métropole médiévale: Pise', *Annales: Économies, Sociétés, Civilisations*, vol. 17 (1962)

MALLETT, M. E., *The Florentine galleys in the fifteenth century* (Oxford, 1967)

MALLETT, M. E., 'Pisa and Florence in the fifteenth century: aspects of the period of the first Florentine domination', in Rubinstein, N., *Florentine Studies*, cited below, p. 358

Florence

SCHEVILL, F., *Medieval and Renaissance Florence* (revised version of his *History of Florence*, 1961; published by Harper Torchbooks, 2 vols., 1963)

RUBINSTEIN, N., ed., *Florentine Studies: politics and society in Renaissance Florence* (London, 1968)

OTTOKAR, N., *Il comune di Firenze alla fine del Dugento* (Florence, 1926)

FIUMI, E., 'Fioritura e decadenza dell' economia fiorentina', *Archivio Storico Italiano, anni* 115–17 (1957–9)

BECKER, M. B., *Florence in transition* (2 vols, Baltimore, Md, 1967–8)

BRUCKER, G. A., *Florentine politics and society, 1343–1378* (Princeton, N.J., 1962)

RODOLICO, N., *I Ciompi: una pagina di storia del proletariato operaio* (Florence, 1945). But cf. the remarks of G. A. Brucker on the same subject in Rubinstein, ed., *Florentine Studies*, cited above.

BRUCKER, G. A., *Renaissance Florence* (New York, 1969)

MOLHO, A., 'Politics and the ruling class in early Renaissance Florence', *Nuova Rivista Storica*, vol. 52 (1968)

MOLHO, A., 'The Florentine oligarchy and the *Balìe* of the late Trecento', *Speculum*, vol. 43 (1968)

GUTKIND, C. S., *Cosimo de' Medici, Pater Patriae (1389–1464)* (Oxford, 1938)

RUBINSTEIN, N., *The government of Florence under the Medici, 1434 to 1494* (Oxford, 1966)

MARTINES, L., *Lawyers and statecraft in Renaissance Florence* (Princeton, N.J., 1968)

RUBINSTEIN, N., 'Florence and the despots: some aspects of Florentine diplomacy in the fourteenth century', *Transactions of the Royal Historical Society*, series 5, vol. 2 (1952)

PARTNER, P., 'Florence and the Papacy, 1300–1375', in Hale, *Europe*; continued in a further essay in Rubinstein, ed., *Florentine Studies*, cited above.

BARON, H., 'A struggle for liberty in the Renaissance: Florence, Venice and Milan in the early Quattrocento', *American Historical Review*, vol. 58 (1952–3)

DE ROOVER, R., *The rise and decline of the Medici bank, 1397–1494* (Cambridge, Mass., 1963)

MALLETT, M. E., *The Florentine galleys in the fifteenth century* (Oxford, 1967)

DE ROOVER, F. EDLER, 'Andrea Banchi, Florentine silk manufacturer and merchant in the fifteenth century', *Studies in Medieval and Renaissance History*, vol. 3 (1966)

Siena

SCHEVILL, F., *Siena: the history of a medieval commune* (new edition, with an introduction by Bowsky, W. M., New York, 1964)

BOWSKY, W. M., 'The *Buon Governo* of Siena (1287–1355): a medieval Italian oligarchy', *Speculum*, vol. 37 (1962)

BOWSKY, W. M., 'The medieval commune and internal violence: police power and public safety in Siena, 1287–1355', *American Historical Review*, vol. 63 (1967)

BOWSKY, W. M., 'Medieval citizenship: the individual and the state in the commune of Siena, 1287–1355', *Studies in Medieval and Renaissance History*, vol. 4 (1967)

BOWSKY, W. M., *The finance of the commune of Siena, 1287–1355* (Oxford, 1970)

BOWSKY, W. M., 'The impact of the Black Death upon Sienese government and society', *Speculum*, vol. 39 (1964)

RUTENBERG, V., 'La vie et la lutte des Ciompi de Sienne', *Annales: Économies, Sociétés, Civilisations*, vol. 20 (1965)

HICKS, D. L., 'Sienese society in the Renaissance', *Comparative Studies in Society and History*, vol. 2 (1959–60)

HICKS, D. L., 'The Sienese state in the Renaissance', in Carter, C. H., ed., *From the Renaissance to the Counter Reformation: essays in honour of Garrett Mattingly* (London, 1966)

Tuscany

FIUMI, E., 'Sui rapporti economici tra città e contado nell' età comunale', *Archivio Storico Italiano*, anno 114 (1956)

JONES, P. J., 'From manor to mezzadria: a Tuscan case-study in the medieval origins of modern agrarian society', in Rubinstein, ed., *Florentine Studies*, cited above, p. 358.

HERLIHY, D., *Medieval and Renaissance Pistoia: the social history of an Italian town, 1200–1430* (New Haven, Conn., and London, 1967)

FIUMI, E., *Storia economica e sociale di San Gimignano* (Florence, 1961)

FIUMI, E., *Demografia, movimento urbanistico e classi sociali in Prato dall' età comunale ai tempi moderni* (Florence, 1968)

Religious Life and the Church

BRENTANO, R., *Two Churches: England and Italy in the thirteenth century* (Princeton, N.J., 1968)

SABATIER, P., *Life of St Francis of Assisi* (London, 1894)

MOORMAN, J. R. H., *A history of the Franciscan order from its origins to the year 1517* (Oxford, 1968)

LAMBERT, M. D., *Franciscan poverty: the doctrine of the absolute poverty of Christ and the apostles in the Franciscan order, 1210–1323* (London, 1961)

BENNETT, R. F., *The early Dominicans* (Cambridge, 1937)

VOLPE, G., *Movimenti religiosi e sette ereticali nella società medioevale italiana (secoli XI–XIV)* (first published 1922; reprint, Florence, 1961)

LEFF, G., *Heresy in the later Middle Ages: the relation of heterodoxy to dissent, c. 1250–c. 1450* (2 vols., Manchester, 1967)

LEA, H. C., *The Inquisition of the Middle Ages: its organization and operation*, ed. with an introduction by Ullmann, W. (London, 1963)

GUIRAUD, J., *Histoire de l'Inquisition au Moyen Âge*, vol. 2 (Paris, 1938)

MONTI, G. M., *Le confraternite medioevale dell' alta e media Italia* (2 vols., Venice, 1927)

Movimento dei Disciplinati nel settimo centenario dal suo inizio (Perugia–1260), Appendice 9 to *Bollettino della Deputazione di Storia Patria per l'Umbria* (Spoleto, 1962)

RAYMOND OF CAPUA, *The life of St Catherine of Siena* (London, 1960)

FERRERS HOWELL, A. G., *S. Bernardino of Siena* (London, 1913)

ORIGO, I., *The world of San Bernardino* (London, 1964)

MORÇAY, R., *Saint Antonin, Archevêque de Florence (1389–1459)* (Paris, 1914)

TASSI, I., *Ludovico Barbo (1381–1443)* (Rome, 1952)

GILL, J., *The Council of Florence* (Cambridge, 1959)

CIPOLLA, C. M., 'Une crise ignorée: comment s'est perdue la propriété ecclésiastique dans l'Italie du Nord entre le XIe et le XVIe siècle', *Annales: Économies, Sociétés, Civilisations*, vol. 2 (1947)

STELLA, A., 'La proprietà ecclesiastica nella Repubblica di Venezia dal secolo XV al XVII', *Nuova Rivista Storica*, vol. 42 (1958)

NELSON, B. N., 'The usurer and the merchant prince: Italian businessmen and the ecclesiastical law of restitution, 1100–1550', *Journal of Economic History*, vol. 7 (1947), Supplement 7

DE ROOVER, F. EDLER, 'Restitution in Renaissance Florence', *Studi in onore di Armando Sapori*, vol. 2 (Milan, 1957)

MILANO, A., *Storia degli ebrei in Italia* (Turin, 1963)

PULLAN, B., *Rich and poor in Renaissance Venice: the social institutions of a Catholic state, to 1620* (Oxford, and Cambridge, Mass., 1971)

Concepts of the Renaissance: General Surveys

BURCKHARDT, J., *The civilization of the Renaissance in Italy* (in many editions)

HUIZINGA, J., 'The problem of the Renaissance', in his *Men and ideas: history, the Middle Ages, the Renaissance* (New York, 1959)

FERGUSON, W. K., *The Renaissance in historical thought: five centuries of interpretation* (Boston, Mass., 1948)

CHABOD, F., 'The concept of the Renaissance', in his *Machiavelli and the Renaissance* (London, 1958)

HAY, D., *The Italian Renaissance in its historical background* (Cambridge, 1961)

LARNER, J., *Culture and society in Italy, 1290–1420* (London, 1971)

Literature and Ideas

WILKINS, E. H., *A history of Italian literature* (London, 1954)

MIGLIORINI, B., *The Italian language*, ed. Griffith, T. G. (London, 1966)

BARBI, M., *Life of Dante*, ed. Ruggiers, P. G. (Berkeley-Los Angeles, 1954)

KRISTELLER, P. O., *Renaissance thought: the classic, scholastic and humanist strains* (New York, 1961)

KRISTELLER, P. O., *Renaissance thought II: papers on humanism and the arts* (New York, 1965)

WEISS, R., *The dawn of humanism in Italy* (London, 1947)

WEISS, R., *The Renaissance discovery of classical antiquity* (Oxford, 1969)

WILKINS, E. H., *Life of Petrarch* (Chicago, 1961)

GEANAKOPLOS, D. J., *Greek scholars in Venice: studies in the dissemination of Greek learning from Byzantium to western Europe* (Cambridge, Mass., 1962)

RUBINSTEIN, N., 'The beginnings of political thought in Florence: a study in mediaeval historiography', *Journal of the Warburg and Courtauld Institutes*, vol. 5 (1942)

RUBINSTEIN, N., 'Some ideas on municipal progress and decline in the Italy of the communes', in Gordon, D. J., ed., *Fritz Saxl, 1890–1948: a volume of memorial essays from his friends in England* (London, 1957)

BURKE, P., 'The sense of historical perspective in Renaissance Italy', *Journal of World History*, vol. 2 (1969)

BARON, H., 'Franciscan poverty and civic wealth as factors in the rise of humanistic thought', *Speculum*, vol. 13 (1968)

BARON, H., 'Cicero and the Roman civic spirit in the Middle Ages and early Renaissance', *Bulletin of the John Rylands Library*, vol. 22 (1938)

BARON, H., *The crisis of the early Italian Renaissance: civic humanism and republican liberty in an age of classicism and tyranny* (new one-volume edition, Princeton, N.J., 1966)

SEIGEL, J. E., '"Civic humanism" or Ciceronian rhetoric? The culture of Petrarch and Bruni', *Past and Present*, no. 34 (1966)

BARON, H., 'Leonardo Bruni: "professional rhetorician" or "civic humanist"?' *Past and Present*, no. 36 (1967)

GARIN, E., *Italian humanism: philosophy and civic life in the Renaissance* (Oxford, 1965)

GARIN, E., *L'educazione in Europa (1400–1600): problemi e programmi* (Bari, 1957)

WOODWARD, W. H., *Studies in education during the age of the Renaissance, 1400–1600* (Cambridge, 1906)

Art, Architecture and Society

PANOFSKY, E., *Renaissance and Renascences in western art* (Paladin Books paperback edition, London, 1970)

MURRAY, P., *The architecture of the Italian Renaissance* (enlarged edition, London, 1969)

WHITE, J., *Art and architecture in Italy, 1250 to 1400* (Penguin, 1966)

WIERUSZOWSKI, H., 'Art and the commune in the time of Dante', *Speculum*, vol. 19 (1944)

RUBINSTEIN, N., 'Political ideas in Sienese art: the frescoes by Ambrogio Lorenzetti and Taddeo di Bartolo in the Palazzo Pubblico', *Journal of the Warburg and Courtauld Institutes*, vol. 21 (1958)

LARNER, J., 'The artist and the intellectuals in fourteenth-century Italy', *History*, vol. 54 (1969)

MEISS, M., *Painting in Florence and Siena after the Black Death* (Princeton, N.J., 1951)

GADOL, J., *Leon Battista Alberti: universal man of the early Renaissance* (Chicago–London, 1969)

LOPEZ, R. S., 'Hard times and investment in culture', in *The Renaissance: a symposium* (New York, 1953): reprinted in Molho, A., ed., *Social and economic foundations of the Italian Renaissance* (London–New York, 1969)

The Florentine Renaissance

HOLMES, G., *The Florentine Enlightenment, 1400–50* (London, 1969)

BRUCKER, G. A., *Renaissance Florence* (New York, 1969)

BECKER, M. B., *Florence in transition* (2 vols., Baltimore, Md, 1967–8)

ULLMAN, B. L., *The humanism of Coluccio Salutati* (Padua, 1963)

GARIN, E., 'I cancellieri umanisti della Repubblica Fiorentina da Coluccio Salutati a Bartolomeo Scala', *Rivista Storica Italiana*, vol. 71 (1959)

MARTINES, L., *The social world of the Florentine humanists, 1390–1460* (London, 1963)

GOMBRICH, E. H., 'The early Medici as patrons of art', in *Ady Studies*

Index

Naples
florence
venice
milan
Papal States